The Womanist Preacher

To: Rev. Dr. Brenda Carter Oldham

I pray that this Womanist
work will bless you in
all that you do
for the body of Christ.

Love Always!

Kim S.

Rhetoric, Race, and Religion

Series Editor

Andre E. Johnson, University of Memphis.

This series explores and examines the intersection of rhetoric, race, and religion. Volumes in this series demonstrate how language both shapes race and/or religion and how race and/or religion shapes the language or rhetoric we use. Scholars examine these phenomena from a historical and contemporary perspective.

Titles in this Series

What Movies Teach about Race: Exceptionalism, Erasure, and Entitlement, by Roslyn M. Satchel.
Women Bishops and Rhetorics of Shalom: A Whole Peace, by Leland G. Spencer
The Womanist Preacher: Proclaiming Womanist Rhetoric from the Pulpit, by Kimberly P. Johnson.

The Womanist Preacher

Proclaiming Womanist Rhetoric from the Pulpit

Kimberly P. Johnson

LEXINGTON BOOKS
Lanham • Boulder • New York • London

Published by Lexington Books
An imprint of The Rowman & Littlefield Publishing Group, Inc.
4501 Forbes Boulevard, Suite 200, Lanham, Maryland 20706
www.rowman.com

Unit A, Whitacre Mews, 26-34 Stannary Street, London SE11 4AB

British Library Cataloguing in Publication Information Available

Library of Congress Cataloging-in-Publication Data
The hardback edition of this book was previously catalogued by the Library of Congress
as follows:

Names: Johnson, Kimberly P. (Assistant Professor of Communications), author.
Title: The womanist preacher : proclaiming womanist rhetoric from the pulpit
/ Kimberly P. Johnson.
Description: Lanham : Lexington Books, 2017. | Series: Rhetoric, race, and
religion | Includes bibliographical references and index.
Identifiers: LCCN 2017023191 (print) | LCCN 2017025460 (ebook) | ISBN
9781498542067 (Electronic) | ISBN 9781498542050 (cloth : alk. paper)
Subjects: LCSH: Preaching. | Womanist theology. | African American women
clergy. | Womanism--Religious aspects--Christianity.
Classification: LCC BV4222 (ebook) | LCC BV4222 .J64 2017 (print) | DDC
251.0082--dc23
LC record available at https://lccn.loc.gov/2017023191

ISBN 978-1-4985-4205-0 (hardback : alk. paper)
ISBN 978-1-4985-4207-4 (pbk. : alk. paper)
ISBN 978-1-4985-4206-7 (ebook)

♾™ The paper used in this publication meets the minimum requirements of American
National Standard for Information Sciences—Permanence of Paper for Printed Library
Materials, ANSI/NISO Z39.48-1992.

Printed in the United States of America

Permissions

I am grateful for permission to reprint in part or in whole the following copyrighted material.

Claudette A. Copeland, "What Shall We Do for Our Sister?" Transcribed by Kimberly P. Johnson. Reproduced by permission of Claudette A. Copeland.

Elaine M. Flake, "The Power of Enough." Reprinted from Elaine M. Flake, *God In Her Midst: Preaching Healing to Wounded Women* (Valley Forge, PA: Judson Press, 2007) 41–47. Reproduced by permission of the publisher.

Cheryl Kirk-Duggan, "Women of the Cloth." Transcribed by Kimberly P. Johnson. Reproduced by permission of Cheryl Kirk-Duggan.

Gina Stewart, "Enough is Enough!" Reprinted from Ella Pearson Mitchell and Valerie Bridgeman Davis (eds.), *Those Preaching Women: A Multicultural Collection* (Valley Forge, PA: Judson Press, 2008) 9–13. Reproduced by permission of the publisher.

Melva Sampson, "Hell No!" Reprinted from Ella Mitchell and Valerie Bridgeman Davis (eds.), *Those Preaching Women: A Multicultural Collection* (Valley Forge, PA: Judson Press, 2008) 27–31. Reproduced by permission of the Publisher.

To my Mom,
who taught me what it means to be a womanist,
before we even knew the term that so adequately
described our human convictions.

To my Grandmothers and Aunts,
who taught me what black girl power really looks like.
To my Twin Sister, my womb mate, my BFF,
who has shown me what perseverance looks like.
To all the womanists and proto-womanists,
whose shoulders I proudly stand on.

To my Dad,
Who is now part of that Great Cloud of Witnesses,
you recognized early on, when I was a little girl, that I
was "The Boss." Your employees would even tell you,
"The Boss is on the phone," whenever I called.

And to all the men in my family, especially my
Brothers and Uncles who show the world that they can
handle being around strong black women.

Contents

Acknowledgments

I will be forever grateful to the late Michael Charles Leff (my Northwestern University and University of Memphis professor), Barbara A. Holmes, and Frank A. Thomas for convincing me to pursue a PhD in Communication, through the Rhetoric Program, at U of M. Leff, you were the reason I chose UofM. Barbara, thank you for giving me access to all of the womanist resources at Memphis Theological Seminary even though I was a UofM student. Frank, you have been my pastor since I was a little girl, you were my preaching professor at McCormick Theological Seminary, you were my colleague and classmate at U of M, you are my mentor, my "Dad in the Ministry," and, most importantly, you are family. Words cannot express how much you mean to me.

I am greatly indebted to my PhD committee at the University of Memphis: Sandy Sarkela (my major professor), Tony de Velasco, Katherine G. Hendrix, Ladricka Menson-Furr, Valerie Bridgeman, and the late Michael Leff, who missed seeing me walk across the stage to receive my degree by a matter of months. All of you were amazing! Thank you for pushing me until I could come up with my own answers. And, thank you for the tremendous love and support that you all have shown through the years. Sandy, I could have never made it through the program without you. Thank you for not only being my advisor, but for being my friend. Valerie, thank you for helping me figure out that womanist preaching and womanist rhetoric is what I wanted to study all along. I just did not have the words for it until I got to Memphis.

To Richard Ranta, former dean of the College of Liberal Arts at the University of Memphis, thank you for your constant support during the time that I served as your graduate assistant and even after I graduated from the program. I was humbled to be offered that position and thankful at the same time because it gave me the opportunity to write the initial draft of this project—the dissertation.

To the five womanist preachers reflected in this project—Elaine M. Flake, Gina M. Stewart, Cheryl Kirk-Duggan, Melva L. Sampson, and Claudette A. Copeland—along with Stacey Floyd-Thomas, the womanist scholar whose framework I borrow, I want to thank you for allowing me to analyze your work, ask you questions, interview you, email you, and text you. Our rich conversations have helped me to formulate what I want to say about womanist preaching and womanist rhetoric.

To Renita Weems, I want to say thank you because you know that words are powerful. I am so grateful that our dear friend, Eugene L. Gibson, Jr., who put us together on the same roster at Olivet Fellowship Missionary Baptist Church, in Memphis, Tennessee, (Thanks Geno!). I was the lecturer and you were the preacher for their Survivors Weekend. After I finished lecturing, you publicly complimented me on my womanist scholarship and thanked me for sharing it with everyone. I have hidden those words in my heart to provide fuel whenever I have gotten weary on this journey toward my first monograph publication.

To the "Mother of Womanism," Alice Walker, thank you for coining such a beautiful term. I could not have done any of this work without you.

To my dear friend and personal editor, Katara Washington Patton, Esteem Publishing founder and executive editor, thank you for editing and proofreading the dissertation so I could get it into shape enough to submit as a book proposal to Lexington Books.

To Angela G. Ray, associate professor at Northwestern University, thank you for giving me plenty of tips on how to go about converting a dissertation into a book that is ready for publication. You were right, this is a lot of work, but I am so pleased with the finished product.

To Andre Johnson, editor of the *Rhetoric, Race, and Religion* series published through Lexington Books, thank you for encouraging me to submit a book proposal.

To Nicolette Amstutz, associate acquisitions editor of Communication, Education, and Latin American Studies at Lexington Books, an imprint of Rowman & Littlefield, and Jimmy Hamill, your assistant editor, thank you for working with me to make my dream of publishing academic books come true.

To my colleagues at Tennessee State University, especially James Stephens, thank you for going the extra mile to actually read what I originally wrote in my dissertation, and then for being a listening ear to help me think through what I want to say and how I want to organize it.

To my circle of friends that I surround myself with, both near and far, you know who you are. Thank you for encouraging me, praying with me, and for me, every step of the way. I tell you all the time that I love you, and I mean it.

To my pastor, Judy D. Cummings, thank you for loving me (and my family), for encouraging me, providing a listening ear, checking up on me, reading some of my work and then offering your critique, praying for me and with me, not just through this writing process, but through life in general, for opening your pulpit to me to preach the Gospel, and for just allowing me to do ministry with you. Most importantly, thank you for allowing me to include part of your story in the last chapter. You mean the world to me and I love you!

To my twin sister, Niki, thank you for taking the image that I purchased for the cover of this book and turning it into a masterpiece. Your work is magnificent! I love you throughout eternity!

To my Aunt Avis, it has been just you and me in Tennessee for the last ten years. I miss living right up the street from you, watching you show up for my academic and ministry functions. I especially miss hanging out with you all the time—being two hundred miles away makes a drastic difference. Thank you for your love and support all along the way! I love you!

And, to my Uncle George and Aunt Joan, thank you for being two of my biggest cheerleaders and for supporting me throughout all my endeavors. Uncle George, I will never forget that time when I was a PhD student and I called you up because I had writer's block. You stopped what you were doing, told people you would call them back, and proceeded to speak life into me. You reminded me that I just need to have faith, God will give me the words to say. I swear you are an undercover evangelist! I love you both beyond words!

Introduction

In 1831, Maria W. Stewart asked, "How long shall the fair daughters of Africa be compelled to bury their minds and talents beneath a load of iron pots and kettles?"[1] Stewart urged women to use their influence as mothers to plant seeds of creativity into the minds of their children and kernels of equality to cultivate a pure heart. She must have recognized that the ongoing invisibility and silencing of African American women would maintain their social inequality, and so she encouraged women to redefine themselves by discovering their own identity. As those women began defining themselves and living out their own definitions of who they were and what they considered to be socially acceptable, they also began to gain their visibility and their voice. However, even in the twenty-first century, African American women continue to ask, "How long shall the fair daughters of Africa be compelled to bury their minds and talents beneath the load of racism, sexism, classism, and all other forms of oppression? How long will we have to live out the definitions of who other people say that we are? When do we get to define ourselves and our own lived realities?"

THE SIGNIFICANCE OF WOMANISM

Coining the Term "Womanist"

Alice Walker questioned these same oppressive paradigms, but she found strength and courage through the civil rights movement to redefine herself from being a feminist to being a womanist. She believes it was the heroism of Dr. Martin Luther King, Jr., along with the advancements of the civil rights movement, that gave her a reassurance that blacks could become whatever they want and live wherever they want that sparked an awakened faith within her and opened the doorway for her to truly become herself. She explains that Dr. King warned them that their activism would more than likely cost them time in prison, but that freedom would finally come.[2] The movement is what gave Walker a reason to look beyond herself and her gender. The movement inspired her to become a community activist as well as a global activist so that she could fight for all oppressed people. The movement awakened her understanding in the capacity of the human spirit to be in relationship across racial barriers. The movement gave blacks a sense of community and a purpose because it created black heroes that little black boys and girls could look up to and follow. She says that because the movement still lives in us, it will not die.[3] Walker helps us to understand that "to fight is to exist and existence means knowing the difference between what you are and what you were, being capable of looking after yourself both intellectually and financially, knowing when you are being wronged and by whom, being able to protect yourself and the ones you love, being part of the world community, being alert to which part of the community you have joined, and knowing how to change to a different part if that part does not suit you."[4] Walker understood freedom as the ability to redefine one's own existence and as the ability to choose to not be coerced into supporting the civil rights movement over the feminist movement.

Womanism originated as a result of the racial divide in the feminist movement and gender divide in the civil rights movement. It was also due to the "refusal to take differences among women seriously that lies at the heart of feminism's implicit politics of domination."[5] The feminist movement put African American women in a "crisis relationship" with their male counterparts because it required them to put black men "in their place" at the expense of supporting their white feminist sisters.[6] "As long as black men are unable to break the strongholds of a white patriarchal society, they will continue to see feminism and feminist movements as a threat to their upward mobility. Likewise, the more women are expected to stay silent in exchange for the advancement of the black male, the less likely is the idea that women's liberation will ever be achieved."[7] bell hooks argues that Elizabeth Cady Stanton even suggested, in her article, "Women and Black Men," that "manhood suffrage" was designed to create antagonism between all women and black men.[8] While men sympathized with the cause of women's rights activists, they were not willing to risk their own political advancement for the right to vote. Consequently, black women were forced to support either women's suffrage or manhood suffrage.[9] "To align themselves with the women's suffrage movement would partner them with white feminists who were already openly racist against black men. Yet, if they aligned themselves with manhood suffragists, civil rights activists, this would cause them to endorse a patriarchal social order that would inevitably continue to silence women."[10]

Audre Lorde claims, "Women of Color in America have grown up within a symphony of anger, at being silenced, at being unchosen, at knowing that when we survive, it is in spite of a world that takes for granted our lack of humanness."[11]

Alice Walker first used the term *womanist* in her 1979 publication of a short story, "Coming Apart." It was not until the 1983 publication of *In Search of Our Mother's Gardens: Womanist Prose* that Walker created the meaning of her newly defined womanist existence. The four tenets of Walker's definition are as follows:

1. From womanish. (Opp. Of "girlish," i.e., frivolous, irresponsible, not serious.) A black feminist or feminist of color. From the black folk expression of mothers to female children, "You acting womanish," i.e., like a woman. Usually referring to outrageous, audacious, courageous or *willful* behavior. Wanting to know more and in greater depth than is considered "good" for one. Interested in grown-up doings. Acting grown up. Being grown up. Interchangeable with another black fold expression: "You trying to be grown." Responsible. In charge. *Serious.*

2. *Also*: A woman who loves other women, sexually and/or nonsexually. Appreciates and prefers women's culture, women's emotional flexibility (values tears as natural counterbalance of laughter), and women's strength. Sometimes loves individual men, sexually and/or nonsexually. Committed to survival and wholeness of entire people, male and female. Not a separatist, except periodically, for health. Traditionally universalist, as in "Mama, why are we brown, pink, and yellow, and our cousins are white, beige, and black?" Ans.: "Well, you know the colored race is just like a flower garden, with every color flower represented." Traditionally capable, as in: "Mama, I'm walking to Canada and I'm taking you and a bunch of other slaves with me." Reply: "It wouldn't be the first time."

3. Loves music. Loves dance. Loves the moon. *Loves* the Spirit. Loves love and food and roundness. Loves struggle. *Loves* the Folk. Loves herself. *Regardless.*

4. Womanist is to feminist as purple is to lavender.[12]

According to Walker, a womanist is a black woman or woman of color who identifies with feminism and is committed to the survival and wholeness of all people regardless of race, class, gender, or sexuality. Womanists love being grown, love the fight, love the Spirit, and, most importantly, love themselves. Stephanie Mitchem, describes Walker's definition as a "conduit for expression of what it means for black women to be women" and what it means for black women to be feminist.[13] Walker's definition captures the inclusive measures by which women are able to embrace the diversity of all people. Her definition claims that a womanist represents the African American feminist who fights for the natural rights and equality of all people. The focus extends beyond the female gender to include genders of all nationalities in a world that oppresses most people. Implicit in Walker's work is the understanding that feminists isolate themselves, whereas womanists do not—except periodically when it comes to women's health.[14] Furthermore, womanists understand that the civil rights movement will never be over; as long as they live, the fight for equality of all people—not just women—must continue for the sake of future generations. And, womanists acknowledge the call to fashion a blueprint for personal and communal survival. I believe it was this desire to be "committed to survival and wholeness" of all people which eventually motivated African American women, who were Christian theologians and Christian ethicists, to merge Walker's womanist strategies with their theological and ethical understanding of Christianity.

The Genesis of Womanist Theology

Womanist theology developed out of the dissatisfaction with feminist theology, which neglected to look at issues of race and class, and black liberation theology (and black preaching), which neglected to consider the issue of gender.[15] Similarly, Valerie Bridgeman claims, "womanist work began as a protest to the realities that North American feminism did not attend to issues of race and class and that North American liberation theologies (especially done by black men) did not attend to gender. In this 'in-between' space, womanist thought arose and found its voice."[16] African American women needed a theology that would address and confront all of the sins that oppressed them and the black community. In 1985, womanist theology emerged as a methodological perspective of religious scholars. In the American Academy of Religion, Katie Geneva Cannon, Jacquelyn Grant, and Delores Williams are recognized as the founders of womanist theology.[17] These three women questioned what Christianity has to say to oppression. Together, they "discovered that economic exploitation, discrimination, racism, sexism, and segregation require African American women to construct their own set of values and virtues that will allow them to conduct themselves with moral integrity in the midst of suffering. As a result, they began to follow in the footsteps of Walker by not letting society define who they are; and so, they redefined themselves within their own theological understanding of Christianity."[18]

The Relationship to Feminism and Feminist Theology

Similar to womanists and womanist theologians, feminists and feminist theologians have also questioned the patriarchal understandings of

Christianity. Elizabeth Cady Stanton, leader of the nineteenth-century women's rights movement, was an activist for the natural rights of women. Stanton argues, "It is the inalienable right of all to be happy. It is the highest duty of all to seek those conditions in life. . . . If that be the heavenly order, is it not our duty to render earth as near to heaven as we may?"[19] Her philosophy of natural rights is centered on the idea that men and women are created equal, with equal rights and privileges. Stanton used both sacred and secular platforms to communicate her message of equality. Likewise, she also questioned the injustices against women in the Bible. Her way of combating religious patriarchy was to become the editor and chief contributing author to both volumes of *The Woman's Bible* (1895, 1898).[20] Additionally, feminist theologians, such as Elisabeth Schüssler Fiorenza, describe feminist theology as a hermeneutical approach that deconstructs the patriarchal paradigms of biblical interpretation and reconstructs those interpretations into non-oppressive paradigms.[21] This tradition recognizes that women's voices have been historically silenced in the church and in the Bible. Feminist theology recovers the biblical heritage of women by its revisionist aim. Feminist theology recovers the forgotten traditions about women. Scholars isolate various biblical texts to determine their proper translation and detect whether the interpretation has been influenced by a patriarchal worldview.

What differentiates a womanist approach from a feminist approach is that womanism is situated from the standpoint of the African American female experience whereas feminism has been traditionally situated from the standpoint of North American middle-class white women. Feminists have historically appropriated their agenda onto African American women, which essentially allows them to maintain power over black women by silencing the voices of black women. Delores Williams argues that "womanist theology also critiques white feminist participation in the perpetuation of white supremacy, which continues to dehumanize black women. Yet, womanist theology is organically related to black male liberation theology and feminist theology in its various expression (including African women's, Mujerista, Jewish and Asian women's theology)."[22] In *White Women's Christ and Black Women's Jesus*, Jacquelyn Grant discusses the inadequacy of a white feminist Christology and suggests that "Christology must emerge out of the condition of the least" since Jesus located the Christ with the outcast—the least.[23] When we examine the hierarchy of our patriarchal society, African American women are at the bottom of the totem pole. We are considered the least, which is why "womanist theology attempts to help black women see, affirm and have confidence in the importance of their experience and faith for determining the character of the Christian religion in the African-American community."[24]

THE RISE OF WOMANISM

From a communication standpoint, the field of rhetoric recognizes a feminist criticism, but has yet to acknowledge a womanist criticism. Marsha Houston and Olga Idriss Davis are the first to expand the canonical world of language and rhetoric to include feminist and womanist discourse, thus providing a "new angle of vision." Their pioneering collection of essays analyzes African American women's communication, acknowledging black women as the voice of authority for our own history. Houston and Davis argue that by positioning the "intellectual traditions of African American women *at the center* of our analyses . . . produces an angle of vision on Black women's communication that is rare, if not wholly new, in communication studies" because it bears witness to the existence and vitality of a language that mainstream linguistics and communication studies have traditionally ignored, which theorizes experience.[25]

According to Davis, most traditional rhetorical theories reflect a patriarchal bias that values competition, control, and domination. She labels these types of rhetorical theories as rhetoric of patriarchy because they suggest that certain belief systems and experiences are adequate and significant while others are not. Thus, the public sphere (the rhetor's power over the audience) and private spheres (the distancing between the rhetor and the audience that casts the audience as other) are separate in this kind of rhetorical paradigm because the paradigm embraces both domination and control. Davis concurs with Frances Smith Foster that values of domination and control are antithetical to the cultural, intellectual, and rhetorical traditions of African American women.[26] She proposes a discourse of experience that "celebrates the construction of knowledge and meaning of African American women and situates rhetoric as a site of struggle for inclusion and survival. It emphasizes the ongoing interplay between Black women's oppression and Black women's activism within the matrix of domination as a response to human agency."[27] She echoes the words of Earnest Wrage, who argued in the late 1940s, "oratory is a repository of ideas" and she claims, along with Houston, that Wrage's argument

> supports a discourse of experience by illuminating how the power of ideas influences the liberatory dimension of human discourse. Offering a space to engage in the values of self-definition, change, and empowerment, a discourse of experience then, centers African American women's ethnic culture as the central organizing concept for theory and research.[28]

From a theological standpoint, there is not much information on womanist preaching. Various works will reference a "womanist hermeneutic and preaching in the black church," or "a womanist reading of (whatever biblical passage)," but rarely will scholarly work combine the words womanist and preaching together to clearly say womanist preaching.[29] Why are seminaries and divinity schools teaching Womanist Art, Literature, Media, Music, Musings, Theology, and Ethics but not producing material that justifies a womanist art of preaching?

Additionally, a few colleges have published womanist journals to further educate people on the importance of womanist thought. For example, University of Georgia's Institute for African-American Studies published four volumes of *Womanist Theory and Research* and Mills College currently publishes *The Womanist, Women of Color Journal*.

From a biblical studies standpoint, Renita Weems is considered one of the progenitors of womanist biblical criticism.[30] Her 1995 book, *Battered Love: Marriage, Sex, and Violence in the Hebrew Prophets*, examines the violence against women that is embedded in the Hebrew prophetic tradition with its use of metaphors and imagery that perpetuates biblical patriarchy and violence against those who are socially marginalized. Weems argues that by appealing to the metaphors of marriage, parenting, slavery, imperial status, and legal standing, the prophets were reinforcing four principles about the divine-human relationship between God and Israel. Those principles are as follows:

> First, the prophets insisted that the bond between God and Israel was that of a relationship. . . . Second, the prophets maintained that the relationship between deity and people was not an egalitarian one but was one of hierarchy and authority. . . . Third, the prophets argued in their use of these five metaphors that the relationship between God and Israel was marked by mutual obligations and mutual responsibilities, that both parties had tasks and responsibilities appropriate to their roles in the relationship, but that the burden of the relationship rested firmly on the shoulders of the subordinate partner. . . . Fourth, and finally, each prophet insisted that failure by the subordinate to fulfill her or his responsibility virtually guaranteed punishment, retribution, or discipline (depending on the metaphor): judges punished defendants; kings banished or executed servants; masters beat slaves; parents disciplined children; and husbands divorced or assaulted wives.[31]

Weems reveals the persuasive hold that certain metaphors and images have over our imagination that allowed the prophets to justify violence and exonerate themselves from any form of guilt. She mostly uses the marriage metaphor to demonstrate how evil becomes justified, which then incites sexist human behavior and violence against the marginalized.

AN OVERVIEW

If we follow in the footsteps of Cannon, Grant, and Williams to question what our religion has to say to our oppression, what happens when we realize that the oppressor is the black church? What can be said when the churches where we worship are intoxicated with patriarchal religious traditions and rhetoric? How can we turn to the church for affirmation, guidance, and strength if the messages that we hear from the pulpit only seem to liberate and affirm the humanity of our male counterparts? Where do we go to get the information on what strategies to use?

This book emerged from simply asking a featured guest preacher a question after she preached at my home church when I lived in Memphis, Tennessee. I asked Rev. Dr. Claudette Copeland if she is a womanist. She said that even though she does identify herself as a womanist, "[she does] not think it comes across clearly in [her] preaching."[32] As I listened, I began to wonder if she can identify as a womanist and yet have difficulty projecting womanist rhetoric in the preaching moment, who is to say that other womanists do not share this same struggle? Her response is what prompted me to investigate the rhetoric of womanist preaching; and because I am an ordained minister of the gospel in the Christian Church (Disciples of Christ), my research reflects a Christian prism of womanist theological public discourse.

The purpose of this book is to bring awareness to the rhetorical art form that exists in womanist preaching and womanist rhetoric because womanism has undoubtedly been under articulated within the academic disciplines. One reason could be that "since the beginning, the womanist frame has been applied more frequently than it has been written about. That is, more people have employed womanism than have described it."[33] In the past, people approached womanism intuitively rather than analytically which explains why womanist discourse is an important and unexplored emerging area of interest in a number of fields, including communication, theology, and preaching, but no significant body of work has been done that researches the verbal expressions of womanist thought. Most womanist scholarship focuses on theory, hermeneutics, methodology or praxis, but not discourse. However, as womanism evolves, womanists are becoming more analytical in their approach so it is time that we start describing how womanists approach rhetoric, thus the need to examine womanist discourse. My goal is to bring awareness for three reasons: (1) so that the academy and especially communication programs along with women's studies and women's history programs can understand and learn about a group of African American women that has been systematically ignored until the late twentieth century; (2) so that rhetoricians and preachers can develop a deeper understanding of how womanist preachers use womanist rhetorical strategies to move their audience to a particular end; and (3) so that audiences will clearly be able to recognize when they hear womanist preaching. The growing body of womanist work in other disciplines demands that womanist rhetoric be studied, identified, and codified.

In this book, I explore how womanist preaching attempts to transform/adapt the tenets of womanist thought to make it rhetorically viable in the church, along with what is gained and lost in womanist sermons. I have identified five women who are considered exemplars of womanist preaching and I analyze their sermons based on the four different categories or phrased tenets that Stacey Floyd-Thomas uses to represent Walker's four tenets of "womanism"—radical subjectivity, traditional communalism, redemptive self-love, and critical engagement—in her anthology, *Deeper Shades of Purple: Womanism in Religion and Society*—because these four phrases effectively describe the goal of its respective tenet. Radical subjectivity refers to the ways in which women have been able to subvert forced hegemonic identities of a racist-sexist-classist world. It is the "radicality" of affirming self and speaking truth to power in the face of formidable odds.[34] Traditional communalism speaks to the ways that cultural traditions have nurtured and supported black women on our individual and collective journey toward liberation, while at the same time calling us back to our foundational values.[35] Redemptive self-love means to unashamedly love self and stand up for self. Finally, critical engagement calls for a critical evaluation of society's cultural norms. This cultural critique engages major questions in a variety of disciplines and social contexts.[36] I apply Floyd-Thomas's conceptual framework to the art of preaching because she helps readers to comprehend what womanist "revolutionary acts of rebellion" look like, and then I use a close textual analysis to uncover what the preachers are actually doing in order to determine whether or not the sermons really do transform/adapt womanist thought.

Chapter 1, "The Emergence of Womanist Preaching," explores the problem with black preaching that led to the emergence of womanist preaching. This chapter lifts up the voices of Katie Cannon, Donna Allen, and Elaine Flake because they developed the hermeneutical and homiletical practices of womanist preaching. They created three womanist typologies to guide us as we write and preach womanist sermons. This chapter lays the foundation for womanist preaching as we currently know it.

Chapters 2 through 5 look at specific examples of womanist preaching that reflect the four different categories that Floyd-Thomas uses to represent the tenets of womanism as described by Alice Walker. Although womanist preaching does not have to address women's issues, all five of the sermons considered in this project specifically focus on women and the scriptures are taken from different versions of the Bible depending on the preacher. Each chapter begins by defining its womanist tenet, followed by a close reading of a sermon, then, a discussion about the major womanist characteristics that the preacher evokes, afterward, I juxtapose the key rhetorical strategies with one of the previous sermons. This critical textual analysis will help me to uncover what rhetorical strategies the preachers are using and to determine what rhetorical patterns, if any, may be necessary in sermons that attempt to fight against oppressive forces. This type of investigation will also reveal how the sermons function, how sermons raise audience awareness, the methods by which sermons are able to transform the beliefs and behaviors of the audience, and what is gained or lost in adapting the tenets of womanist thought to the preaching moment. Additionally, a close textual analysis will allow me to understand how preachers train their audience as well as how audiences know whether or not they are hearing a womanist message.

Chapter 2, "Radical Subjectivity," examines Elaine Flake's sermon, "The Power of Enough," and Gina Stewart's sermon, "Enough Is Enough!" to understand what rhetorical strategies are necessary when a preacher needs to encourage women on their journey toward identity formation, self-love, and self-worth, to make revolutionary changes regarding their current situations. Flake is the co-pastor of the Greater Allen AME Cathedral with her husband, Floyd Flake, and co-founder of the Allen Christian School in Jamaica, New York. Her sermon demonstrates radical subjectivity because it addresses the course of action that a woman had to take in order to affirm herself. Likewise, Stewart, who is the senior pastor of Christ Missionary Baptist Church in Memphis, Tennessee, also demonstrates radical subjectivity and uses the same scripture as Flake. Since both preachers use the same text, I have included both of their sermons to help me to do a comparative analysis that explains the key methodologies used by the preachers and identifies the patterns that exist in radical subjectivity sermons.

Chapter 3, "Traditional Communalism," examines how Cheryl Kirk-Duggan's sermon, "Women of the Cloth" is used to pass down cultural knowledge from one generation to the next. In other words, how do preachers privilege knowledge and what rhetorical strategies are necessary when a preacher needs to protect, nurture, sustain, liberate, reunite or even call people back to their original values while bringing a community together on a particular issue? Cheryl Kirk-Duggan is a professor of Theology and Women's Studies, as well as the director of Women's Studies at Shaw University Divinity School in Raleigh, North Carolina. Her sermon demonstrates traditional communalism by addressing the skewed traditions and circumstances that tend to cripple women in ministry and the need for discernment in recognizing the crippling spirits, while at the same time calling us back to our freedom in Christ Jesus. I juxtapose the traditional communalism sermon with the radical subjectivity sermons to discover the differences between the two forms of womanist preaching.

Chapter 4, "Redemptive Self-Love," examines Melva L. Sampson's sermon, "Hell No!" in an effort to understand what Walker means when she says that we are to love ourselves *regardless*. As we will see in this sermon, regardless does not come without a price. Sampson helps us recognize what rhetorical strategies are necessary for a preacher who needs to confront commonly held stereotypes. Sampson is a PhD graduate from Candler School of Theology at Emory University in Atlanta, Georgia. She is an Assistant Professor of Preaching and Practical Theology at Wake Forest School of Divinity in Winston-Salem, North Carolina and serves as an ordained elder in the Presbyterian Church. Her sermon, "Hell No!" demonstrates redemptive self-love because it expresses the courage of a woman who refused to become objectified by her husband. My comparative analysis establishes a differentiation between redemptive self-love sermons and radical subjectivity sermons.

Chapter 5, "Critical Engagement," examines Claudette Copeland's sermon, "What Shall We Do for Our Sister?" to understand how womanist preachers also function as cultural critics and how they engage major questions in multiple disciplines and social contexts. Copeland is co-pastor and co-founder of New Creation Christian Fellowship in San Antonio, Texas, with her husband, Bishop David M. Copeland. She is also the founder and president of Destiny Ministries, a national and international ministry that empowers women and young girls. Her sermon demonstrates critical engagement because it addresses the cultural misconception that breast cancer only affects the person (or woman) who has it. Copeland explains that breast cancer affects everyone. The effects of the disease do not discriminate; everyone is joined together in the struggle against cancer. Additionally, I juxtapose the critical engagement sermon with the traditional communalism sermon to help us differentiate between the rhetorical strategies used in both forms of preaching.

Chapter 6, "Conclusions about Womanist Preaching and Womanist Rhetoric," serves as a three-part conclusion by (1) explaining what we learn about womanist preaching; (2) revealing the four rhetorical models of womanist preaching that diagram the various rhetorical strategies, sermonic functions, and methodological approaches used by Flake, Stewart, Kirk-Duggan, Sampson, and Copeland; and (3) uncovering what we learn about womanist rhetoric. The first section discusses who can be a womanist and voices which side I fall on in the essentialism versus particularity debate. I also talk about who God is in womanist preaching, how cultural artifacts and personal narratives become sacred texts, who the sermons address, what is gained or lost in womanist preaching, how womanist preaching goes unnoticed, and general womanist preaching characteristics by expanding the general womanist typology. The second section unveils the four rhetorical models that I developed to reflect radical subjectivity sermons, traditional communalism sermons, redemptive self-love sermons, and critical engagement sermons. Each of these models explain what rhetorical strategies were used, the purpose of those strategies, and offer an example from the sermon used in the case study. The last section synthesizes what we learn about womanist rhetoric and discusses the topics or forms of oppression that still need to be explored. In the end, people will ask who can be a womanist preacher and do race, gender, and religion matter? By definition, Alice Walker's womanism requires essentialism but the broader understanding of womanism in the religious academy leaves room to argue that race, gender, and religion are not determining factors, which means that the determinant must be in the discourse.

Appendices A–E offer a print version of all five sermons by the five womanist preachers and Appendix F houses all four rhetorical models together. Appendix A, "The Power of Enough," by Elaine M. Flake is used as one of two rhetorical artifacts in chapter 2. Appendix B, "Enough is Enough!" by Gina Stewart serves as the second rhetorical artifact. Appendix C, "Women of the Cloth," is a transcript of Cheryl Kirk-Duggan's sermon that is used as the rhetorical artifact for chapter 3. Appendix D, "Hell No!" by Melva Sampson is used as the rhetorical artifact in chapter 4. Appendix E, "What Shall We Do for Our Sister?" is a transcript of Claudette Copeland's sermon that is used as the rhetorical artifact for chapter 5. Finally, Appendix F shows the four rhetorical models: radical subjectivity, traditional communalism, redemptive self-love, and critical engagement.

NOTES

1. Patricia Hill Collins, *Black Feminist Thought: Knowledge, Consciousness, and the Politics of Empowerment* (New York: Routledge, 2000), 1.

2. Alice Walker, *In Search of Our Mother's Gardens: Womanist Prose* (Orlando: Harcourt Inc., 1983), 124–125.

3. Ibid., 128–129.

4. Kimberly P. Johnson, "Womanism," in *The Wiley Blackwell Encyclopedia of Gender and Sexuality Studies*, ed. Nancy A. Naples (Oxford: John Wiley & Sons, Ltd., 2016), 1; see also Walker, 125–126.

5. Elizabeth V. Spelman, *Inessential Woman: Problems of Exclusion in Feminist Thought* (Boston: Beacon Press, 1988), 11.

6. Walker, *In Search of Our Mother's Gardens*, 321; See also Johnson, "Womanism," 1–3.

7. Johnson, "Womanism," 1.

8. bell hooks, *Ain't I A Woman: Black Women and Feminism* (Boston: South End Press, 1981), 3.

9. Ibid.

10. Johnson, "Womanism," 1.

11. Audre Lorde, "The Uses of Anger: Women Responding to Racism," in *Sister Outsider: Essays and Speeches* (Berkeley, The Crossing Press, 1984), 129.

12. Walker, *In Search of Our Mother's Gardens*, xi–xii.

13. Stephanie Y. Mitchem, *Introducing Womanist Theology* (Maryknoll: Orbis Books, 2002), 55.

14. Walker, *In Search of Our Mother's Gardens*, 81.

15. Elaine Flake, *God in Her Midst: Preaching Healing to Wounded Women* (Valley Forge: Judson Press, 2007), xiv.

16. Valerie Bridgeman, "Womanist Criticism" in *The Oxford Encyclopedia of the Bible and Gender Studies*, Vol. 2 (New York. Oxford University Press, 2014), 432.

17. Stacey M. Floyd-Thomas (ed.), *Deeper Shades of Purple: Womanism in Religion and Society* (New York: New York University Press, 2006), 4.

18. Johnson, "Womanism," 2.

19. Elizabeth Cady Stanton, "National Woman's Rights Convention Debate, New York City, 1860," in *Man Cannot Speak for Her: Key Texts of the Early Feminists*, Volume II, ed. Karlyn Kohrs Campbell (New York: Praeger, 1989), 192.

20. Elizabeth Cady Stanton, *The Woman's Bible* (New York: European Publishing Company, 1895–1898); see also, Karlyn Kohrs Campbell, *Man Cannot Speak for Her: Key Texts of the Early Feminists*, Volume II (New York: Praeger, 1989).

21. Elisabeth Schüssler Fiorenza, *But She Said: Feminist Practices of Biblical Interpretation* (Boston: Beacon Press, 1992), 20.

22. Delores S. Williams, *Sisters in the Wilderness: The Challenge of Womanist God—Talk* (Maryknoll: Orbis Books, 1993), XV.

23. Jacquelyn Grant, *White Women's Christ and Black Women's Jesus: Feminist Christology and Womanist Response* (Atlanta: Scholars Press 1989), 6.

24. Williams, *Sisters in the Wilderness*, XV.

25. Marsha Houston and Olga Idriss Davis, *Centering Ourselves: African American Feminist and Womanist Studies of Discourse* (New Jersey: Hampton Press Inc., 2002), 7.

26. Ibid., 38; see also Francis Smith Foster, *Written by herself: Literary production by African American Women, 1746–1892* (Bloomington: Indiana University Press).

27. Ibid.

28. Ibid.

29. I found only two books, three chapters, and two articles that solely address womanist preaching or a womanist prophetic voice. Donna E. Allen, *Toward a Womanist Homiletic: Katie Cannon, Alice Walker, and Emancipatory Proclamation* (New York: Peter Lang, 2013); Elaine Flake, *God in Her Midst: Preaching Healing to Wounded Women* (Valley Forge: Judson Press, 2007); Katie Geneva Cannon, "Womanist Interpretation and Preaching in the Black Church," in *Searching the Scriptures: A Feminist Introduction 1*, ed. Elizabeth Schüssler Fiorenza (New York: Crossroads, 1993), 326–337; Katie Cannon, "Womanist Interpretation and Preaching in the Black Church," in *Katie's Canon: Womanism and the Soul of the Black Community* (New York: Continuum, 1996), 69–76; Emilie M. Townes, "Ethics as an Art of Doing the Work Our Souls Must Have," in *The Arts of Ministry: Feminist-Womanist Approaches*, ed. Christie Cozad Neuger (Louisville: Westminister John Knox Press, 1996), 143–161; Renita Weems, "How Will Our Preaching Be Remembered? A Challenge to See the Bible from a Woman's Perspective," in *The African American Pulpit 9*, no. 3 (Summer 2006): 26–29; Teresa Fry Brown, "A Womanist Model for

Proclamation of the Good News," The African American Lectionary, http://www.
theafricanamericanlectionary.org/PopupCulturalAid.asp?LRID=73 (accessed April
24, 2010).

30. Bridgeman, "Womanist Criticism," 432.

31. Renita Weems, *Battered Love: Marriage, Sex, and Violence in the Hebrew
Prophets* (Minneapolis: Fortress Press, 1995), 17–18.

32. A personal conversation with Claudette Copeland on October 7, 2007, at the
Madison Hotel, Memphis, Tennessee.

33. Layli Phillips, *The Womanist Reader* (New York: Routledge, 2006), xxi.

34. Stacey M. Floyd-Thomas (ed.), *Deeper Shades of Purple*, 8

35. Ibid., 9.

36. Ibid., 10.

Chapter 1

The Emergence of Womanist Preaching

The Problem with Black Preaching

> While "black preaching" has traditionally demonstrated a
> commitment to the eradication of sin and the liberation of the
> African American community from racism, social injustice, and
> economic oppression, by and large, it has not included elements
> that are sensitive to the experiences of African American women. If
> anything, preaching in the black church has tended to include biblical
> interpretations that have robbed women of their freedom and authentic
> personhood. Indeed, some have accommodated, even perpetuated,
> African American women's oppression and sense of woundedness.[1]

Womanism has just recently begun to question the role of preaching in the
black church. In its questioning, it developed a connection between womanist
theology and black preaching, which has now led toward what can be called,
womanist preaching. However, I find it necessary to first explain this connection to black preaching since I have already made clear its connection to
feminist theology.

Black preaching emerged out of the invisible church, during slavery, in the
1600s. This religious institution represented the only means by which blacks
could exercise leadership and power. Both the role of the preacher and the
act of preaching were held in highest regard and preaching became the tool
that enslaved black leaders used to influence their fellow laborers.[2] This tool
was used, and continues to be used, to exalt "the word of God above all other
authorities."[3] Cannon claims,

> Black preaching is a running commentary on scripture passages, showing how
> the Bible is an infinite resource that provides hearers with ways in word and
> deed for overcoming oppressive situations. . . .

. . . The sermon is a combination of serious exegesis and imaginative elabora-
tion of the stories in the Pentateuch, the sayings in wisdom literature, the prophetic writings, and the New Testament. It is an unhampered play of theological
fantasy and at the same time an acknowledgment of the cultural maturity and
religious sophistication of traditional themes.[4]

The black preacher mediates between God and the congregation in order to
instruct the listeners on how to interpret, define, and solve life's problems.
Grant argues, "How can a Black minister preach in a way which advocates
St. Paul's dictum concerning women while ignoring or repudiating his dictum
concerning slaves? Many Black women are enraged as they listen to 'liberated'
Black men speak about the 'place of women' in words and phrases similar to
those of the very White oppressors they condemn."[5] James H. Cone admits,
"The difficulty that black male ministers have in supporting the equality of
women in the church and society stems partly from the lack of a clear liberation criterion rooted in the gospel and in the present struggles of oppressed
people. . . . It is truly amazing that many black male ministers, young and old,
can hear the message of liberation in the gospel when related to racism but
remain deaf to a similar message in the context of sexism."[6] The problem that
African American women have found with black preaching is that the black
preaching tradition has not taken seriously the sin of sexism. Elaine Flake suggests that black preaching has in fact perpetuated women's oppression by its
use of biblical interpretations that rob women of their freedom and authentic
personhood.[7]

THE EMERGENCE OF WOMANIST PREACHING

From a homiletical standpoint, three women have examined the characteristics of womanist preaching: Katie Cannon, Donna Allen, and Elaine Flake.
Cannon's work represents the first attempt of systematically identifying
womanist interpretive strategies that are necessary for the preaching moment.
She created a womanist hermeneutic for preaching that focuses on the arguments, or what Aristotle calls *logos*, also known as logical appeals, which
represents the rational arguments that a speaker invents to prove, or at least
appear to prove, the speaker's position.[8] Allen even claims that Cannon is
mostly concerned with the logos—the words, content, and reasoning—of
black preaching because Cannon focuses on the interpretative strategies of
a womanist hermeneutic that can both challenge and uncover the religious
patriarchy that exists in black preaching.[9] Cannon argues that "the essential
task of a womanist hermeneutic consists in analyzing how black sermonic
texts 'participate in creating or sustaining oppressive or liberating theoethical
values and sociopolitical practices.'"[10]

Katie Cannon. According to Cannon, this genre of sacred rhetoric "requires sacred orators to be responsive to the emotional, political, psychic, and intellectual implications of our message. . . . Therefore, we must identify the qualities of an 'ideal' Black churchwoman and a 'realized' Christian woman."[11] A womanist hermeneutic "challenges conventional biblical interpretations that characterize African American Women as 'sin-bringing Eve,' 'wilderness-whimpering Hagar,' 'henpecking Jezebel,' 'whoring Gomer,' 'prostituting Mary Magdalene,' and 'conspiring Sapphira.' . . . Eliminating the negative and derogatory female portraiture in Black preaching" by exposing the "phallocentric" concepts embedded in black preaching and "encouraging an ethic of resistance."[12] Womanist preachers have to be "responsive to the emotional, political, psychic, and intellectual implication of our message" and maintain "a balanced tension between the accuracy of the spoken word—organization, language, fluidity, and style—and the expressed political aim of our sermonic content"[13] Cannon claims, that a womanist hermeneutical lens places the periscope in the real-life cultural context that produced it.[14] Through this examination of the rhetorical situation, the preacher must educate the audience by providing "visions of liberation" that transcend oppression. The preacher can use imagery to invite the listeners to participate in dismantling patriarchy by guiding them on how to resist being marginalized.[15] A womanist hermeneutic also "removes men from the 'normative' center and women from the margins."[16]

Donna Allen. Allen uses Cannon's womanist hermeneutical methodology outlined in "Roundtable Discussion: Christian Ethics and Theology in Womanist Perspective" and "Womanist Interpretation and Preaching in the Black Church," in *Katie's Canon*, as her method for critiquing sermons. She claims that "Cannon's womanist critique of Black sacred rhetoric is an attempt to understand and improve the use of labels in the Black preaching tradition."[17] She notes, on several different occasions, that Cannon's womanist typology is influenced by the convergence of Elisabeth Schüssler Fiorenza's feminist hermeneutical approach and Isaac R. Clark's work on black preaching, but that Cannon adds emphasis to race and class in order to formulate a womanist interpretation.

According to Allen, The following list identifies Cannon's central homiletical concerns for a womanist analysis:

1. Eliminate "negative and derogatory female" images. Identify and refute the "androcentric, phallocentric . . . stereotypes that are dehumanizing, debilitating, and prejudicial to African-American women."
2. Address the marginalization of women in the biblical text and context. "A Womanist hermeneutic seeks to place sermonic texts in the real-life context of the culture that produced them. . . . Images used throughout the

sermon can invite the congregation to share in dismantling patriarchy," and create an emancipatory response.

3. Eliminate discriminatory language and the marginalizing of women characters in the sermon that in the biblical text are central figures. To challenge the sermonic retelling of the biblical story in such a manner that women are inferior to men. "What happens to the African-American female children when Black preachers use the Bible to attribute marvelous happenings and unusual circumstances to an all-male cast of characters?"

4. Monitor the impact of images to empower women and create "an ethic of resistance" to oppression. "As Womanist theologians, what can we do to counter the negative real-world consequences of sexist wording that brothers and sisters propagate in the guise of Christian piety and virtue?"

5. Womanist hermeneutic considers the sociocultural context of the preaching event. Examine the words of the preacher and the context of the community. What are the leadership roles of women within the church community? "This practice removes men from the normative center and women from the margins."

6. African American clergywomen must have praxis of resistance. The faith communities' response to the "proclaimed word" is the emancipatory praxis.[18]

Cannon's first item serves as an example of how one might refute the masculine stereotypes and demeaning images of women that seem to dominate both the biblical text and black preaching. Cannon's second point invites preachers to insert women into the biblical text as a means of moving women from the fringes of society into the center of mainstream society by giving women a voice and a presence in the Bible. Cannon's third matter explains how one would go about reconstructing the biblical text to retell the story in a manner that affirms women. Cannon's fourth item emphasizes that the preacher must guard against the negative images of the text and then counter those images with empowering images. Cannon's fifth point serves as a necessary reminder that it is the responsibility of preachers not only to question and dismantle the patriarchal and oppressive forces that exist in the world, but also to question and dismantle those same oppressions that exist within their own religious institution. Finally, Cannon's last item explains that the proclaimed message represents an emancipatory praxis because it is a discursive act of resistance and liberation. Cannon explicates this point by arguing that it is the preacher's responsibility to teach their congregation how to trace out the liberating strategies of a sermon that have the ability to transform oppression.[19] In other words, the preacher must help the listeners recognize the transformative aspect, or rhetorical agency,[20] of the preached message. Rhetorical agency is the power that guides readers or listeners to a particular end. Therefore, the rhetorical agency of the preached message lies in the prophetic words, gestures, and the overall performance of the sermon.

Although Allen does not use the terminology of rhetorical agency, she does allude to what rhetorical agency looks like in black preaching when she discusses the communal act of preaching. Allen claims that Cannon's rhetorical criticism of African American preaching suggests that more critical dialogue is needed between the preacher and the congregation. The preaching moment is a dialogue that takes place between the preacher and the congregation.[21] Preaching has a rhetorical agency that makes it communal and participatory, invented, artistic, effected through change, and as Karlyn Kohrs Campbell says, "perverse" at the same time. Or, as Cannon says, "preaching . . . is both sacred and profane, active and passive, life-giving and death-dealing."[22] The preaching event is a time of shared reflection where the preacher, the congregation, tradition, language, and culture all work together to shape and place limitations on "new meaning." The preacher speaks not as the originator of the message, but as the point of articulation or presumed mouthpiece for God. The preacher has to negotiate, during delivery, all of the available means of persuasion and has to discriminate when to use logical appeal, emotional appeal, and ethical appeal. Then, the words that are conveyed through the message have the power to guide people toward a particular end, a particular understanding or belief. Finally, preaching becomes perverted when it demeans, belittles, or oppresses any person or group of people.

At the same time Allen praises Cannon's work toward identifying a womanist homiletic, Allen also identifies some problems. Allen claims that Cannon's womanist critique is not exhaustive because it only focuses on imagery, biblical interpretation, and the emancipatory praxis of the preached message as they relate to women. Furthermore, Allen points out that Cannon only examines the linguistic violence—the derogatory words that demean women—used in sacred rhetoric, whereas Clarice Martin explores the linguistic sexism—the instances in the Bible where women were removed from the text. Therefore, Allen proposes that a rigorous womanist critique would call for a combination of both Cannon's and Martin's hermeneutical paradigms.

Allen believes that a womanist homiletic must reflect all three of the Aristotelian proofs: logos, ethos, and pathos, whereas Cannon only focuses on logos. Allen links logos, pathos, and ethos to Walker's womanist definition and she uses this connection to help her expand Cannon's womanist heuristic in order to develop her own womanist preaching typology. In terms of logos, Allen makes some rhetorical clarifications by inserting into her typology that womanist rhetoric must challenge heterosexism and homophobia along with all of the constructs that inform human sexuality.[23] Allen also explicitly challenges womanists to use inclusive language when discussing the Trinity by using non-gendered or gender-inclusive terms in their God talk.

In regard to pathos, Allen notes that pathos is not only created verbally, it can be created through performance by using gestures, dance, or movement as a way to embody the sermon. She claims that effective pathos in preaching makes it hard for the congregation to resist connecting with the sermon and that this connection is what leads to an emancipatory response from the congregants to the preached Word.

In relation to ethos, Allen recognizes that both internal and external factors help to create one's credibility. So, when it comes to preaching, the rhetoric and knowledge of the preacher yield internal ethos, while the preacher's credentials, ministerial position, popularity, celebrity status, and the actual invitation extended by senior pastors to preach in their pulpit (for those preaching in a pulpit that is not their own) all contribute to the preacher's external ethos. Allen also acknowledges that ethos can be created through kinesthesia (movement) and shamanism (embodiment). According to Allen, a person who creates ethos through movement would be called a "conjurer" because conjurers magically transform reality through ritual speech and action. Likewise, a person who creates ethos through embodiment would be called a "shaman" because a shaman has the ability to embody the emotional and social problems of the people.[24] Together, Allen uses these findings, along with the womanist rhetorical analysis of Cannon and Walker's definition of womanism, to create her own typology of an emancipatory praxis for womanist preaching:

1. Equip listeners with a systematic process to critically engage the rhetoric of the sermon;
2. The use of non-gendered or gender-inclusive language in our God talk;
3. A non-gendered language for traditional Trinitarian language;
4. An emphasis on the humanity of Christ while not focusing on the gender of Jesus;
5. The adopting of a rhetorical stance to make an effective use of Christian rhetoric;
6. The effective use of multisensory and kinesthetic communication;
7. The Divine presence manifested in shamanistic and conjuring oratory that is performed identity, conflict resolution, and homeopathic;
8. An atonement theology that takes seriously an African American historical experience of sexual exploitation and forced surrogacy that, therefore, affirms the ministerial vision of Jesus' life as redemptive and not his surrogacy in crucifixion; and
9. The dismantling of heterosexism and homophobia; inclusive of an affirmation of the diversity of human sexuality.[25]

For Allen, a womanist homiletic considers both the rhetorical and performative aspects of womanist preaching, which is evidenced in her sermonic analyses of Prathia Hall, a self-proclaimed womanist theologian and ethicist. Even though Allen makes the claim that she is not performing an Aristotelian analysis of Hall's sermons, this is exactly what she does throughout her book. The only difference is that she moves beyond the terminology of artistic proofs to discuss elements of association, disassociation, bringing into view, kinesthesia, conjuration, and shamanism.[26] Allen defines logos as "the words, the content, and the line of reasoning in proclamation"; pathos as "the emotional identifications wrought in preaching"; and ethos as "the embodied communication that devolves from the very person and presence of the preacher."[27] Although she later abandons the logos, ethos, pathos terminology, all of her arguments either explicitly or implicitly point back to one of these three forms of artistic proofs.

Elaine Flake. Flake attempts to develop a more holistic womanist typology by not only challenging the biblical text, but also challenging the oppressive practices of the black church. She argues from the standpoint of a pastor, that black preaching has perpetuated women's oppression by its use of biblical interpretations that rob women of their freedom and authentic personhood.[28] She says, "There can be no real discussion of the eradication of oppression for African Americans without also admitting that one of the oppressors of African American women is the African American Church."[29] She claims, since womanist theology came about due to the dissatisfaction of feminist and black liberation, "If [womanist] preaching is to truly reach the hearts, minds, and souls of African American women, preachers must employ an analysis of Scripture that reconstructs the Word of God in ways that are liberating to women as well as men and that reflects the totality of the African American experience."[30] This type of preaching must not only uncover the various sins of oppression, but also require the preacher to equip the congregation with spiritual and pragmatic strategies that will allow them to dismantle those oppressive forces as well as allow them to heal.[31]

According to Flake, womanist preaching has ten important characteristics. Preaching to heal requires the preacher to:

1. Affirm
2. Show sensitivity
3. Honor tradition
4. Liberate
5. Present Jesus as an Advocate for women
6. Acknowledge African ancestry
7. Avoid male-bashing
8. Tell the truth
9. Inspire action
10. Think outside the box[32]

Flake's typology is a combination of hermeneutical and practical concerns. The first six suggestions address an interpretive methodology and the last three refer to practical considerations. Flake urges womanist preachers to avoid male-bashing because the devaluation of one human being over another is anti-thetical to womanist preaching.[33] While discouraging "bashing," she encourages womanists to tell the truth about some black men in their sermons because womanist preaching mandates that we speak truth to oppressive power structures, even when they come from the abusive and misogynist behavior of our male counterparts.[34] Furthermore, like Allen and Cannon, she wants preachers to inspire action. She claims that womanist preaching is corrective in the fact that it inspires a change of behavior along with a new way of thinking.[35] Finally, she pushes womanist preachers to think outside the box because the work it takes to eradicate African American women's oppression obligates preachers to renew their own minds.[36] Preachers cannot get caught up in conventional interpretations if their task is to truly liberate all oppressed people.

Even though Flake clearly outlines that her womanist preaching typology only has ten characteristics, I believe she should have used her six points from the "epilogue" of her book to make her list more complete—complete in the sense that her list fully matches the claims that she makes in her book. Based on Flake's arguments, her womanist preaching typology should reflect the following:

1. Affirm
2. Show sensitivity
3. Honor tradition
4. Liberate
5. Present Jesus as an Advocate for women
6. Acknowledge African ancestry
7. Avoid male-bashing
8. Tell the truth
9. Inspire action
10. Think outside the box
11. Give women a positive presence in the Bible
12. Identify all forms of oppression in the Bible, our religious practices and the larger community
13. Address violence on systematic levels
14. Employ methodologies that identify toxic relationships
15. All sermons do not need to address the issues of women
16. Convey the promise of hope, joy, and wholeness[37]

Flake needs to include items eleven through sixteen because these are impor-tant claims that give preachers, along with her readers, a clearer understanding of what constitutes womanist preaching. She asserts, "It is the responsibility of womanist theologians to . . . find in the Bible a divine hope and promise that consistently affirm[s] African American women's humanity and gives them a positive presence in the text."[38] Her typology mentions affirmation, but it neglects to address, in items one through ten, this need to give women a positive presence in the Bible. Next, she stresses that preachers, pastors, and academicians need to recognize the oppressive forces that reside in our own culture, politics, and churches.[39] Flake maintains the necessity not just to critique the Bible or the theological language of sermons, but to examine the culture that we live in, our political realities, as well as our church traditions and practices. Therefore, this needs to be reflected in her typology. She also emphasizes that oppressive structures such as gender inequality, rape, and racism along with other forms of violence have to be on the agenda within our own church walls and they must be addressed on systemic levels in order to bring forth healing to wounded individuals.[40] Additionally, Flake contends that preachers must inspire people to identify toxic relationships, attitudes, and behaviors.[41] Womanist preaching must not only inspire people to action through transformation, but also carry the burden of helping people to recognize their own toxic relationships, attitudes, and behaviors. Finally, she explicitly sets the record straight by explaining that womanist preaching is not required to always deal with "women's issues," or even a female biblical character for that matter, but they must convey a message of hope, joy, and wholeness, while ushering in a Divine encounter.[42] This critique is vital because all womanist sermons do not have to be about women, nor does the central character in the biblical text have to be a woman, which is why it is detrimental to have some message of hope, joy, and wholeness because if the sermon is not going to specifically bring wholeness to a particular woman with a certain issue, it must at least bring wholeness to the larger community of believers.

NOTES

1. Elaine Flake, *God in Her Midst: Preaching Healing to Wounded Women* (Valley Forge: Judson Press, 2007), xiii–xiv.

2. Katie Cannon, *Katie's Canon: Womanism and the Soul of the Black Community* (New York: Continuum, 1996), 115.

3. Ibid.

4. Ibid., 115–116.

5. Grant, "Black Theology and the Black Woman" in *Black Theology: A Documentary History, vol. 1 1966–1979*, eds. James H. Cone and Gayraud S. Wilmore (Maryknoll: Orbis Books, 1993), 326.

6. James H. Cone, *Speaking the Truth: Ecumenism, Liberation, and Black Theology* (Grand Rapids: Wm. B. Eerdmans Publishing, 1986), 150.

7. Elaine Flake, *God in Her Midst: Preaching Healing to Wounded Women* (Valley Forge: Judson Press, 2007), xiii.

8. George Kennedy, *The Art of Persuasion in Greece* (New Jersey: Princeton University, 1963), 97.

9. Donna E. Allen, *Toward a Womanist Homiletic: Katie Cannon, Alice Walker, and Emancipatory Proclamation* (New York: Peter Lang, 2013), 12–13.

10. Cannon, 114; see Elizabeth Schüssler Fiorenza, *Revelation: Vision of a Just World* (Minneapolis: Fortress Press, 1991), 9.

11. Cannon, 120.

12. Ibid., 114, 119.

13. Ibid., 120.

14. Ibid., 121.

15. Ibid.

16. Ibid.

17. Allen, 8.

18. Allen, 17.

19. Cannon, 121.

20. Karlyn Kohrs Campbell defines rhetorical agency through a five-part series of propositions. She claims that agency "(1) is communal and participatory, hence, both constituted and constrained by externals that are material and symbolic; (2) is 'invented' by authors who are points of articulation; (3) emerges in artistry or craft; (4) is effected through form; and (5) is perverse, that is, inherent, protean, ambiguous, open to reversal." See Karlyn Kohrs Campbell, "Agency: Promiscuous and Protean," paper presented at the Alliance of Rhetoric Societies 2003 Conference, 3.

21. Allen, 12.

22. Cannon, 120.

23. Allen, 23.

24. Ibid., 36.

25. Ibid., 82.

26. *Association* rhetoric "put[s] together Christian understandings with images of lived experience"; *disassociation* rhetoric "employs familiar rhetorical systems, such as dialectic, antithesis, opposition, and at times, perhaps even charitable giggling [to emphasize our] peculiar double consciousness—a consciousness of being-saved and a consciousness of being-in-the-world"; and finally, *bringing into view* rhetoric brings attention "to understandings of God, of God's mysterious purposes, and of unseen wonders of grace in human lives" that all work to create pathos. See Allen, 29–30; see also David Buttrick, *Homiletic: Moves and Structures* (New York: Harcourt Brace & Company, 1983), 41–42.

27. Ibid., 7.

28. Elaine Flake, *God in Her Midst: Preaching Healing to Wounded Women* (Valley Forge: Judson Press, 2007), xiii.

29. Ibid., vii.

30. Ibid., xiv.

31. Ibid., 12.

32. Ibid., 13–21.

33. Ibid., 18.
34. Ibid., 19.
35. Ibid., 20.
36. Ibid.
37. Ibid., 13–20, 91–93.
38. Flake, 91.
39. Ibid., 92.
40. Ibid.
41. Ibid.
42. Ibid., 93.

Chapter 2

Radical Subjectivity

Radical subjectivity sermons seek to liberate and lead people to a type of self-transformation—physically, spiritually, mentally, and/or emotionally—by re-imaging a victim into a victor. The preacher can rhetorically move a woman from being a victim of circumstance to being victorious over the situation once the moment of epiphany has been identified because an epiphany gives a woman profound insight and divine revelation that allows her to resist her current state of oppression. Radical subjectivity reflects the journey toward identity formation, self-love, and self-worth, along with a moment of epiphany that empowers a woman to escape her oppressive situation.

Radical Subjectivity, the term Stacey Floyd-Thomas uses to describe the first tenet of womanism, expresses a woman's ability to affirm her authentic self in the midst of oppression. I understand it as the journey toward identity formation, the journey toward self-love, and the journey toward valuing self because it represents the process in which identity is formed. It also speaks to the ways in which women are able to subvert domination. Floyd-Thomas defines it as a "process that emerges as Black females in the nascent phase of their identity development come to understand agency as the ability to defy a forced naiveté in an effort to influence the choices made in one's life and how conscientization incites resistance against marginality."[1] According to Floyd-Thomas, "the radicality of affirming the authentic self-hood lies in Black women's ability to speak truth to power even in the face of formidable odds."[2] Exercising the right to speak or speaking truth to power "says something about the power and value of authorizing one's own perspective. To be author of our own reality is to claim the value of our experience, to trust our ability to reason and reflect, and to accept ourselves as we really are."[3] Therefore, identity formation under the guise of radical subjectivity carries with it an acceptance of self, a love of self, and an affirmation of self that allows women to move from being a victim to being a victor through self-transformation. Radical subjectivity requires women to operate out of their own agency.

According to Katie Cannon, this first tenet of womanism challenges the "masterminds of intellectual imperialism" who classify the work of black women scholars in the theological academy as questionable, anecdotal evidence.[4] For her, radical subjectivity does not allow anecdotal evidence to be banished to the margins of religious knowledge. Radical subjectivity is the telling of our subjective truths. Carol Duncan argues that Walker's radicalism is rooted in her assessment of the womanishness quality—acting outside of what is considered normative gender behavior and challenging those behaviors that restrict social relationships.[5]

Similarly, Debra Mubashshir Majeed advocates a broadening of boundaries by challenging the ways in which womanism privileges Christianity. She argues that womanist discourse must encompass religious plurality. For Majeed, radical subjectivity is the emergence of a Muslim Womanist Philosophy that gives voice, expression, and legitimacy to the embodied experiences and knowledge of African American Muslim women.[6] Like Cannon, her form of radical subjectivity appears to be a resistance to silence or a refusal to be relegated to the margins of religious knowledge.

In the same way, Diana Hayes argues that black Catholic women suffer from a quadruple oppression of race, class, gender, and devout faith.[7] She confesses that she straddles in and out of the black community, the university/scholarly setting, and the Roman Catholic Church. She says women who challenge the teaching of the church are viewed as radical, sometimes as heretic, and never fully as authentically Catholic.[8] Her understanding of radical subjectivity appears to be reflected in her efforts to affirm self, authenticate self, and to legitimize her work as a black female professional by removing the masks of ignorance that covers the three communities that she finds herself in, and then by challenging those communities with a different perspective. According to Hayes, who views herself as an "outsider-within," black Catholic women enlighten the womanist dialogue by bringing images of black women (i.e., Hagar) who act counter-cultural to the dominant perspective.[9] Although Hagar was abused by her mistress and her master, she is a model of strength, perseverance, and love.[10] I believe the narratives of biblical characters who contradict the dominant perspective are stories that help describe the essence of Floyd-Thomas's term, radical subjectivity. Women who come face-to-face with patriarchy and other forms of oppression, who are able to reach deep within themselves in a manner that affirms self and then change their situation or at least change their perception of their situation demonstrate radical subjectivity and create agency.

When Alice Walker discusses the first tenet of her womanist definition, she explicitly states that a womanist is:

From womanish. (Opp. Of "girlish," i.e., frivolous, irresponsible, not serious.) A black feminist or feminist of color. From the black folk expression of mothers to female children, "You acting womanish," i.e., like a woman. Usually referring to outrageous, audacious, courageous or *willful* behavior. Wanting to know more and in greater depth than is considered "good" for one. Interested in grown-up doings. Acting grown up. Being grown up. Interchangeable with another black folk expression: "You trying to be grown." Responsible. In charge. *Serious.*[11]

This first tenet immediately qualifies who can fit into the womanist category by attaching race and color to the term "feminist." Next, we gain an understanding of womanist behavior. To be a womanist is to express "outrageous, audacious, courageous or willful behavior" and to be "responsible," "in charge," and "serious" at the same time. Here, Walker applies these characteristics to a girl who is "trying to be grown," which expands our understanding that womanism has a revelatory component that pushes girls/women to resist conforming to the dominant social structures. Ultimately, Walker's and Floyd-Thomas's perspectives on womanism are rooted in identity formation of young girls and women, and how one comes to understand and affirm her own ability to speak, think, and act on behalf of self.

RHETORICAL ANALYSIS OF ELAINE FLAKE'S SERMON, "THE POWER OF ENOUGH"

When the Lord saw that Leah was not loved, he opened her womb, but Rachel was barren. Leah became pregnant and gave birth to a son. She named him Reuben, for she said, "It is because the Lord has seen my misery. Surely my husband will love me now."

She conceived again, and when she gave birth to a son she said, "Because the Lord heard that I am not loved, he gave me this one too." So she named him Simeon.

Again she conceived, and when she gave birth to a son she said, "Now at last my husband will become attached to me, because I have borne him three sons." So he was named Levi.

She conceived again, and when she gave birth to a son she said, "This time I will Praise the Lord." So she named him Judah. Then she stopped having children.

Genesis 29:31–35, NIV

Elaine Flake's sermon, "The Power of Enough," was published in her book, *God in Her Midst: Preaching Healing to Wounded Women.* She has preached versions of this sermon at her home church, Greater Allen AME Cathedral, in Jamaica, New York, and at numerous women's conferences in the last fifteen years. When she delivered this sermon, which is approximately forty minutes, at Greater Allen AME Cathedral during one of the three Sunday morning services, she preached to an audience of about two thousand people, the majority of whom were African American men and women.

"The Power of Enough" is a sermon that celebrates a woman's ability to begin to love and value herself in a manner that enables her to move from being a victim to a victor. Flake demonstrates the necessity of self-transformation and the integral role it plays in helping us to defy a forced naiveté—a coercion into thinking that one deserves abuse, unfaithfulness, and even a loveless marriage. This sermon challenges us to learn how to love ourselves, to be honest with ourselves, to recognize when we have had enough, and to be proactive about our situation. Flake moves her audience to a state of maturity in realizing "Enough is enough!" so that they can defeat their oppressive forces.[12]

The title of the sermon comes from the movie, *Enough*, starring Jennifer Lopez. When asked, why she paired this film with the sermon, she said:

Because the woman was in an abusive situation and she needed to be freed for herself, she needed to be freed for her child. I just happened to have been watching that movie and I was so taken by that movie even much more than I was "What's Love Got to Do With It?" because to see that woman run, run, run, and every time that man found her. . . . And then I saw *Delores Claiborne* where she said, "An accident can be a wife's best friend." Just the fact that she ran and said, "Shoot, I'm not running anymore." That girl went and trained. And so, for me, that was like a woman taking charge of her life. . . .

She just had enough of trying to please this man and you know, coming to an understanding that it is what it is—I can't make him love me, but I can make me love me.[13]

Flake explained that she talks to so many women who are so bitter over divorce that they can't move on. So when she pairs the movie with the sermon and does an altar call at the end, she claims:

It's a very liberating experience because whether they've had enough of a teenager disrespecting them, or whether they've had enough of a grown son living with them and not carrying his load, or a daughter-in-law. You know, whatever enough is—a boss, or being abused on your job—but we all have to get to the point where we've had enough. And when you reach that point, which is what I say in my sermon, when you get to the point that you say, enough, that means that you have been empowered beyond measure. That empowers you. And it's not until you reach that point, then that's when your life begins to change.[14]

Her audience responds extremely well to this sermon every time she preaches it, which is why she continues to preach it at women's conferences and retreats all across the nation.

ANALYSIS

After providing the focal text, Genesis 29:35, "She conceived again and bore a son, and said, 'This time I will praise the Lord,'" Flake opens the sermon with her scene-by-scene replay of the movie. Lopez plays a character named Slim who falls victim to the domestic abuse of her husband. Flake strategically paints the picture of how Slim's storybook courtship, wedding, and honeymoon turned into a nightmare. She explains the cycle of abuse that consisted of beatings, cheating, repentance, and declarations of love. The more Slim's husband abuses her, the more he convinces her that she deserves his beatings and unfaithfulness.

Flake challenges the notion that domestic abuse is limited to physical abuse. In talking about Slim, she says, "Not only is this woman abused physically, but she is also abused verbally. Emotionally and mentally manipulated, she is constantly told: 'It's your fault. You deserve it. You make me have to hit you.'"[15] This simple act of naming the various aspects of abuse is a strategy that not only helps her listeners identify with the character, but also gives them insight so that they too may recognize if they are also victims of domestic violence.

As Flake begins to deconstruct this idea that married women deserve to be abused, she strategically uses language that will draw out value judgments from her listeners. When she builds the imagery of a fairytale wedding and marriage gone wrong, she intentionally groups words together that will create a positive and negative association with survival and developmental motives. Flake utilizes what Michael Osborn calls light-dark metaphors.[16] Flake uses the light-dark combinations of: (1) storybook (fairytale) with nightmare; and (2) marriage with prisoner to express the stark difference between where Slim's relationship with her husband started and where it ended. The relationship began as a storybook. It was a fairytale and the marriage started off being everything that Slim had hoped for, but then the marriage became a nightmare and the union that freely brought the two together had now become a union that had enslaved her causing her to be a prisoner in her own marriage. Both light-dark combinations symbolically represent Slim's past as light and her present as dark because the goal is to demonstrate that Slim needs

Table 2.1 Flake Rhetorical Tools

Rhetorical Tools	Purpose of Rhetorical Tools
Enthymematic identification	To create identification between the movie character and biblical character using same premise
Uses light-dark metaphors, and then the reversal—dark-light metaphors	To express the difference between where she started and ended. To emphasize the future that is in store
Names domestic violence and rejection	To confront the oppressive forces of power
Cause-effect relationships	To show that what happened to her (the abuse) has caused something to take place within her
Fight/war language and imagery	To show the extremes of the abuse and the perversion of the abuser
Linguistics	To show the tragedy of Leah's suffering embedded in the names of her children
Jacob metaphor	To help people identify their own oppressor
Embodiment	To create identification with the audience by expounding on what the biblical character possibly said about her situation

Table created by Kimberly P. Johnson.

to transform her future into a new form of light. Light-dark combinations are useful according to Michael Osborn "when speakers find it expedient to express an attitude of *inevitability* or *determinism* about the state of present affairs or the shape of the future. Change not simply *should have* occurred or *should* occur, but *had to* or *will* occur."[17] Hence, Slim's moment of radical subjectivity, or as Flake says, "change of attitude," happens when she decides that she has had enough abuse. It is in that moment that she begins to understand how to move from her dark and dreary present into a much brighter future. Flake's dichotomy between storybook (fairytale) and nightmare, and the dichotomy between marriage and prisoner build up to the overarching metaphor of Slim's struggle for survival in moving from victim to victor.

In addition to the light-dark metaphors, Flake uses war metaphors and verbs that coincide with the movie to help demonize the enemy—the husband—by visualizing the unthinkable. She discusses how Slim stages her "attack on him," how she "removes all of the guns in his arsenal," that it is either "crush or be crushed," and she describes the husband as a tormentor.[18] Then, Flake proceeds to mention that the time has come "for him to kill her" and that he is going to "bludgeon her to death."[19] All of these descriptions create an image that is in stark contrast to the victimized wife because the husband is unmistakably viewed as the abuser—the oppressive force that Slim must overcome.

At the end of the movie, Slim develops a plan to fight back in self-defense but her husband dies, by accident. So, Flake clarifies for her listeners:

> I'm not celebrating the death of the abuser; however, I do celebrate this woman's realization that she has to take charge of her messy and miserable life and find a better way to live. I celebrate the fact that when she decides that she has lived with violence, weakness, and unhappiness long enough, she reaches down into her untapped inner resources and finds a power that has been hidden from her by her circumstances.[20]

Although womanist preaching does not support male-bashing, celebrate violence, or liberate one group at the expense of another, the ending scene of the movie narrative appears to do so. I get the point that Flake is making about Slim taking charge of her life, but the movie narrative appears to overshadow Flake's self-empowerment message with an anti-womanist message that liberates one person at the expense of another, which is why Flake qualifies what she is celebrating. Unfortunately, with this movie selection, there is no way to get around unintentionally communicating that it is okay to liberate one at the expense of another. However, I know that she fundamentally believes and even argues in her book that the "devaluation of African American men or any human being in order to affirm and heal African American women is antithetical to womanist preaching."[21] Therefore, this part of her sermon reflects a point of difficulty that Flake encounters when preaching womanist sermons.

Moving beyond the point of difficulty, Flake seems to spiritualize the movie when she talks about Slim's transformation, in order to (1) emphasize the power of God at work when one says she has had enough, which also demonstrates the power of God at work during moments of radical subjectivity; (2) create a sense of identification between her audience and Slim; and (3) prophesy a message to all the women who identify with Slim. Here, Flake explains how Slim transforms from victim to victor—Slim's moment of radical subjectivity. It is in Slim's moment of desperation that "Everything that has happened *to* her finally causes something to happen *within* her." Flake orally emphasizes the words, "*to*" and "*within*" to highlight the cause-effect relationship between the abuse that Slim experienced and her ability to finally reach deep within herself to decide that she has had enough and that she can do better. As Flake goes on to explain Slim's inward change she says, "Something inside Slim makes her realize that if she does not overcome some inner weaknesses, she will never move out of her place of oppression. She is clear that her husband is not going to give up or change, so the only way she is going to be free requires her to change."[22] The radicality of being able to say, "Enough is enough," I'm not going to take this anymore and I'm not going to let him oppress me anymore because I deserve better is what makes this sermon an example of radical subjectivity—it represents the journey of a woman who gives herself permission to love and value self. This is radical because entirely too many African American women suffer from low self-esteem due to a lack of self-affirmation and self-love.

In the book, *Feminism is for Everybody*, bell hooks explains this point by discussing the devastating effects of sexism and how women had to unlearn self-hatred. She says:

> We all knew firsthand that we had been socialized as females by patriarchal thinking to see ourselves as inferior to men, to see ourselves as always and only in competition with one another for patriarchal approval, to look upon each other with jealousy, fear, and hatred. Sexist thinking made us judge each other without compassion and punish one another harshly. Feminist thinking helped us unlearn female self-hatred.[23]

When one has been socialized into practicing self-hatred, the idea of learning how to value one's self can be quite challenging. Likewise, when a woman is in an abusive relationship, the abuser conditions the woman to fear and she oftentimes begins to develop a warped image of herself.

If we look closer at Slim's transformation, we see more instances in which Flake spiritualizes the movie, *Enough*. I believe the "untapped inner resources" refers to the power of the Holy Spirit at work inside of Slim. Every time Flake makes reference to the Holy Spirit, she uses terminology such as "something inside Slim" or "untapped inner resources." By alluding to the presence of the Holy Spirit at work in Slim, Flake is able to then deliver the prophetic message that God has for those who find themselves in similar situations. She states:

> The word of the Lord to every woman who has spent too much time settling for relationships, jobs, and situations that are not fulfilling, nurturing, or true to your potential is that there is power in deciding you have had enough. . . . God is calling for brave and determined women to adopt an attitude of intolerance for those things in their lives that abuse, confuse, and restrict. Our divine Provider is just waiting for some of us to say, "I am not going to go on like this. I am ready to walk in my privilege and break through to a new way of being." God is just waiting to work in us and with us to replace fear with self-confidence, guilt and shame with the determination to be better, and low expectation for self to a conviction that says, "I am better than this, so I can do better than this."[24]

Once again, Flake employs light-dark metaphors, but here, she switches the order of the metaphor to dark-light in order to place emphasis on the future that is in store for her listeners. She says, "God will replace fear with *self-confidence*, guilt and shame with the *determination to be better*, and low expectation for self to *a conviction that says, 'I am better than this, so I can do better than this.'"*[25]* Overall, the movie functions on two levels: (1) as a narrative to illustrate the power of an epiphany and (2) as a rhetorical artifact that the preacher is able to preach from in place of a biblical text. Flake's entire introduction operates as a sermon within the sermon. She uses the movie as one of her sermonic texts; she establishes the plot to illustrate the situation, complication, and resolution of the character, and then delivers a prophetic message for Slim and all the Slims in the congregation. Slim, the character becomes a metaphor for the women (or Slims) in the congregation.

After Flake finishes dissecting the movie, to make her first main point, that "there is power in deciding you have had enough," she immediately transitions to the story of Leah in Genesis 29 to reveal the point at which Leah decides that she has had enough.[26] Similar to how she outlined the plot of the movie, she outlines the plot of this biblical story. She conveys that Leah was Jacob's first wife and that he never loved her because he loved her younger sister, Rachel. Flake explicitly names rejection as one of the sources of Leah's pain. As a result of this rejection, Leah became a woman of convenience, whom Jacob chose to sleep with, but not love. Flake develops Leah's character as a victim of a love-impoverished marriage. Flake says, "[W]hen God saw that Leah was not loved, God opened her womb. Perhaps the blessing of reproduction was designed to make her see that sometimes you have to create new life for yourself apart from the one that cannot give you what you need."[27] This idea about the blessing of reproduction helps Flake to establish the point at which Leah decides that she has had enough. Flake describes Leah's mental and emotional condition during the first three pregnancies. She says:

> When Leah gave birth to her first son, her thoughts were only of Jacob and her misery. She named him Reuben, which means "surely my husband will love me now." Her son's name is an indication of her desperation. She had another son, but his birth gave Leah no joy or self-appreciation. All she could see in the midst of divine creation was "because the Lord saw that I am hated, God gave me Simeon." She had a third son, but still she was controlled by fear, poor judgment, and emotional dysfunction, and she was never able to celebrate the creative process that was God's gift to her to motivate her to emotionally connect to herself. Instead, her response to God's blessing upon the birth of Levi was "Now my husband will become attached to me because I have given him three sons."[28]

Flake parallels Leah's condition to Slim's condition without explicitly saying that she is doing this. Here, Leah, quite like Slim, feels hated, desperate, and she finds herself a prisoner of fear, poor judgment, and emotional dysfunction. Just as Slim's change of attitude, or moment of epiphany, came "in the midst of her depression and despair," Leah's change of attitude/defining moment came in the midst of her emotional dysfunction, fear, poor judgment, self-denial, and people (Jacob) pleasing behavior.[29] Furthermore, Flake uses similar language when describing Leah's change of attitude. For Leah, Flake claims, "One day a defining moment gave birth to a change of attitude. This change of attitude changed her focus and reshaped her inner reality. . . . She had enough of trying to deny who she was and trying to be who Jacob wanted her to be."[30] For Slim, she says, "One day, in the midst of her depression and despair, Slim has a change of attitude. Everything that has happened to her finally causes something to happen within her. . . . But one day she experiences the inner power that comes with saying, 'Enough.'"[31] Flake creates enthymematic identification between the biblical character Leah and the movie character Slim. She uses the same premise in Slim's struggle of survival to describe Leah's struggle, thus creating identification between the two characters. Both Slim and Leah eventually arrive at the point where they are able to see their situations for what they are and decide to do something about it. The only difference is that Slim's struggle is a physical battle and Leah's struggle is a spiritual battle. Slim has to physically fight to save her life, whereas Leah has to internally fight in a spiritual war against the "spirit of fear and defeat" to save herself from emotional dysfunction.[32]

Flake argues, when Leah gave birth to her fourth son, "Leah gave birth to a new Leah."[33] Leah's transformation into a "new Leah" lends itself to radical subjectivity because she finally gave herself permission to love self and to find her value in God. Flake argues, this time, Leah realized that she could not make Jacob love her, but "she could make Leah love Leah. The new Leah vowed with the birth of Judah, 'This time I will praise the Lord.'"[34] Flake briefly embodies the biblical character to show that Leah finally realized her life was so much bigger than Jacob and she came to the understanding that she would have to put Jacob in proper perspective. Flake uses Leah's change of attitude to bring the identification full circle. She has already identified Slim with her listeners, then Leah with Slim, and now, as she makes her second main point, "So many women have some "Jacobs" in their lives that they need to put in proper perspective." Here, Jacob becomes a metaphor to identify Leah with her listeners. According to Flake, Jacob represents whatever is capable of preventing a woman from appreciating who she is and discovering her purpose. She says, "For every Leah who is ready to be free of bad habits, negative attitudes, and ungodly behaviors that keep her in bondage, things can change when she draws the line and begins to walk in godly strength. . . . Become a real fighter and force with which to contend in this spiritual war for your life."[35] By using the words, *fighter* and *spiritual war*, Flake continues to draw parallels between

Leah and Slim, for her listeners to figure out. By the time that she arrives to her final main point, "Sometimes we cannot wait for deliverance; we have to fight for it," the listeners have already figured out that Leah's plan of action was to engage in a spiritual fight that would free her to love herself, and Slim's plan of action was to engage in a physical fight that would free her from abuse.

In this sermon, Flake has used the movie character, Slim, and the biblical character, Leah to encourage us to "break away from the stuff that ushers us into dangerous territory," to stop waiting for deliverance, and to fight for it ourselves.[36] The sermon teaches people to "adopt an attitude of intolerance for those things in our lives that abuse, confuse, and restrict."[37] Flake affirms self, authenticates self, and legitimizes self by conveying to her individual listeners that "there is power in deciding you have had enough," by helping them to understand that "when [they] are really walking with the Lord, [they] will eventually get to the place that [they] know that [their] survival and growth depend on [their] ability to say, 'No more!'," and by re-envisioning the characters from victim to victor.[38] In other words, she moves her audience to operate out of their own agency, or their own individual radical subjectivities, so they can fight for their own deliverance.

The Womanist Characteristics

According to Flake, womanist preaching preaches healing to African American women. She claims that womanist preaching is

> responsible for sending messages that transform a culture of violence into a culture of healing. . . . [It] must challenge the notion that violence against women is in any way justified. . . . [It names] the sins of . . . male perpetrators and dismantle[s] all antifemale attitudes, even those perpetuated in scripture. . . . [F]or victims of violence [it] must alleviate guilt, blame, and shame; minister healing to their wounded hearts, minds, and spirits; and empower them to lead fulfilled and productive lives.[39]

Flake has interpretive methods and preaching methodologies that help her to live up to her understanding of womanist preaching. Ministers who want to preach healing to wounded women must affirm, show sensitivity, honor tradition, liberate, present Jesus as an Advocate for women, acknowledge African ancestry, avoid male-bashing, tell the truth, inspire action, and think outside of the box.[40]

Throughout Flake's sermon, she either demonstrates or names some of these characteristics Without a doubt, the affirmation to value self and inspiration to act on behalf of self is seen in both the movie narrative and the biblical narrative because both characters come to a realization that they deserve better and then they fight for what they believe they deserve. Flake models sensitivity by the way she discusses the suffering and the circumstances surrounding the suffering of Slim and Leah, and by the way she broadens the definition of domestic abuse to include "settling for relationships, jobs, and situations that are not fulfilling, nurturing, or true to [one's] potential."[41] Her commitment to not ignore or justify the abuse of both characters reflects her obligation to tell the truth. Flake's words of liberation to an authentic human existence are mirrored in her discussions surrounding Slim's change of attitude that helps her develop courage and self-esteem along with Leah's change of attitude that allows her to find the Lord and finally love herself. Flake's movie narrative comes close to male-bashing because it demonizes the abuser by illustrating that the male antagonist dies at the end of the movie. More than this, Slim kills him—accidentally, but she kills him nevertheless, as a result of her newfound strength. However, this is why she does qualify that what she is celebrating is Slim's ability to take charge of her life, which then attempts to take the celebratory focus off the demise of the abusive husband. Finally, in terms of thinking outside of the box, if we take time to look at the main character of the movie narrative, we will see that Flake opened her sermon already thinking outside of the box by telling a story about a Latina, instead of an African American, a point which I will address later.

The overall quality that makes Flake's sermon a womanist sermon expressing radical subjectivity is the fact that it affirms women and it empowers them to change themselves and to change their oppressive situations. Flake's sermon reflects the process of learning to accept the truth about one's self and one's circumstances along with the journey to self-love, self-confidence, self-worth, a healthy self-esteem, and the actualization of the ultimate agency—defeating one's oppressor, which is what categorizes her message under this first tenet of radical subjectivity. The process that the characters go through to get to the point of loving and valuing themselves demonstrates that they have achieved an elevated sense of consciousness that finally allows them to resist their oppression. Radical subjectivity helps women to overcome male domination by empowering them to change their perception so they can change their situation. Let us examine how another womanist preacher approaches the same text.

RHETORICAL ANALYSIS OF GINA STEWART'S SERMON, "ENOUGH IS ENOUGH!"

She conceived again, and when she gave birth to a son she said, "This time I will praise the Lord." So she named him Judah. Then she stopped having Children.

Genesis 29:35, NIV

Gina Stewart's sermon, "Enough is Enough!," was first delivered in 2006 for a women's revival, at Berean Baptist Church, in Memphis, Tennessee.[42] She preached this forty-minute sermon to a predominantly African American audience of approximately one thousand women. Stewart continues to preach this sermon and different versions of it all across the country to women and men. "Enough is Enough!" celebrates the defining moment when a woman decides that she does "not have to participate in [her] own oppression," that she is "better than [her] situation, and [she] can do better."[43] The sermon is about a woman who suffers from a "wounded self-esteem" because she lives her life and sees herself through the eyes of her unloving husband. Eventually, she decides to stop participating in her own oppression and start valuing herself. She has a defining moment which changes her attitude and allows her to realize that her value is not determined by what another person thinks; her value comes from God. Stewart, like Flake, uses a movie character and a biblical character to demonstrate how the defining moment of realizing, "enough is enough," and walking away from "love-deficient relationships" can free us from emotional dependence and a "wounded self-esteem."[44] This sermon challenges us to learn how to love ourselves, how to value ourselves aside from what other people think, to realize when "Enough really is Enough," and to develop our love relationship with God.[45] Stewart moves her audience to a state of maturity in realizing "Enough is Enough!," which also serves to liberate and heal them from their emotional dependence, "wounded self-esteem," impaired vision, and holes in their souls.[46]

ANALYSIS

The sermon opens with a scene from the movie, *What's Love Got to Do with It?* where Tina Turner runs across the parking lot to a motel, after being beaten by her husband, Ike Turner. She tells the clerk that she only has 36 cents and a Mobil card, but if he gives her a room, she will pay him back. Stewart refers to Tina Turner's ability to walk away from "a life of physical, emotional, and mental abuse," as Turner's defining moment, which I refer to as her moment of epiphany because in that moment she finally affirmed herself in a way that allowed her to escape her abuse.[47] She says, "When Tina decided she had had enough and decided to say no to an unproductive, unhealthy relationship, she opened the door to a new and exciting chapter in her life."[48]

Stewart uses Turner's defining moment as her transition into the biblical text so that she can show Leah's unproductive, unhealthy relationship(s), and then identify Leah's defining moment. The movie analogy serves as a contemporary example of what is going on in scripture. As she moves into the text, she confesses that "Tina's story" reminds her of the character in the Genesis text. Stewart immediately defines the meaning of Leah's name as "wearied" or "afflicted one," so that she can paint the picture of Leah's suffering and distress in order to make her first main point, "Leah invested a lot of time and mental and emotional energy trying to gain Jacob's affection."[49] Here, she addresses the tragedy of Leah's relationship with Jacob, including his lack of love and attraction for her, along with the fact that her father had to trick him into marrying her. Stewart strategically uses the meaning of Leah's name, the names of her first, second, and third-born sons, and then the name of her fourth-born son to help develop all three main points.

Table 2.2   Stewart Rhetorical Tools

Rhetorical Tools	*Purpose of Rhetorical Tools*
Analogy	To compare the movie character's emotional and psychological prison to that of the biblical character
Emotional and psychological prison language	To develop the imagery and depth of Leah's spiritual battle
Linguistics	To show the tragedy of Leah's suffering embedded in the meaning of her name as well as the names of her children
Names domestic violence, rejection, and patriarchy	To confront the oppressive forces of power
Cause-effect relationships	To show how Leah's dependence on Jacob caused her to suffer from low self-esteem
Embodiment	To create identification with the audience by expounding on what the biblical character possibly said about her situation
Repetition	To reiterate points and make them clear to the audience
Jacob/Laban metaphors	To help people identify their own oppressor
Universal "I"	To help all women and men to see themselves in the biblical text

Table created by Kimberly P. Johnson.

Next, Stewart names and describes the unapologetic patriarchal social structure that Leah is subjected to, which attaches a woman's worth to her ability to reproduce. She claims that a woman's redemption was in producing children to preserve the male family name. According to Stewart, "Leah had something that Rachel didn't have. Leah could produce."[50] But the irony of the situation is that it did not matter how many sons Leah had, Jacob's feelings for Leah never changed. Stewart explains how Leah's expectation of Jacob increased with the birth of each son.

> When Leah gave birth to her first son, she named him Reuben, meaning the "Lord has seen" my misery. She thought, *Surely Jacob will love me now*. She had another son and named him Simeon, which means "because the Lord heard" that I am unloved. She had a third son and named him Levi and said, "Now this time my husband will become attached to me, because I have borne him three sons."[51]

Unfortunately for Leah, her expectations were never met, "Jacob never heard, never saw, and never connected."[52] Leah allowed her dependence to rob her of her self-worth. I believe Stewart's portrayal of Leah being robbed of her self-worth reflects an individual who fell into the trap of naiveté. Although Leah's self-worth has to do with her own value of herself, she allowed her cultural tradition to dictate who could assign her value, and unfortunately for her, Jacob never followed through.

Stewart uses the cultural practices of the patriarchal society along with the names of Leah's first three sons to support her second main point, "Leah suffered a wounded self-esteem. She relied too much on Jacob's estimation and evaluation."[53] Once she makes this point, Jacob and Laban becomes metaphors that allow her to relate Leah's condition to the condition of her listeners in an effort to help them identify with Leah. She states:

> Like Leah, so many of us suffer from wounded self-esteem because of someone else's evaluation of us. Although self-esteem refers to our estimation of our own worth, many of us inherited our initial perception of ourselves from other sources: from Jacobs and Labans in our lives. We never consulted God about our worth. So we suffer from impaired vision, holes in our soul, insecurity, and mistaken identities.[54]

The fact that Stewart makes the point about Leah suffering from "wounded self-esteem" due to Leah's dependence on Jacob and then ties it to the women in the congregation is a strong indication that this is one of her main points. In Stewart's explanation, she sheds light on all the women in her audience who naively inherited their perception of themselves based on what another person thought. She does this to expose the naiveté of her audience members.

After establishing Leah's situation and complication, the next movement of the sermon deals with Stewart's third main point, the defining moment or moment of epiphany that helps Leah resolve her problems, or at least change her attitude about her problems. "One day, Leah decided that enough is enough."[55] This defining moment changed Leah's focus and gave her a new perspective of herself—"she realized that she could no longer live her life dependent upon the ongoing nurture and approval of Jacob. . . . She finally realized that she couldn't make Jacob love Leah, but she could love Leah, and most of all, God loved Leah."[56] The "radicality" of this defining moment is in Leah's decision to finally love herself, to affirm herself, and to stop looking for the approval or affirmation of others to give her self-worth. Stewart identifies the birth of Leah's fourth son, Judah, as Leah's defining moment because this birthing process allowed Leah to give birth to a new Leah. When Leah gave birth to Judah, she said, "This time I will praise the Lord."[57] Leah's moment of radical subjectivity enables her to (1) finally resist self-hatred, (2) resist having her worth determined by people in her life, (3) love herself, and (4) turn to God, to find her value in the One who gives her worth.

Stewart uses her homiletical imagination, as she assumes the role of Leah, to further expound on what she thinks Leah said during the defining moment that changed her life. Speaking in first person, Stewart embodies the cries of Leah's heart as Leah gives birth to her first three sons—"I had Reuben and he didn't see me. I had Simeon, and he didn't hear me. I had Levi, and he wouldn't become attached to me."[58] She reestablishes the problem in order to restate her main points, but this time, from the first-person standpoint. She says, "I cannot experience my potential as long as I keep investing my emotional and mental energy in love-deficient relationships," which corresponds to her original point, "Leah invested a lot of time and mental and emotional energy trying to gain Jacob's affection."[59] Next, she states, "I can't give myself away trying to measure up to somebody else's idea of what acceptable is," which alludes to the point that Leah had low self-esteem because she "relied too much on Jacob's estimation and evaluation."[60] Then, she makes the claim, "Jacob may not change, but I can change," which evokes her third point, "Leah decided enough is enough."[61]

Stewart uses repetition again, but this time to restate her points from the perspective of first-person plural. She acknowledges first that "many of us have Jacobs in our lives," second, that "we believe [Jacob] is essential for our sense of security and self-worth," and third, that "we have to do what Leah did—and say enough is enough."[62] The purpose of reiterating her points and moving from first person, as Leah, to first-person plural and then to the universal "I" of first person is to put the congregation of women into her sermon so that they become the individual who finally realizes, "I do not have to settle for less. I do not have to participate in my own oppression. . . . I am better than this situation, and I can do better. . . . The God I serve will get me to the point where I can say enough is enough." And then, decide "Enough really is enough."[63]

In this sermon, Stewart uses Tina Turner from the movie *What's Love Got to Do with It?* and the biblical character Leah to encourage us to consult God about our worth and to stop being emotionally dependent on other people to construct our sense of security, self-worth, and self-esteem. The sermon teaches women to stop settling for less and to stop playing a role in their own oppression. We see the characteristics of radical subjectivity through the manner in which Stewart affirms self, nurtures self to a particular level of maturity, and in her embodiment of Leah. As Stewart re-envisions the characters in her sermon from that of victim to victor, she also moves her audience to operate out of their own radical subjectivities by deciding "Enough really is Enough!" in order to free themselves from their own "emotional and psychological prison."[64]

The Womanist Characteristics

According to Stewart, womanist preaching liberates women, is sensitive to women's experiences, challenges traditional interpretations, constructs alternative realities, and validates women's experiences and perspectives.[65] She believes that while this form of preaching serves to liberate women, it must also be sensitive to people's experiences. When expounding on this idea, she mentions the woman at the well in the Gospel of John chapter four, and says, "Jesus never talks to her about her husbands, Jesus talks to her about thirst."[66] In other words, Jesus does not demonize this woman, instead he liberates her. Stewart argues that "womanist preaching challenges us in new ways of interpreting scripture. Often, when we preach [Genesis 21], Hagar is the villain instead of the victim.[67] Womanist preaching helps us construct alternative realities."[68] This type of homiletical approach allows the preacher to re-image the text in a manner that illustrates Hagar the victim as opposed to Hagar the villain, which serves to then validate the experiences and perspectives of women. Stewart claims the top womanist themes that arise out of her preaching are "valuing of self and self-worth; self-esteem; giving yourself permission to love yourself; giving yourself permission to walk away from destructive, non-productive toxic relationships; liberation; and gender justice."[69]

After examining Stewart's sermon, we clearly see a number of these qualities reflected in her message. From the character in the movie selection to the character in the biblical narrative to the women in the congregation, the sermon is a message of liberation that seeks to liberate all women who suffer in the areas of low self-esteem. She does not demonize Leah for thinking so poorly of herself. Instead, she contextualizes Leah's circumstance and then creates identification with the women in the pews to show that Leah is not alone because many of us do this too. This is her way of demonstrating sensitivity to a situation that she points out as negative, by making the claim that so many of us suffer from the same situation, which is what also helps her at the end to empower the women in the pews to change their situations. A sermon not focused on sensitivity would not even acknowledge that others share the same wounded self-esteem experience as Leah, which would rhetorically condemn Leah as a sinner and cause the listeners to place judgment against Leah. This sermon undoubtedly validates the experiences and perspectives of women because it is a sermon about a woman's experience and the preacher looks at the text from Leah's perspective. Stewart even takes it a step further when she begins to speak in first person because then she rhetorically takes on the role of Leah and begins to speak as Leah.

The overarching quality that makes Stewart's womanist sermon a sermon that can be classified as an example of radical subjectivity is the fact that it empowers women to validate themselves and to finally give themselves permission to love themselves. This sermon ultimately communicates that self-worth is not tied to what another person thinks. Stewart strategically demonstrates the various phases of Leah's identity development and then celebrates Leah's realization that her value and self-worth come from God. She also celebrates Leah's decision to finally start loving herself. Stewart's contextualization of Leah's state of oppression reveals how Leah inherited a low self-esteem. She implies that Leah's father did not think Leah was marriage material, hence the trickery of marrying Leah off to Jacob. She discusses the patriarchal social structure that attaches value to one's ability to reproduce and even though Leah could produce, Jacob never loved her—he never gave her value. Then, she provides the illustration of the birth of Leah's sons, which voices Leah's agony of her love-impoverished relationship. But, when she arrives at the birth of Leah's fourth son, Stewart emphasizes Leah's attitude change, the point of Leah's process where Leah realizes that she can change—she experiences her own transformation and stops participating in her oppression. The fact that this sermon addresses the journey toward self-esteem, self-love, and self-worth is what makes this sermon an example of radical subjectivity.

CONCLUSION: A COMPARISON AND CONTRAST OF RHETORICAL STRATEGIES

The most obvious rhetorical similarity, besides the use of the same scripture/ biblical narrative or the title resemblance, is that both sermons begin with a movie narrative. Flake's movie choice, *Enough*, clues the congregation into how she came up with the title of her sermon, whereas Stewart's movie title does not present the same connection with her sermon title. What is different about Flake's inclusion of the movie, *Enough*, is that the main character of the movie is a Latina, not an African American woman. Is Flake thinking outside of the box by including this movie narrative even though the starring role is not played by an African American woman? Is she pushing the envelope on the womanist debate surrounding essentialism versus particularity? Essentialism argues that a womanist can only be an African American female, while particularity argues that it is not essential for a womanist to be an African American female. It is the particular experiences of an individual that allows the individual to relate to the oppressive experiences of black women, which qualifies that person to be a womanist. On the one hand, Flake's construction of womanism and womanist theology, in her book, confines womanism to African American women, which leads to essentialism. Yet, on the other hand, when she discusses the practical methodologies that preach healing to wounded women, she opens the discussion to men and women, which creates room for the particularity argument. In an interview, Flake brought clarity to this very issue. She said, "Womanist preaching can come from males and females. I don't necessarily think that a black man can be a womanist, but I do feel that Jim [James] Cone and some of the others would see themselves as one sympathetic to womanism and maybe even more."[70]

Another similarity between the preachers is that they challenge people's understanding of domestic violence by broadening the scope of abuses that fall under the category of domestic violence. The term domestic violence is most often used to refer to the physical abuse or assaults that women experience by their spouse or significant other. However, Flake and Stewart help their audience members recognize that emotional, psychological, and verbal abuse also fall under the umbrella of domestic violence. The reason they bring their audience to this level of understanding is that they are both specifically targeting women who have been emotionally, physically, psychologically, and verbally abused in order to empower them to change their situation and finally decide for themselves that "enough is enough." Furthermore, in addition to naming domestic violence as one of the evils that plague African American women, Flake explicitly names rejection and Stewart names patriarchy as additional sources of pain. Naming domestic violence, rejection, and patriarchy is necessary because womanism seeks to confront all oppressive forces of power, and the only way to confront a problem is to name the problem.

Flake and Stewart use metaphor and identification to help their audience recognize themselves in the sermon so that they too can begin to name the sources of their pain. Both movie narratives describe their character as a prisoner. Jennifer Lopez's character, Slim, becomes a "prisoner in her marriage and her home" who is "living in the emotional prison of low self-esteem" and she is not able to break out of this prison until she decides she has had enough.[71] Similarly, Stewart's recap of the scene from *What's Love Got to Do with It?* portrays Tina Turner as an escaped prisoner who just walked away from an emotional and psychological prison. Both characters took up residence in the prison of low self-esteem, so for the audience to see them come to a point where they give themselves permission to love and value themselves, this permission gets transferred onto the audience through identification. Additionally, the Jacob metaphor for Flake and the Jacob and Laban metaphors for Stewart help the audience to identify the various sources of their oppression. According to Flake, Jacob represents a person, experience, or memory; and according to Stewart, "Jacob does not have to be a man. He could be a woman or some primary person in our lives."[72] Likewise, the same holds true for Laban.

The more Flake and Stewart identify the source of Leah's pain, the more they try to relate it to the pain of their audience members through identification. Oftentimes, when the preachers make a point, they tie that point to their audience. For example, Flake does this by interjecting, "The word of the Lord to every woman who has spent too much time settling for relationships. . . . So many women have some 'Jacobs' in their lives that they need to put in proper perspective. . . . Being women of God requires that we recognize our own oppression and our own destructive and ungodly behavior."[73] Stewart connects with her audience by saying, "Like Leah, so many of us suffer from wounded self-esteem. . . . Like Leah, many of us have Jacobs in our lives. . . . But, at some point, we have to do what Leah did—and say enough is enough."[74] This form of identification empowers the audience to act just like Leah at the end of the sermon and declare for themselves that enough really is enough. The reason being, if the audience can see themselves as Leah, and logically understand how detrimental it was to Leah's survival for her to have a change of attitude or defining moment, then they too will realize how detrimental it is for them so they also have a change of attitude or defining moment. Plus, Leah's scenario gives them a glimpse of how their own future will pan out to be a brighter future as long as they are courageous enough to have their own defining moment by realizing that "enough is enough" and bold enough to use their own human agency to change their situation.

Another major similarity is that both sermons talk about Leah's defining moment that transformed her life. The preachers not only refer to this as a defining moment, they also use the words change of attitude and personal transformation to describe this life-changing moment. They both construct their sermons as a physical war for Slim/Tina Turner and a spiritual war for Leah. Slim and Turner are fighting for freedom, whereas Leah, is fighting for deliverance, according to Flake, or for self-worth in learning how to value self, according to Stewart. In both cases, Leah fights to get out of her situation. Stewart claims that Leah's change of attitude in deciding she could no longer be dependent upon Jacob "changed her focus and reshaped her perspective and inner reality."[75] Likewise, Flake argues that Leah's "change of attitude changed her focus and reshaped her inner reality. . . . She had enough of trying to deny who she was and trying to be who Jacob wanted her to be."[76] All in all, they use some of the same language throughout their sermon to make similar points.

In addition to identifying contrasting sources of pain and varying movie narratives, the major difference between these two sermons is that Stewart employs repetition and embodies the biblical character significantly more than Flake. Stewart's homiletical imagination allows her to take on the role of Leah to reiterate her points in first person. Then, as she switches back and forth between first-person plural and first-person singular (but from the perspective of the universal "I"), she restates her argument from the standpoint of Leah, from the standpoint of the audience, and from the standpoint of one included, among all people, in the proposed actions of the sermon—the universal "I." Flake, however, primarily preaches in second person and then chooses to further emphasize her main points by providing more examples. Flake only embodies Leah in a total of five sentences because she consistently maintains the role of a prophet to affirm the divine power that we have within ourselves to change our situations. On the contrary, Stewart moves from the role of "prophet" to the "embodiment of Leah" to help her audience see themselves in the biblical narrative so they can envision their own deliverance.

Overall, these sermons illustrate how radical subjectivity is communicated through the preached message and what rhetorical strategies are used to convey radical subjectivity. In both cases, the preachers illustrated the radical subjectivity of Leah through their narration of Leah's process from victim to victor. Their narrative demonstrated the abuse that Leah experienced, which led to low self-esteem, and then described the defining moment that empowered Leah to change her situation and to start loving herself. Both sermons revealed a moment of epiphany that empowered Leah to act. This does not mean that all sermons attempting to reflect radical subjectivity must address domestic violence. Radical subjectivity reflects the heightened awareness that one develops that empowers her to escape from her oppressive situation. Furthermore, we have recognized that radical subjectivity sermons are very intentional about naming the source of pain for wounded women, using identification, and various metaphors, to help the audience members see themselves in the message or form their own value judgments about the character(s) in the sermon. Plus, radical subjectivity sermons are deliberate about using empowering/transformative language to not only detail the character's epiphany, but to authorize and encourage the audience to act on behalf of self—via their own human agency.

NOTES

1. Floyd-Thomas, *Deeper Shades of Purple*, 16.

2. Ibid., 8.

3. Mary Donovan Turner and Mary Lin Hudson, *Saved from Silence: Finding Women's Voice in Preaching* (St. Louis: Chalice Press, 1999), 12.

4. Katie Cannon, "Structured Academic Amnesia: As If This True Womanist Story Never Happened," in *Deeper Shades of Purple: Womanism in Religion and Society*, ed. Stacey Floyd-Thomas (New York, NY: New York University Press, 2006), 19, 27.

5. Carol B. Duncan, From "Force-Ripe" to "Womanish/ist:" Black Girlhood and African Diasporan Feminist Consciousness in *Deeper Shades of Purple: Womanism in Religion and Society*, ed. Stacey Floyd-Thomas (New York, NY: New York University Press, 2006), 31.

6. Debra Mubashshir Majeed, "Womanism Encounters Islam: A Muslim Scholar Considers the Efficacy of a Method Rooted in the Academy and the Church," in *Deeper Shades of Purple: Womanism in Religion and Society*, ed. Stacey Floyd-Thomas (New York, NY: New York University Press, 2006), 44.

7. Diana L. Hayes, "Standing in the Shoes My Mother Made: The Making of a Catholic Womanist Theologian," in *Deeper Shades of Purple: Womanism in Religion and Society*, ed. Stacey Floyd-Thomas (New York, NY: New York University Press, 2006), 66.

8. Ibid., 70.

9. Ibid., 68; see Patricia Hill Collins, *Black Feminist Thought: Knowledge, Consciousness and the Politics of Empowerment* (New York: Routledge, 2000), 11–13.

10. Hayes, "Standing in the Shoes My Mother Made," 67.

11. Walker, *In Search of Our Mother's Gardens*, xi.

12. Elaine Flake, *God in Her Midst*, 47.

13. Elaine Flake, personal interview by Kimberly P. Johnson, November 4, 2009, Memphis, Tennessee.

14. Ibid.

15. Flake, *God in Her Midst*, 41.

16. Michael Osborn, "Archetypal Metaphor in Rhetoric: The Light-Dark Family" in *Readings in Rhetorical Criticism, Third Edition*, ed. Carl R. Burgchardt (State College, PA: Strata Publishing, Inc, 2005), 307.

17. Ibid., 308.

18. Flake, *God in Her Midst*, 41.

19. Ibid., 43

20. Ibid.

21. Ibid., 18.

22. Ibid., 42.

23. bell hooks, *Feminism is for Everybody: Passionate Politics* (Cambridge, South End Press, 2000), 14.

24. Flake, *God in Her Midst*, 43–44.

25. Ibid.

26. Ibid., 43.

27. Ibid., 44.

28. Ibid., 44–45.

29. Ibid.

30. Ibid., 45.

31. Ibid., 42.

32. Ibid., 47.

33. Ibid., 45.

34. Ibid.

35. Ibid., 46.

36. Ibid., 47.

37. Ibid., 43.

38. Ibid., 47.

39. Ibid., 4.

40. Ibid., 13–20.

41. Ibid., 43.

42. Gina Stewart, "Enough is Enough" in *Those Preaching Women: A Multicultural Collection*, eds. Ella Pearson Mitchell and Valerie Bridgeman Davis (Valley Forge, PA: Judson Press, 2008), 13.

43. Ibid., 13.

44. Ibid., 11.

45. Ibid., 13.

46. Ibid., 11.

47. Ibid., 9.

48. Ibid.

49. Ibid., 9–10.

50. Ibid., 10.

51. Ibid., 11.

52. Ibid.

53. Ibid.

54. Ibid.

55. Ibid.

56. Ibid., 11–12.

57. Ibid., 12.

58. Ibid.

59. Ibid., 12, 10.

60. Ibid., 12, 11.

61. Ibid.

62. Ibid., 12.

63. Ibid., 13.

64. Ibid., 9.

65. Gina Stewart, personal interview by Kimberly P. Johnson, October 20, 2009, Christ Missionary Baptist Church, Memphis, Tennessee.

66. Ibid.

67. A few chapters prior, in Genesis 16, the Lord promised Abram, who later became Abraham, that he would have many offspring. The problem was that his wife, Sarai, who later became Sarah was barren. Sarai decided that her maidservant, Hagar, should sleep with Abram so they could build their family. Hagar gave birth to a child named Ishmael. By the time we get to Genesis 21, Sarah is finally pregnant by Abraham and gives birth to a son, Isaac. Sarah becomes disturbed with Ishmael and decides that she does not want him sharing in the inheritance of her son, so she orders Hagar and Ishmael to be sent away. In the unfortunate occasion when ministers preach that Hagar is a villain, it is usually because they are addressing the fact that Hagar slept with another woman's husband. They miss the fact that Hagar was in servitude to Sarai, which means that Hagar had no say in the matter. Renita Weems argues, in her book, *Battered Love: Marriage, Sex, and Violence in the Hebrew Prophets* (Minneapolis: Fortress Press, 1995), 18, that "Failure by the subordinate to fulfill her or his responsibility virtually guaranteed punishment, retribution, or discipline. . . ." Therefore, Hagar really was a victim.

68. Gina Stewart, personal interview by Kimberly P. Johnson, October 20, 2009, Christ Missionary Baptist Church, Memphis, Tennessee.

69. Ibid.

70. Elaine Flake, personal interview by Kimberly P. Johnson, November 4, 2009, Memphis, Tennessee.

71. Flake, *God in Her Midst*, 41.

72. Gina Stewart, personal interview by Kimberly P. Johnson, October 20, 2009, Christ Missionary Baptist Church, Memphis, Tennessee.

73. Flake, *God in Her Midst*, 43–47.

74. Stewart, "Enough is Enough," 11–12.

75. Ibid., 11.

76. Flake, *God in Her Midst*, 45.

Chapter 3

Traditional Communalism

Traditional communalism sermons seek to heal and liberate both self and community through its rhetorical Jeremiad that calls people back to the beliefs and values of one's own community. The preacher must reconcile individuals and communities back to their original beliefs and values through a self/communal healing that will free the people up so that they can go back to being in authentic relationship with one another. Traditional communalism reflects a Jeremiad.

Traditional communalism, the term that Floyd-Thomas uses to describe the second tenet of womanism, speaks to the ways in which cultural traditions have nurtured and supported black women on our individual and collective journey toward liberation.[1] I understand traditional communalism as life-giving relationships that empower, protect, and nourish us in ways that help us to stay on the course toward authenticity, freedom, justice, and equality. According to Floyd-Thomas, traditional communalism also encompasses "the moral principles and practices of Black women living in solidarity with and in support of those with whom they share a common heritage and contextual language . . . [it is] 'in/visible dignity' and 'un/shouted courage' (adapted from Cannon) which furthers the survival and liberation of *all* Black women and their communities."[2] She describes it as a "synthesis of double consciousness" that comes not only from the ability to address and readdress, deconstruct and reconstruct, but also from the ability to subvert hegemonic power structures that seek to devastate communities and destroy lives.[3] Floyd-Thomas defines traditional communalism as:

[T]he affirmation of the loving connections and relational bonds formed by Black women—including familial, maternal, platonic, religious, sexual, and spiritual ties. Black women's ability to create, re-member, nurture, protect,

37

sustain, and liberate communities which are marked and measured not by those outside of one's own community but by the acts of inclusivity, mutuality, reciprocity, and self-care practiced within it (opposite of the biological deterministic assumption that a woman's role is to serve as nurturer and protector).[4]

Traditional communalism is an inherited and shared legacy that is passed down through the generations and it has the ability to rescue women from various forms of internalized oppression and self-deception and reestablishes a sense of self-awareness, communal pride, and collective memory.[5]

According to Dianne M. Stewart, traditional communalism calls black women back to their roots.[6] Her idea of communalism is influenced by her cultural understanding of solidarity, honor, and character.[7] She employs the "limbo dance," from her father's characterization of the Jamaican limbo, as a metaphor to describe the continuous process of negotiating space and boundaries on both the personal and communal levels.[8] She argues that the African diaspora story brings to light how meanings of blackness deprive us from being sensual beings and from using our sensual power as a tool for liberation.[9] The limbo becomes a "dance of resistance," a "boundary crossing," and an "encoding of an exilic people's" aspiration of going home.[10] For Stewart, the communal aspect of privileging her father's voice and experience with dancing limbo in Jamaica, and the preserving of ancestral (male and female) narratives and/or memories, is that they enhance our cultural flexibility and dexterity, and offer texture and detail to our collective memories and cultural knowledges that seem to disappear with time.[11] She argues that the natural memories of our foreparents have the ability to free us from alienation and dehumanization. Thus, traditional communalism represents the life-giving ancestral narratives that tell us who we are and remind us from where we come.

Similarly, "Hospitality, Haints, and Healing: A Southern African American Meaning of Religion," by Rosemary Freeney Harding with Rachel Elizabeth Harding, examines narratives but also explores rituals, healing practices, and the hospitable practices of the Harding family over a period of five generations. The stories that Harding tells relate to the ethics and spirituality displayed in Alice Walker's womanist definition.[12] For the Harding family, traditional communalism appears to be the coming together of family, friends, and co-laborers to encourage each other, to laugh, to address the absurdities and humiliations that come with oppression, to pray with/pray for each other, and most importantly, to expand the confines in which we live by stretching its boundaries and transforming the air so that we can finally breathe.[13]

Rosetta E. Ross's take on traditional communalism also examines space. She echoes Katie Cannon by claiming that womanist religious thought establishes the intellectual space to unearth the hidden treasures buried in the lives of black women.[14] Ross claims that much of her work reveals the life-giving normative beliefs that are already embedded in the moral practices of black women.[15] She critiques the lack of communalism within what she calls, "customary black Christianity." This term refers to the thoughts and actions of active members who regularly attend black churches.[16] Ross argues that the failure of "customary black Christianity" to include critical-analytical and spiritual capacities in its routine religious practices leaves a gaping psychological void that needs to be/and is being filled by content that will help individuals make sense of and assign meaning to their lived experiences.[17]

I think what Ross is trying to establish is that traditional communalism is a pragmatic spirituality that recognizes the need for practices and traditions to evolve, but at the same time is able to attach a communal meaning to the lived experiences of black people as well as respond in a communal fashion to the challenges that face us. In a sense, traditional communalism is rooted in human agency. It helps people realize that they have the power within them to overcome oppression. In other words, traditional communalism helps people recognize their commonality, even with the less fortunate, which tells me that embedded within traditional communalism is the understanding that what affects one affects everyone.

Nancy Lynne Westfield's idea of Walker's second tenet entails ethical considerations that push beyond the pre-established boundary lines of one's chosen community to include a dimension that cares for not only the oppressed but also the oppressors.[18] She claims that this epistemology of hope allows one to discern the gospel message no matter whose mouth it comes from.[19] She argues that black women have rejected the feeble dichotomy—care for self versus care for others—because we live in a both/and reality that requires us to care for self *and* others at the same time. The beauty of this "both/and" vantage point is that it allows old paradigms of hopelessness to be replaced with new paradigms of liberation, forgiveness, and redemption.[20]

As Alice Walker explains the second tenet of her womanist definition, she explicitly states that a womanist is:

> *Also*: A woman who loves other women, sexually and/or nonsexually. Appreciates and prefers women's culture, women's emotional flexibility (values tears as natural counter-balance of laughter), and women's strength. Sometimes loves individual men, sexually and/or nonsexually. Committed to survival and wholeness of entire people, male and female. Not a separatist, except periodically, for health. Traditionally universalist, as in "Mama, why are we brown, pink, and yellow, and our cousins are white, beige, and black?" Ans.: "Well, you know the colored race is just like a flower garden, with every color flower represented." Traditionally capable, as in: "Mama, I'm walking to Canada and I'm taking you and a bunch of other slaves with me." Reply: "It wouldn't be the first time."[21]

This second tenet clearly says that womanism supports and affirms heterosexual and homosexual relationships. Therefore, when Walker says that a womanist is "Committed to survival and wholeness of entire people," she is not just referring to race, class, or gender. Womanism also fights for the survival and wholeness of all people, including the civil rights of those who are transgendered as well as those engaged in gay and lesbian relationships. For Walker, this second tenet is about the coming together of a people, sustaining a legacy, restoring pride, being hospitable, renewing our courage, and supporting each other in ways that promote authenticity. Traditional communalism, involves providing basic needs, knowledge, encouragement, comfort and nurture, purpose, protection, and liberation to those within one's community and I would even go as far to include those outside of one's community because of its "both/and" vantage point. Traditional communalism has the power to call us all back together.

RHETORICAL ANALYSIS OF CHERYL KIRK-DUGGAN'S SERMON, "WOMEN OF THE CLOTH,"

Now Jesus was teaching in one of the synagogues on the Sabbath. And just then, there appeared a woman with a spirit that had crippled her for eighteen years. She was bent over and quite unable to stand up straight. When Jesus saw her, he called her over and said, "Woman, you are set free from your ailment." When he laid his hands on her, immediately she stood up straight and began praising God.

Luke 13:10–13, NIV

Cheryl Kirk-Duggan's sermon, "Women of the Cloth,"[22] was delivered on March 23, 2006, at Austin Presbyterian Theological Seminary's Shelton Chapel in Austin, Texas, for their Women of the Cloth Conference—Celebrating 50 years of the Ordination of Women to Word and Sacrament—in the Presbyterian Church. Those in attendance were administrators, faculty, staff, students, ministers, and other people from the Austin metropolitan area. Kirk-Duggan is an alumna of Austin Presbyterian Theological Seminary (APTS), so she uses her experience, her knowledge about the seminary, and several humorous moments to relate to her audience. Although Kirk-Duggan has not preached this sermon again, she has preached "five to six versions of the Luke 13:10–13 text."[23] This sermon is approximately twenty-two minutes in length.

ANALYSIS

"Women of the Cloth" is a sermon that boldly addresses the attitudinal and behavioral practices that seem to cripple many of us who are in ministry. The sermon begins with the reading of the scripture which recounts the story of how Jesus healed a woman who had been crippled by a spirit and unable to stand up straight for eighteen years. From that text, Kirk-Duggan provides her subject, "Weaving New Cloth: Confronting the Chorus of Bent Over Women," and her thesis, "Each moment we have an opportunity to shift from being busted and bent over to embracing God's anointing as we let go of our brokenness, dream dreams, listen to prophetic voices, and build community," according to the Bob Shelton tradition of homiletics.[24] After announcing the thesis, she sings the hymn, "There is a Balm in Gilead," in an operatic voice. The hymn functions as a narrative to help reiterate the claim of her thesis that if we embrace God's anointing, we can shift from being "busted and bent over."[25]

Following the hymn, Kirk-Duggan offers greetings to her audience and immediately establishes her credibility by creating identification with her personal testimony about how she was called to ministry twice and upon the second call, became a student at APTS. This type of identification breaks the ice between a stranger addressing an audience full of students who may not know Kirk-Duggan versus the realization that Kirk-Duggan has walked the same halls, had some of the same professors, and shared in many of the same experiences. She becomes a credible source who can impart wisdom that will help and inspire the current student body, faculty, and administrators.

In the testimony about Kirk-Duggan's calling to the ministry, we see the first instance in which she brings humor into the sermon. She says, "[T]he first time God called me, I said, "No way! If this really is you, you're going to have to do this again" [laughter]. And God did, and a week later I was here on campus wondering what I had gotten myself into."[26] The reason the humor and laughter are significant is that they give us an idea about the audience's reception. The laughter shows us that Kirk-Duggan's words were received by the audience with a positive response. This tells us (1) that the audience was listening, (2) that the audience was amused, and (3) that audience was laughing with her because she even chuckles and smiles herself.

Following the introduction, Kirk-Duggan directs her attention to the woman in the Luke 13 scripture. She begins to speculate that the woman could have been bent over physically, but she quickly points out that "the text says, that she was bent over by a spirit."[27] Here, the word spirit refers to a demon or a supernatural force that has possessed the woman and crippled her. Therefore, Kirk-Duggan argues that the woman was crippled by a spirit and that the woman's handicap is also a spiritual handicap. Kirk-Duggan takes the crippling spirit and uses it as a metaphor to address the societal oppressions that currently cripple us. We see this in her first main point: "Point one: Sexism, heterosexism, racism, classism, faux churchism, and skewed traditions cripple and bust the joy, an image of God in God's people."[28] She

Table 3.1   Kirk-Duggan Rhetorical Tools

Rhetorical Tools	Purpose of Rhetorical Tools
Sings a hymn	To develop a narrative of a sin-sick soul that needs to embrace God's anointing
Personal testimony	To create identification with the students and establish credibility
Humor	To ease her audience, and it tests their receptiveness
Crippling spirit metaphor	To show the spiritual impact of social oppression
Language of sickness	To identify our current condition and what cripples self/community
Names sexism/patriarchal sexism, heterosexism, racism, classism, faux churchism, and the game of passive-aggressive	To confront the oppressive forces of power and to overcome the pathological behaviors
Re-images biblical character	To create enthymematic identification
Cause-effect relationships	To describe the spiritual impact of each form of social oppression
Rhetorical/interrogatory questions	To deepen the dialectical exchange between the preacher and the listeners by engaging the audience's capacity to think about their own lives when they listen for inspiration
Inclusive language	To allow people to image or see God for themselves in a manner that advances their faith
Cultural critique	To critique society's cultural norms and offer a perspectival corrective
"Two Sundays without women" analogy	To explain that women still have the power to change their circumstances, even in the church
Rhetorical Jeremiad	To call people back to their cultural beliefs and values
Freedom/salvation/liberation imagery	To encourage people that they can overcome their situation and become the person that God called them to be
Blessing/benediction	To affirm what the people will experience when they choose to be set free from their crippling spirits

Table created by Kimberly P. Johnson.

makes the argument that all of the above are crippling spirits that spiritually handicap us from experiencing God in our lives, which she calls, joy. Kirk-Duggan points out a causal relationship between the crippling spirit and the woman's relationship with God by saying, "The woman had a crippling spirit. It was stopping the manifestation of God in her life."[29] In other words, the cause of the crippling spirit affected the presence/experience of God in the woman's life and the effect was that signs of God were not evident in her life. This first point coincides with Luke 13:11a, "And just then, there appeared a woman with a spirit that had crippled her for 18 years."

Kirk-Duggan uses her homiletical imagination to create further identification with the students, but this time by identifying the students with the biblical character. She re-images the woman in the text as "a poor seminary student who was confused . . . and had difficulty in exegesis [laughing] and wasn't too clear about what it meant to be a Presbyterian in 2006 [laughing]. She might have been a Presbyterian woman on the journey for 20 or 30 years and still trying to figure out, 'God, was this your joke on me? [laughter] What's going on? I don't quite get it?'" To re-image the woman of the text tells us that Kirk-Duggan was targeting the students. This allows the students to see themselves in the text because the crippled woman is now a poor seminary student who is having difficulty in her exegetical class while trying to figure out Presbyterian polity at the same time (students learn what it means to be part of their denomination in a polity class). Once she said, "poor seminary student who was confused," the audience started laughing and didn't stop until she said, "I don't quite get it."[30] Kirk-Duggan even smiles at what she is saying several times throughout this section of her sermon. Between her facial expressions and the laughter of the audience, we can deduce that she successfully reached her target audience for this portion of the sermon and that it created a form of enthymematic identification—the seminarians were able to finish the poor seminary student narrative for themselves.

After appealing to the students, Kirk-Duggan draws in the rest of her audience to help them identify with the woman in the text. She states, "Well you see, most people in the world, including church people and seminary professors, are bent over. . . . Beloved, we all have issues [Amen]. Some of us are better at hiding them than others [laughter]. Some of us are less bent over than others."[31] She tries to get her listeners to understand that everybody is bent over to some degree, and therefore, challenges them to "look in the mirror and take a risk and get to see, do you really know who you are?"[32] Kirk-Duggan is asking her audience not only to see that they too are crippled, but to also recognize the type of crippling spirit(s) in their life.

Similar to how verse 11 identifies that the woman had a crippling spirit, Kirk-Duggan names the crippling spirits in our lives that block our experiences of God. Here, she begins to culturally critique the various "isms" that cripple people. Kirk-Duggan argues (italics added):

Sexism is a crippling spirit that violates and needs to control gender. *Heterosexism* is a crippling spirit that fears God's gift of sensuality and sexualities. *Racism* mocks and violates God's precious, magnificent color and cultural palate of peoples. How dare we not like someone because of the color of their skin. When you think about it, it must really grieve God and it really makes us quite stupid [laughter]. *Classism* violates and has disdain for the poor and those with less status. And let us be really clear, we don't really want the poor people from the wrong side of the track, who may be a little smelly, sitting on those pews that my mama, or the group from the session, bought for this church. After all, this is First Presbyterian Church; we have our standards [laughter]. And I tell you, because of that attitude, not only in Presbyterian, but Catholic, and Baptist, and Methodist, and all kinds of churches, Jesus would not be welcomed if he showed up on Sunday. Because *faux churchism* limits our experience of God and condemns the experience of others.[33]

As opposed to just saying that discrimination is morally wrong or that our conscience should suggest that it is unjust, Kirk-Duggan examines the spiritual impact or violation of each crippling "ism," which helps us understand the underlined cause-effect relationship. Sexism "violates gender" because it seeks to differentiate between the sexes when equality originally existed, and sexism "needs to control gender" because the person with this spirit is really after power. The spiritual impact of heterosexism is that it "fears God's gift of sensuality and sexualities."[34] People who think that homosexuality is wrong and sinful are hung up on the fact that God created a female partner for Adam and that the Bible says that homosexuals will not inherit the Kingdom of God.[35] The spirit of racism mocks God—it makes fun of God and disappoints God because it intentionally chooses not to like everybody and to only like a few people based on the color of their skin. Racism also violates God's "color[ful] and cultural palate of peoples" because it causes us to not love all people the same, or at least the way that God loves them.[36] Classism creates a hierarchal structure based on economic status, which also violates God's unconditional love for everyone. Kirk-Duggan defines faux churchism as having "false church."[37] In my mind, it would be equivalent to the times when people play church and pretend to be super spiritual when they are only acting out or mocking what they see others do during church service. By mocking the experiences of others, "faux churchism" inadvertently condemns the experiences of others as well.

In her attempt to heal all the individuals who have crippling spirits, Kirk-Duggan gives a second challenge to her audience, but this time she is not asking, "Do you really know who you are?"[38] Instead, she wants people to ask themselves, "Who is God in my life? Who am I?" Not what you do, but, "Who are you? Who am I? And, what is God calling you to do today?" For, if you knew that today was the last day of your life on this planet, what would you be doing and what kind of minister would you be?"[39] All of the questions raised have a dual meaning that helps the audience to identify with what is going on in the text. "Who is God in your life" poses the questions," Is God your healer? And, is God your liberator? Jesus, who represents God in the flesh, healed the woman in the text through the laying on of hands and liberated the woman by setting her free from her illness. Hence, this question gets at the identity of God in one's life. "Who am I?" is a twofold question because Kirk-Duggan spends the beginning of her sermon establishing the fact that the woman in the text is a woman with a crippling spirit and then she uses her first point to name the crippling spirits that handicap us. Therefore, the question first asks: Are you a person with a crippling spirit or a person who can stand up straight? Secondly, it inquires as to whether or not we are sexist, heterosexist, racist, classist, or even one who engages in faux churchism or skewed traditions. "What is God calling you to do today?" really raises the questions: Is God calling you to be healed? And, are you willing and ready to let God set you free? Verses 12–13 read, "When Jesus saw her, he called her over and said, 'Woman, you are set free from your ailment.' When he laid his hands on her, immediately she stood up straight and began praising God."[40] In other words, Jesus called the woman over to deliver her from the evil spirits and the woman willingly came and allowed him to lay hands on her and heal her. Kirk-Duggan is asking if we are willing to do the same. Finally, she asks, "What kind of minister would you be?" I believe this question asks, would you be a minister who goes around teaching, preaching, calling out demons, healing the sick and fighting against sexism, heterosexism, racism, classism, faux churchism, and the crippling spirit of skewed traditions? Kirk-Duggan stays true to her subject matter, "Weaving New Cloth: Confronting the Chorus of Bent Over Women," because her points as well as her rhetorical questions all weave back to the scripture and help to confront the crippling spirits that cause us to become bent over. The weaving process is not a visual image that Kirk-Duggan develops throughout the sermon. Instead, the weaving process takes place as we come to a self-awareness in confronting our own "bent overness."

What we also see in Kirk-Duggan's first point is that she uses inclusive language. She does not assign a masculine pronoun to God. Instead, she uses the possessive form of God to say, ". . . an image of God in God's people."[41] Kirk-Duggan does this throughout the sermon. The only time she attaches a "he" pronoun to the Godhead is when she is referring to Jesus. So, she recognizes the masculinity of Jesus, but does not attach any type of masculinity to God. This decision to use inclusive language when talking about God allows the hearers, both males and females, to see themselves as being made in the image of God. Inclusive language also supports the belief that God is a spirit, not a human being with genitalia. Therefore, to take away the masculinity that conventionally gets assigned to God enables women to not just see themselves as being made in God's image, but it allows us to relate to God on a more intimate level. For example, to image God as a father to a woman who was physically abused by her father could serve as a significant hindrance to a woman's spiritual development. But to disassociate gender allows people to image or see God for themselves in a way that will advance their own faith.

Moving on to the second main point, Kirk-Duggan claims, "Many of us are bent over by circumstances, fear, and family pathologies."[42] Her first main point names the spirits that cripple us and now her second main point explains how so many of us have become crippled and bent over. She culturally critiques the gender inequality that still exists in some of our churches and argues against conventional views by saying, "women are where we are today and our churches are where we are . . . where they are today because of the other women—it's not so much the men keeping us down."[43] In other words, women's oppression is not a consequence of patriarchy, but rather a result of the complacency of women. This is a significant argument because far too often women have argued that our male counterparts along with our church disciplines and religious traditions are responsible for the continued oppression of women in the church. Yet, Kirk-Duggan points out that the problem is with the women. She implicitly argues that the women have the power to change their circumstances. The problem appears to be that the women who attend churches that do not support female ordination or leadership have lived with the traditions and practices for so long that they have become complacent with how churches are operated.

In an effort to explain how women become bent over by circumstance, Kirk-Duggan shares the advice that she offers to her Baptist and Catholic women friends about using their own power to change their circumstances. She says:

> I would dare them, two Sundays in a row, just two, to not show up and to not spend a dime, to not send that tithe, and you want . . . you think Joseph Smith had a revelation, it would be no kind of revelation [clapping, laughing, and shouting]. It would be no kind of revelation compared to what would happen in the American Baptist, Southern Baptist, and the Roman Catholic Church. Pope Benedict would have to make a new encyclical in a heartbeat [laughter]. Because without women in the church, we do not have church.[44]

What is striking about this particular counsel is that we have a minister (and former pastor) who is telling church members to take two Sundays to not go to church and to not financially support the church in order to see how their power will instantly dismantle the hegemonic structures within the church. Pastors and preachers are known for taking up offerings or "begging for money." But here, Kirk-Duggan solicits the opposite because she is well aware of the fact that women make up the church, which means that women finance the budget. If women stop giving for an extended period of time, the churches will have no choice, but to close down. The idea is that the male leadership, or in this case, Pope Benedict, would rather give up the antiquated practices than subject the church to have to shut its doors forever.

This analogy implicitly communicates to the audience that they too have the power to collectively change their circumstances but the reason people fail to do so is that they are complacent and scared. Their fear has crippled them. Kirk-Duggan claims, "[T]he problem is, because of patriarchy and misogyny, we as women have been so bent over for so long that we've learned to play the game of passive-aggressive. . . . [W]e haven't learned how not to do the passive-aggressive thing. And since we haven't learned how to do that, we are often catty among women," which begins to explain some of our pathological behaviors.[45] So, women have become crippled by circumstances due to their passive-aggressive behaviors because they are afraid of being aggressive, which has led to the passing down of pathological behaviors through generations. We have passed down our catty behavior of backbiting, cutting each other's throat, and humiliating each other. Plus, we have also chosen to be "closer friends with men than women," which means that we ourselves perpetuate this same behavior against our own gender.[46] She reminds her audience that Jesus would not have behaved in the same way that we do.

Kirk-Duggan posits that "the church [and the academy] cannot move forward until we name, what [she] call[s] patriarchal sexism."[47] "Patriarchal sexism" refers to the "I am jealous syndrome. It's fueled by patriarchy—women don't realize the power they have."[48] She testifies that she "has had some of [her] most difficult times with women who were already in the Academy and should have known better. But, they didn't 'cause they were so bent over from the pain that they went through as students during their doctoral programs that they didn't know how to relate to [her], so [she] proved a threat."[49] She intimidated the other professors to the point where they attempted to hinder her own success as a professor. She tells her audience, "But, what they didn't realize is I have a cloud of witnesses in glory and a cloud of witnesses here. And so do you! [shouting] And therefore, I fear no one!"[50]

Up until this point, we have only heard the names of the spirits that cripple us and been taught how we become crippled by circumstance, fear, and family pathologies. It is only now that we begin to recognize that we can resist becoming crippled and bent over through the power of faith and courage. Implicit within Kirk-Duggan's testimony is the idea that she was able to overcome her struggles through faith and courage. The "cloud of witnesses," which comes from the Hebrews 12:1 text, "Therefore, since we are surrounded by such a great cloud of witnesses, let us throw off everything that hinders and the sin that so easily entangles, and let us run with perseverance the race marked out for us," represent a multitude of people in heaven who can testify to their own perseverance in the Christian faith. Hence, she has people, both living and deceased, that she can lean on and look toward for strength and encouragement that she too will persevere. Next, she states, "I'm up here because of the invitation, but the invitation was given because God called me to preach and teach, I really wasn't interested [laughter]."[51] This statement also resorts back to faith because she had to believe and have faith in what God called her to do. Then, she presents her third challenge by saying, "And I challenge you [laughter continues], I challenge you to look and see, what is your call and are you still interested? If you're not interested, then maybe it's time for you to do something different. God's people ought not suffer because we're bent over, busted up, and burned out."[52] In essence, she tells her audience that they too have a cloud of witnesses, but in order to avoid becoming bent over, they must have faith—faith that they can persevere and faith in what God has called them to do—along with courage—courage to not be afraid and courage to walk away from ministry when it is time for them to do something different.

As a prelude into her third main point, Kirk-Duggan makes the claim, "Jesus did not condemn the bent over woman, but he saw her and he named her freedom."[53] In other words, he did not tear down the woman's spirit because of her condition. Instead, he recognized her bondage and set her free. Kirk-Duggan then poses the question to her audience, "How many times have we seen people bent over due to depression, drugs, alcohol, sex, gambling, and we refuse to acknowledge them?"[54] She even suggests that when we go to the grocery store, we "act like the cashier is an extension of the cash register," and that we neglect to thank the garbage men for faithfully doing their job.[55] Notice, the term "garbage men" is used as opposed to the more inclusive and more politically correct term, sanitation workers or garbage workers. Maybe, Kirk-Duggan is attempting to balance her feminine examples with a few masculine examples. Whatever the reason, this appears to be the only occupational reference that is attached to a masculine noun. Regardless, the whole point of inquiring whether or not we acknowledge the people around us was for her to get her audience to see that, "God's church cannot be the church until we name the bent overness and help to set people free."[56]

As Kirk-Duggan delves deeper into family pathologies, she argues:

Many women remain bent over because of their patriarchal and misogynistic conditioning. They've never gotten over the fact that they're not the son that their dads wanted. They've not got the healing and therapy that they needed because they were molested or raped. They've become bitter and so bent over like . . . when they stand up straight, it's still like they're bent over touching their toes. And, when you're bent over and touch your toes, you cannot see what's before you. You can only see what's beneath and behind.[57]

To identify the "bent overness" as patriarchal and misogynistic conditioning is not male-bashing because she is not degrading men, Kirk-Duggan is simply naming the source of the problem. Hence, she qualifies her comment by saying, many women have "never gotten over the fact that they're not the son that their dads wanted," or "They've not got the healing and therapy that they needed because they were molested or raped," which means that these women were rejected by their fathers to a certain extent, they were abused, and objectified—the women were "bent over." Here, Kirk-Duggan calls attention to the fact that "when you're bent over and touch your toes, you cannot see what's before you. You can only see what's beneath and behind."[58] Women who are not healed and have not come to grips with being raped or molested can only see what is beneath and behind because they are in bondage to their present condition and past situation. In the black community, and especially in ministry, it is considered taboo for individuals, even ministers, to seek psychological or psychiatric counsel. One is expected to be strong in challenging situations and to have enough faith to overcome catastrophe. So, to even suggest that people need therapy is liberating in itself.

Kirk-Duggan emphasizes the necessity of liberating people from what binds them to their past. She claims people who are "bent over" are in bondage to their past and present situation. This is why verses 12–13 of the Luke text are so significant, "When Jesus saw her, he called her over and said, 'Woman, you are set free from your ailment.' When he laid his hands on her, immediately she stood up straight and began praising God." Jesus set the woman free. The woman was no longer in bondage to a crippling spirit. The woman could stand up straight because she could finally see beyond her past and present condition. This helps to illustrate Kirk-Duggan's point that "set[ting] people free is the fundamental key of salvation."[59] As she provides further biblical examples, she says, "Jesus did not sit down and write a ten-volume set of dogmatics [laughing]. Jesus said, they're hungry, let me kind of multiply some of this fish and bread. They can't see, let me slap some mud on their eyes so they can. What are you doing to feed the hungry—spiritually hungry, physically, mentally, emotionally hungry?"[60] When Jesus saw a need, he met the need. She says, "it's not enough to teach and preach Jesus is Lord because if their stomachs are growling too loud, if they're hurting too bad, the noise of their pain will drown out any message of the gospel that you preach."[61] Therefore, one must also live the gospel message because, according to Kirk-Duggan, "Freedom is more than eschatology, it is lived reality."[62]

The discussion of freedom as a "lived reality" provides a segue into Kirk-Duggan's last main point because her goal is to get her audience to embrace this "lived reality" by naming and dealing with our own "bent overness." She argues:

Point three: as friends, faculty, staff, and students of Austin Presbyterian Theological Seminary, let us press on to embrace the legacy of women who hear the call of God and experience ordination to a variety of ministries. As we choose to be set free in Christ Jesus, as we name the pathologies, and work for justice through the power of the Holy Spirit. To be church means, discerning all the bent overness and deal with them. Starting first with ourselves.[63]

This final point is structurally more complex than the first two main points because Kirk-Duggan uses multiple compound sentences to make her argument instead of one simple sentence or one complex sentence. Here, she names the various groups of people in her audience so that they will know that she is calling the entire community to action—"to embrace the legacy of women who hear the call of God and experience ordination to a variety of ministries. . . . To be set free in Christ Jesus, . . . [to] name the pathologies, and work for justice through the power of the Holy Spirit."[64] Then, she provides her own definition of what it means "to be church." So, she is not only calling the entire community to action, she wants them to fully understand what it means to be part of that community. To be church, they must discern and deal with all of the "bent overness" including their own. Kirk-Duggan offers examples of how we neglect to recognize our own "bent overness" by imprisoning ourselves to drugs, alcohol, people, other people's opinions, big churches, big cars, and all that stuff. She notes, "you aren't really saved, 'cause you're not really free," which ties into her earlier statement that, "That is pathological, that is not salvation."[65] In other words, being imprisoned to someone or something is not freedom because freedom is salvation. So, she helps the audience to name their pathologies.

Next, Kirk-Duggan explains that "we can't talk about being the people of God [or the church] if we don't live the people of God."[66] Here, she calls the community back into accountability. She reminds the wealthy parishes to look beyond the good work that they are doing and she reminds the seminary students that it is a privilege to go to school, "So, if you're going to be here, choose to be here, choose to learn."[67] She also reminds the faculty members that they need to familiarize themselves with new ways of teaching because she considers teaching a privilege as well. Here, her purpose is to help the entire community, the students, and the faculty to recognize their "bent overness," deal with it, and to get over it. Throughout this entire section of the sermon, the audience laughs with her and shouts in agreement with what she is saying because they know that what she says is true.

Then, as Kirk-Duggan begins to close out her sermon, she takes her audience back to the passive-aggressive behavior that comes from patriarchy and misogyny but this time it is the passive-aggressive behavior of the church. She admits, "I love to wax eloquently with theory, but if my theory cannot somehow be converted to praxis, I'm in trouble and I'm not helping anybody."[68] After which, she poses the question, "So, what are we willing to do to be free from our 'bent overness?'" What will each of you do today—not tomorrow—because you may be dead tonight?"[69] She is asking, are you willing to name the pathologies, are you willing to work for justice, are you willing to discern all the "bent overness," not just yours, but the "bent overness" of the church, and are you willing to deal with it? Her question indicates a sense of urgency because she is asking about their actions for today, not tomorrow. It is so easy to say that we will perform a deed tomorrow, but the problem is that tomorrow does not always come. Likewise, Kirk-Duggan is concerned about today because any one of us could be dead tonight and not take the opportunity to be set free in Christ Jesus from our own crippling spirits and "bent overness."

Following this inquiry, Kirk-Duggan quotes Dr. Cynthia Campbell, who said that morning, "We are bent over when others are silenced around us and when we do not pay attention to race and class and culture."[70] This means that we will not be free until all of us are free—until everyone is granted a voice to speak. We will also not be free until we stop neglecting or being passive-aggressive about the injustices that people experience due to race, class, and culture.

The sermon ends with Kirk-Duggan's blessing upon the people. She says, "Beloved, this is our day—tomorrow, standing up straight, tomorrow grace, tomorrow freedom, tomorrow love. What are you willing to do for there is a balm in Gilead? God bless you (Amen)."[71] To declare, "this is our day" and then lead with a blessing that talks about tomorrow is not a negation of the importance of today. I believe this serves as an affirmation of what the people will experience when making the decision to be set free from their "bent overness." As a result of their decision today, she informs them that tomorrow, they will stand up straight; tomorrow, they will experience grace, freedom, and love. Another reason why I think this is a blessing of affirmation is because she then repeats her question, "What are you willing to do," but this time, she avows "for there is a balm in Gilead." She strategically connects the lyrics of her opening hymn with the rhetorical question to remind her audience that there is someone who can make them whole. And, with her final words, "God Bless you," she blesses them again.[72]

In this sermon, Kirk-Duggan has sought to nurture, protect, and liberate the women of the cloth from their crippling spirits that keep them bound to their past and present situations. The sermon educates people in ministry about their internal societal oppressions, or internal "isms," and pathological behaviors which hinder their future growth. Kirk-Duggan liberates her audience by helping them to realize that they have the power to overcome their oppression and by encouraging them to embrace their salvation by living out the message of the gospel. She claims, "To be church means discerning all the 'bent overness' and deal with them."[73] In order for the audience to truly be the church, they must be free from bondage—they must individually deal with their internal oppressions and pathological behaviors to free themselves so they can be the church and set others free. Traditional communalism is about affirming, nurturing, protecting, and liberating self/and community, so that the community as a whole will be reconciled and set free.

The Womanist Characteristics

According to Kirk-Duggan, womanist preaching "involves 'illustrative story-preaching' that tells of God's activity in the world, meant to affirm, inspire, provide hope, and confirm God's nearness to an oppressed people."[74] She says, "Womanist preaching is living ritual, committed to deep change and healing."[75] "To preach from a womanist perspective means to live a life of proclaimed justice, joy, peace, humbleness, with prophetic candor, and innocent delight amid complex issues and sometimes dangerous people. Womanist preaching may expose the wrongdoing of those who would rather live a lie."[76] She argues that this form of preaching "incorporates Womanist biblical hermeneutics towards searching to help people be responsible, engaging their capacities to think as they are inspired where they can listen, and then incarnate freedom, dignity, and justice of all people, communally and individually."[77]

One of the most important characteristics of womanist preaching is naming the oppressive forces that confront women—identifying the source(s) of oppression. We see this in all three of her main points. She identifies and then culturally critiques the oppressive forces that continue to cripple God's people. To name oppression allows one to confront oppression. Kirk-Duggan claims that "Womanist preachers must be willing to name, expose, and call out the harm, the evil, the wrong doing" because she sees womanist preachers as agents of change.[78] In doing so, her goal is to shift her audience from being people who are bent over to actually being people who can embrace God's anointing. In order to do this, she names the crippling spirits, explains how we become crippled, and then encourages us to embrace the legacy of those who have gone before us. Kirk-Duggan also names the pathological behaviors that get passed down through the generations by discussing the alienation that exists between genders.

Although the sermon is entitled, "Women of the Cloth," Kirk-Duggan discusses the crippling effects of each "ism" in such a way that the sermon becomes applicable to everyone. The universality of the sermon identifies it as a sermon that is committed to the survival and wholeness of all people in ministry—male, female, black, white, Hispanic, Native American, Asian, Catholic, Baptist, Methodist, or Presbyterian. What helps to make the message universal is the relevant subject matter, the line of questioning that Kirk-Duggan uses, the narratives she employs, the pronouns she uses, and the inclusive language that she uses in her line of questioning. Every culture, race, ethnicity, religious group, and academic body has traditions that hinder them from future success. In the sermon, Kirk-Duggan identifies what prevents the people of God (the church) from truly being the people of God (The Church) and what prevents those in the academy from doing what they have been called to do. In terms of the line of questioning, Kirk-Duggan believes "Womanist preaching is interrogatory in that the entire process is one of dialogue and questions, of questions and dialogue."[79] As a result, she asks questions that are not predicated on gender because she is trying to free all of her audience members from their "bent overness" so that they might free others. To do this, she incorporates first person and first-person plural pronouns (I, my, we, us) along with the second person and second-person possessive pronouns (you, your) in her questions to the audience. She poses more than thirty questions to her audience members that mostly ask: are we, are you, what is your, and do you? This way, everyone in the audience is invited to answer the questions that are raised.

Another womanist characteristic is the fact that the sermon speaks from a "both/and" vantage point. Like Westfield, Kirk-Duggan recognizes that we must both care for ourselves and others. Therefore, she does not narrow her focus to only target the women. While each of her challenges require introspection, she also asks questions such as, "[A]re you willing to be free so that you can help others to be free?" and "When was the last time you had a Native person or a Hispanic or an African American person preach at your church? Teach at your church? How many of you all have Black neighbors or Brown neighbors or Asian neighbors that you really talk to?"[80] There is this sense of probing going on that wants to find out not only what are we doing for ourselves, but also, what are we doing for other people?

CONCLUSION: A COMPARISON AND CONTRAST OF RHETORICAL STRATEGIES BETWEEN TRADITIONAL COMMUNALISM AND RADICAL SUBJECTIVITY

The major rhetorical similarities between the two types of sermons—the traditional communalism sermon by Cheryl Kirk-Duggan and the radical subjectivity sermons Elaine Flake and Gina Stewart—is their aim to heal those who are wounded or crippled, which requires people to take a similar form of action (there is an agency component), and they rely heavily on identifying the biblical character with the experiences of their audience members.

Agency, the ability to work or act on behalf of self or community, appears to have a strong role in womanist preaching. Kirk-Duggan's sermon constantly inquires of its audience members by asking them to assess themselves, by asking them if they are they willing to be set free so that they can help set others free, by asking them what are they doing for other people, and by asking them to transform their behavior. Flake's sermon moves people to action by affirming the power that lies in deciding that we have had enough, telling us to put our Jacobs in proper perspective, and then telling us that sometimes we have to fight for our deliverance. Stewart points out some of our faults—that we sometimes invest too much time and energy into relationships and that we suffer from wounded self-esteem because we mistakenly base our own worth on what others think about us. So, she encourages us to take our power back by changing our attitude and deciding that enough is enough.

Furthermore, the preachers are able to create identification between the biblical characters and their audience members through the use of metaphors. Kirk-Duggan uses the "crippling spirit" metaphor to discuss the negative effects of sexism, heterosexism, racism, and faux churchism that currently affect those in ministry. In other words, she re-images the text to make the crippling spirits fit today's experiences. Flake talks about domestic violence in such a way that she creates images of war with the help of the storyline from the movie, *Enough*, which pits husband against wife and uses language to establish that the couple is fighting back and forth and the husband is trying to kill the wife. She relates to women who are in abusive relationships and then uses light-dark metaphors such as fairytale/nightmare and love/abuse to show the past as positive existence and the present as a dreary and negative existence so that we will choose to transform our lives back into a more positive existence. Stewart uses the name of the biblical character, Jacob, as a metaphor, which Flake does as well, to symbolize the people that we allow into our lives to give us our self-esteem. They all use imagery to connect to the real-life experiences of today.

The major difference between traditional communalism and radical subjectivity is that with traditional communalism the focus is simultaneously on self and community, whereas when it comes to radical subjectivity, the focus is always on self. In looking at the element of agency, traditional communalism has a "both/and" vantage point that pushes people toward improving self and improving their relationship with others (community) so that communities or groups of people can and will continue to thrive. With radical subjectivity "self" is always the subject. How is the person improving self? What is the person doing to mature? Has the person come to an epiphany about self? Radical subjectivity spends a lot of time affirming self, while traditional communalism has a broader reach because it not only affirms "self," it also affirms the relational bonds with other people. Radical subjectivity sermons lend themselves toward moving the audience from victim to victor, whereas traditional communalism sermons lend themselves toward some form of communal healing and communal remembrance to live out the Christian faith. In rhetorical terms, this is like a Jeremiad because this type of sermon calls people back to their cultural beliefs and values after they have broken the covenant of their community.

NOTES

1. Floyd-Thomas, *Deeper Shades of Purple*, 9.
2. Ibid., 78.
3. Ibid.
4. Ibid., 78.
5. Ibid.
6. Diana M. Stewart, "Dancing Limbo: Black Passages through the Boundaries of Place, Race, Class, and Religion," in *Deeper Shades of Purple: Womanism in Religion and Society*, ed. Stacey Floyd-Thomas (New York, NY: New York University Press, 2006), 82–83.
7. Ibid., 83.
8. Ibid.
9. Ibid.
10. Ibid., 88.
11. Ibid., 94–95.
12. Rosemary Freeney Harding with Rachel Elizabeth Harding, "Hospitality, Haints, and Healing: A Southern African American Meaning of Religion," in *Deeper Shades of Purple: Womanism in Religion and Society*, ed. Stacey Floyd-Thomas (New York, NY: New York University Press, 2006), 99.
13. Ibid., 109.
14. Rosetta E. Ross, "Lessons and Treasures in Our Mothers' Witness: Why I write about Black Women's Activism," *Deeper Shades of Purple: Womanism in Religion and Society*, ed. Stacey Floyd-Thomas (New York, NY: New York University Press, 2006), 115.
15. Ibid.
16. Ibid., 116.
17. Ibid.
18. Nancy Lynne Westfield, "Mama Why...?" A Womanist Epistemology of Hope," in *Deeper Shades of Purple: Womanism in Religion and Society*, ed. Stacey Floyd-Thomas (New York, NY: New York University Press, 2006), 134.
19. Ibid.
20. Ibid., 135.
21. Walker, *In Search of Our Mother's Gardens*, xi.
22. Since this sermon has never been published, I have included in my transcription of the sermon, Appendix C, commentary brackets that note the response of the

audience from a DVD recording (i.e., clapping, laughing, and shouting). A DVD of this sermon is available in the library of Austin Presbyterian Theological Seminary in Austin, Texas.

23. Cheryl Kirk-Duggan, phone interview by Kimberly P. Johnson, December 8, 2009.

24. Cheryl Kirk-Duggan, "Women of the Cloth," March 23, 2006, Austin Presbyterian Theological Seminary, Austin, Texas. (Transcribed by Kimberly P. Johnson, see Appendix C).

25. Ibid.
26. Ibid.
27. Ibid.
28. Ibid.
29. Ibid.
30. Ibid.
31. Ibid.
32. Ibid.
33. Ibid.
34. Ibid.
35. See Genesis 2:22, 1 Corinthians 6:9.
36. Appendix C.
37. Ibid.
38. Ibid.
39. Ibid.
40. Ibid.
41. Ibid.
42. Ibid.
43. Ibid.
44. Ibid.
45. Ibid.
46. Ibid.
47. Ibid.
48. Cheryl Kirk-Duggan, phone interview by Kimberly P. Johnson, December 8, 2009.
49. Appendix C.
50. Ibid.
51. Ibid.
52. Ibid.
53. Ibid.
54. Ibid.
55. Ibid.
56. Ibid.
57. Ibid.
58. Ibid.
59. Ibid.
60. Ibid.

61. Ibid.

62. Ibid.

63. Ibid.

64. Ibid.

65. Ibid.

66. Ibid.

67. Ibid.

68. Ibid.

69. Ibid.

70. Ibid.

71. Ibid.

72. Ibid.

73. Ibid.

74. Cheryl Kirk-Duggan, "Prophesied, Sanctified Performed Praxis: Womanist Preaching," (working paper, Womanist Preaching, Faculty of Theology and Women's Studies, Shaw University Divinity School, Raleigh, 1999), 13.

75. Ibid., 12.

76. Ibid., 5.

77. Ibid., 10.

78. Ibid., 5, 13.

79. Ibid., 5.

80. Appendix C.

Chapter 4

Redemptive Self-Love

Redemptive self-love sermons seek to redeem a woman by removing
the socially perceived shame of a woman away from her actions.
The preacher must offer a perspectival corrective that re-images the
woman from being a villain to being a heroine by identifying the
integrity and morals by which the woman lives to lift the shame,
dishonor, disgrace, and condemnation that society has placed upon the
woman. These sermons also require the preacher to encourage women
(both in the text and in the audience) to match their human agency and
moral agency with a rhetorical agency. Redemptive self-love reflects
the ability to unashamedly love self and stand up for self regardless of
what anyone else thinks.

Redemptive self-love, the term that Floyd-Thomas uses to describe the third
tenet of womanism, employs autobiographical and/or spiritual trajectories to
speak to the ways in which womanists are able to develop a deep sense of
self-love. Floyd-Thomas defines this tenet as "[A]n assertion of the humanity, customs, and aesthetic value of Black women in contradistinction to the
commonly held stereotypes characteristic of white solipsism. The admiration
and celebration of the distinctive and identifiable beauty of Black women.
'I'm black and beautiful O ye daughters of Jerusalem.'" Song of Solomon
1:5, NRSV.[1] Redemptive self-love examines the ability to unashamedly
love self and stand up for self, even against the stereotypes held by those
in power/white power. I recognize that this individual is not on a journey
toward self-love because she already loves herself *regardless*. Regardless
of what anyone else thinks, this individual is going to enjoy life, stick to her
beliefs, and look out for herself to make sure that she is not taken advantage
of. This individual has a strong sense of who she is, so she guards against

others trying to make her into who she is not. The redemptive aspect is that it lifts the shame, dishonor, disgrace, and condemnation that society has placed upon this woman. Consequently, redemptive self-love sermons urge women to match their human agency and moral agency with a rhetorical agency—an emphatic oral expression—in order to reclaim their voice.

According to Kelly Brown Douglas, womanism affirmed that it was okay for her to be black, female, and authentic at the same time because it gave her the voice to speak from her own experiences of pain and struggle—womanism validated the authoritative power of the black female voice.[2] It allowed black women to stand in solidarity with their black female sisters as they all struggled to discover their own voice and their own path in life.[3] She explains how reading Alice Walker's definition connected with her in her places of pain, struggle, trying to fit in, and trying to be herself and love herself, "regardless."[4] For Douglas, the most significant aspect of womanism is its dialogical nature, which is found in the second tenet of Walker's womanist definition—"'Mama, why are we brown, pink, and yellow, and our cousins are white, beige, and black?' Ans.: 'Well, you know the colored race is just like a flower garden, with every color flower represented' and . . . 'Mama, I'm walking to Canada and I'm taking you and a bunch of other slaves with me.' Reply: 'It wouldn't be the first time.'"[5] Douglas addresses the "dialogical nature" of womanism primarily that of the later excerpt in order to make meaning out of redemptive self-love.

In "Twenty Years a Womanist: An Affirming Challenge," Douglas argues that womanist dialogue (redemptive self-love) must privilege the everyday experiences of black women, reflect the privileged dialogue of black women in the black church, necessitate a moral agency as well as an existential moral commitment, counter the normative view of sexuality, and affirm the voices of the weak and powerless.[6] This type of "epistemological privilege" that womanism gives to everyday black women challenges notions of knowledge, and at the same time, forces scholars to recognize that knowledge legitimated by white patriarchal academic institutions may not be knowledge at all.[7] Womanist dialogue also elucidates the meaning of moral agency. Douglas defines moral agency quite like human agency, which is human engagement or even a self-motivated political engagement, because we have to use our physical, emotional, and spiritual energy to fight off oppressive forces.[8] Womanist dialogue (redemptive self-love) must forthrightly engage in "frustrating" and "debunking" heterosexism and homophobic rhetoric so that people can love whom they choose to love—love starts by loving one's self, regardless.[9] This is done by challenging views of sexuality that only affirm "reproductive" sexual expression. Womanist dialogue affirms those who have been marginalized, it does not matter what gender, race, ethnicity, class, or sexuality womanism seeks to redeem and uplift the oppressed.

Throughout Douglas's article, she constructs a framework to describe her own understanding of what womanist scholarship looks like if it is attempting to reflect this third tenet of womanism. She claims that womanist scholarship (redemptive self-love) must affirm *authentic* knowledge, uncover discourses of power, engage in work that responds to the voices of those who have been pushed to the margins, oppose all forms of human oppression, address the difficult issues and challenges of sexuality that permeates black churches, and reconcile the bond between sexual intimacy and loving relationships.[10] For Douglas, womanist scholarship, more specifically, womanist dialogue that reflects redemptive self-love must affirm authentic knowledge, confront discourses of power, oppose all forms of oppression, and restore the viewpoint that sexuality is not sinful, it is sacred.

Karen Baker-Fletcher's understanding of redemptive self-love is explained in her article, "A Womanist Journey," which discusses her voyage from self-identifying as a feminist to self-identifying as a womanist. She argues from the essentialist perspective that a white woman or white feminist cannot be a womanist because womanism emerged from what Katie Cannon refers to as "the real-lived experiences" of black women or women of color in the face of modern-day slavery, racism, segregation, colonization, and globalization.[11] Yet, she is open to other women of color identifying as a womanist as long as they are *"in authentic relationships of mutuality, equality, and respect with black women."*[12] White feminists who attempt to appropriate the womanist identity actually disassociate its original sociohistorical and cultural contexts.[13] Baker-Fletcher claims "[t]he goal is to develop relationships of mutuality while respecting boundaries."[14] Then she gives the example:

> One of my responses to white women who want to *be* womanists, rather than advocate womanist thought, has been, "Are you willing to stop identifying as 'white' and live *every* moment of your life as a black woman?" In order to do this, one would have to be black in *community with black people*, with all that means: self-identity in the workplace, with friends, in the neighborhood, shopping, in worship, with family, etc. It entails giving up *every* vestige of white privilege, including skin color, when mistaken for white I have not met anyone who was willing to give up white racial privilege to this degree.[15]

When white women attempt to become womanists this is seen as "disrespect for the freedom to be collectively self-naming as black women or women of color" because they are ignoring the boundaries of womanism, which then becomes oppressive—they want to control black women's self-identity—which is an issue of power and ownership.[16] For Baker-Fletcher, redemptive self-love appears in her ability to stand by her convictions of not letting others, particularly white feminists, control her self-identity, and her conviction to not worship the earth, but God, whose Spirit is in everything and everybody, including the earth.

Cheryl Kirk-Duggan examines "relationality" rooted in Walker's definition, bell hook's notion of "killing rage," and the Christian value of love in order to bring clarity to her meaning of redemptive self-love. She identifies three categories by which we engage or thwart relationships: a spirituality of aesthetics, an incarnated holistic vision, and parasitic oppression.[17] A *"womanist"* spirituality reveals an embodied, individual and communal, revolutionary way of life and theoretical discourse that is grounded in its resistance to injustice.[18] A "womanist" holistic vision builds on the framework of an aesthetic spirituality to include an imaginative epistemology and a transformative attitude as it constructs a solid methodology that honors all voices. [19] An aesthetic spirituality is one that sees Divine Beauty and a liberating form of resistance incarnated in human form to work toward wellness and transformation. An imaginative epistemology honors the wisdom of our ancestors and a transformative attitude lives in the chaos of hate, but draws on the spiritual richness of love, justice, and tolerance.[20] A "womanist" aesthetic spirituality exposes all forms of oppression, along with the character traits of those in power who manipulate, misuse, and abuse other human beings.[21] Kirk-Duggan echoes the ideas of bell hooks and her notion of "killing rage" by reminding us that "killing rage" is a necessary and powerful tool of militant resistance that transforms denial and complicit oppression by defying victimhood. It does this by engaging in a language of self-determination to dismantle racist, sexist, classist, and heterosexist hegemonic power structures. This tool of resistance is a tool for change because it cultivates healthy relationships that are rooted in love.[22] In other words "killing rage" can be either a destructive or creative force because we have the power to decide if we want to comply or resist, be pessimistic or hopeful, be stagnant or strive for healthy relationships.[23] When "killing rage" becomes a creative force, it empowers us to act out of love, agape love, which is unconditional love.

Kirk-Duggan identifies agape love—unconditional love rooted in Christianity—as a term that epitomizes the Womanist motif.[24] This love ethic requires us to always act out of love, even when it comes to loving our enemies. Agape love is ultimately self-love because it forces us to love others as we love ourselves. Jesus expressed this very notion in teaching the great commandment, "Love the Lord your God with all your heart, mind and soul, and love your neighbor as yourself."[25] Kirk-Duggan argues that the paradox of this type of love is that regardless of behavior, one must be able to see the sacred in others, have the capacity to love others and to love one's self.[26] Ultimately, Kirk-Duggan recognizes that redemptive self-love entails agape love, or unconditional love, because it commands us to love others as we love ourselves. But, what makes this self-love redemptive is how womanists strategize and organize for the uplift of the survival and wholeness both individually and communally.

In Shani Settles's description of redemptive self-love, we begin to understand that in order to love *regardless* and to adhere to Walker's third tenet of the womanist definition, one must walk in one's destiny always conscious of the cloud of witnesses that have gone before us.[27] Settles explores how African Derived Religions (ADRs) can serve as a significant resource to advance womanist thought and praxis since they produce conscientization by demanding a revolutionary type of love, which in turn creates a revolutionary being. The modes of resistance in ADRs equip individuals to be able to claim to themselves and the dominant hegemonic power structures a reconstructed definition of self through an Afrocentric lens.[28]

Settles examines the modes of resistance by exploring the representations and attributes of Osun, a popularly imaged prototypical "love goddess," an "African Venus" or "Afrodite," who is the essence of passion and beauty itself.[29] As a result of ethnic masking, she is situated within the motif of a white "love goddess" whose image and value are constructed via white cultural standards. She becomes an honorary white woman who represents beauty, power, and being.[30] While being reduced to a hypersexual being, Osun also foregrounds the command to eradicate Blackness. Osun empowers black women to dissect and scrutinize the dominant social, patriarchal, and capitalistic power structures that maintain social segregation, political exclusion, and economic degradation.[31] Osun emerges as a source of/for power because her degraded sexuality becomes reimaged into a "revolutionary love" for self. Settles defines revolutionary love as the "life-force" that challenges black women to celebrate and exalt themselves and each other.[32]

Ultimately, Settles recognizes redemptive self-love as (1) the ability to love self at all costs; (2) the ability to reject social constructions; and (3) the ability to redefine, reconstitute or construct self-identity by deconstructing Eurocentric patriarchal codes and structures.[33] In order to love self, one must totally and intensely love one another, humanity, and life itself. This mutual respect for one's multiplicity and the capacity to see a divine presence allows for revolutionary communities to then emerge.[34] Love becomes the transformative key toward liberation.

Alice Walker describes this third tenet of her womanist definition as a woman who "Loves music. Loves dance. Loves the moon. *Loves* the Spirit. Loves love and food and roundness. Loves struggle. *Loves* the Folk. Loves herself. *Regardless*."[35] In other words, redemptive self-love loves self at all costs—even at the expense of being misunderstood, degraded, or vilified.

Redemptive self-love causes individuals to resist the social constructs of others by operating out of who they themselves say that they are.

RHETORICAL ANALYSIS OF MELVA L. SAMPSON'S SERMON, "HELL NO!"

This happened in the days of Ahasuerus, the same Ahasuerus who ruled over one hundred twenty-seven provinces from India to Ethiopia. In those days when King Ahasuerus sat on his royal throne in the citadel of Susa, in the third year of his reign, he gave a banquet for all his officials and ministers. The army of Persia and Media and the nobles and governors of the provinces were present, while he displayed the great wealth of his kingdom and the splendor and pomp of his majesty for many days, one hundred eighty days in all.

When these days were completed, the king gave for all the people present in the citadel of Susa, both great and small, a banquet lasting for seven days, in the court of the garden of the king's palace. There were white cotton curtains and blue hangings tied with cords of fine linen and purple to silver rings and marble pillars. There were couches of gold and silver on a mosaic pavement of porphyry, marble, mother-of-pearl, and colored stones. Drinks were served in golden goblets, goblets of different kinds, and the royal wine was lavished according to the bounty of the king. Drinking was by flagons, without restraint; for the king had given orders to all the officials of his palace to do as each one desired. Furthermore, Queen Vashti gave a banquet for the women in the palace of King Ahasuerus.

On the seventh day, when the king was merry with wine, he commanded Mehuman, Biztha, Harbona, Bigtha and Abagtha, Zethar and Carkas, the seven eunuchs who attended him, to bring Queen Vashti before the king, wearing the royal crown, in order to show the peoples and the officials her beauty; for she was fair to behold. But Queen Vashti refused to come at the king's command conveyed by the eunuchs.

                                                    Esther 1:1–12, NRSV

Sampson's sermon, "Hell No!" was first delivered, in 2007, at Sankofa United Church of Christ (UCC), which is an African-centered ministry in Atlanta, Georgia. On the day of delivery, Sampson preached this 20–25-minute sermon to approximately fifteen people whose ages ranged from 0 to 65 years of age.[36] The second time Sampson preached this sermon was at the American Baptist College for the Nannie Helen Burroughs luncheon.[37] When asked what gave her the courage to title her sermon, "Hell No!" she said:

[She] went to see the musical, *The Color Purple*, when it first debuted in Atlanta, and that there is a title song called "Hell No!" . . . and [she] loves that song. One day [she] was reading over that text [Esther 1:1–12] . . . [which she has] preached . . . before on numerous occasions under different titles and when [she] read the part, verse 12, where the eunuch asks Vashti to come to see the King, [she] remembers saying out loud, Hell No! And, ever since that day, [she] decided if [she] were to ever preach the sermon again, [she] would title it that ["Hell No!"]. Part of it was the shock-and-awe value and the adamant absolute stand against oppressive, nature, order, systems.[38]

When Sampson first preached this sermon at Sankofa UCC, she says, "The congregation was such that [she] knew it [the title] would be acceptable."[39] But, the second time this sermon was delivered, she says "It could have appeared risky . . . [because] when she preached it at American Baptist College, they were shocked. The audience's response at the title was 'What did she say?' . . . and [she] said it again." Although some may be shocked by its title, as Sampson continues to preach this sermon in the future, she will keep the title, "Hell No!"

ANALYSIS

"Hell No!" is a racy sermon that creatively emphasizes the point, "Material gain, position, and status are never worth giving one's soul away."[40] It is the shortest out of all five sermons, but in its brevity, Sampson is able to counter patriarchal dominance, bring a marginalized voice to the forefront, and address the importance of loving and saving one's self. The sermon begins with the focal text verse 12, "But Queen Vashti refused to come at the king's command conveyed by the eunuchs" and is quickly followed by lyrics from the song "Hell No!" in the musical adapted from Alice Walker's novel, *The Color Purple*, and Steven Spielberg's film of the same name.

Girl child ain't safe in a family o' mens.
Sick 'n tired how a woman still live like a slave.
You better learn how to fight back while you still alive . . .
But he try to make me mind and I just ain't that kind . . .
Hell no![41]

These lyrics, which are taken from two different stanzas, call attention to the predatory, oppressive, and abusive nature of some men that women, particularly African American women, encounter. The first line, "Girl child ain't safe in a family o' mens," references the dangers of incest when a little girl is left in the presence of her male relatives. *The Color Purple* sheds light on this unfortunate reality in the African American community of little

girls being raped at the hands of their fathers. The story is about a young
girl named Celie, who writes letters to God because her father beats her and
rapes her. As a result of the incest, Celie gives birth to a daughter and son.
She later becomes a battered wife and eventually learns how to stand up for
herself and fight back. So when the musical character, Sofia, sings about how
little girls are not safe, which is a saying that has been passed down through
so many black families, the danger is incest and the result is that these little
girls become pregnant. The second line, "Sick 'n tired how a woman still live
like a slave" invokes the tragedy of slavery, when the white male was the
master over blacks, and it implies that the role of African American men has
changed to the point that they now act as masters over their wives/women.
Whatever the man says goes and the woman must always oblige. Then, Sofia
sings this third line, "You better learn how to fight back while you still alive .
. ." because she is trying to encourage Celie to stand up for herself and to stop
taking the abuse. The fourth line of this musical excerpt pertains to Sofia's
own life. Sofia is referring to her husband, Harpo, who tries to box her in to
make her act a certain way, but she refuses to conform. Hence, her emphatic,
"Hell No!"

Sampson uses excerpts from the "Hell No!" lyrics as a bridge in her narrative anecdote of sitting around her grandmother Nez's, kitchen table. Here,
she defines what "Hell no!" means. She says that in her family, "'Hell no!'
signaled an emphatic refusal used to express discontent toward a person,
place, or thing. . . . 'Hell no!' was a saying or righteous indignation, the
opposite of blasphemy but an acknowledgment of the reverence for ourselves
as wholly holy and without restraint to resist whatever sought to silence
our voices. . . . [It was] grown woman's talk."[42] Next, she provides real-life
situations when Sampson, her grandmother, and her mother responded with
an emphatic "Hell no!" The womanist dialogue begins with the time big
momma, Nez, said 'Hell no!' when asked if she would "honor and obey" her
husband. Sampson's "mother said, "Hell no!" when the pastor summoned
. . . her to consider staying with [Sampson's] father."[43] And finally, when
Sampson was asked "if [she] would preach from the floor because the pulpit
was reserved for male authority, . . . [she] vehemently replied, 'Hell no!'"[44]

Sampson uses all of these "Hell no!" sayings from the musical and from
the women in her family, who were influenced by Nez, to theoretically justify the plausibility of her anecdote—"When I read Vashti's story, I think of
Nez, who, if she had been with Vashti after hearing the king's request, surely
would have looked at the queen and given her the royal nod to repeat after her
and say, 'Hell no!'"[45] Immediately, Queen Vashti becomes familiar to Sampson because she places Queen Vashti on a first name basis, similar to what she
does with the women of her family (i.e., Nez). Then, by creatively inserting
Nez into the biblical text not only encourages Queen Vashti in her attempt

Table 4.1 Melva Sampson Rhetorical Tools

Rhetorical Tools	Purpose of Rhetorical Tools
Provocative language	To encourage women to go for the shock-and-awe value by matching their actions and decisions with an emphatic oral response
"Hell No!" Lyrics from the musical, *The Color Purple*	To call attention to the predatory, oppressive, and abusive nature of some men that leads to rape/incest
Anecdote of sitting around Nez's kitchen table	To establish the meaning of "Hell no!"—an emphatic refusal used to express discontent toward a person, place, or thing
"Hell no!" testimony	To show us how we must resist whatever tries to silence our voices
Embodiment	To encourage Queen Vashti and all of us to go ahead and say the words, "Hell no!" when we find ourselves in a "Hell no!" moment
Metaphorical "Hell no!"	To give Queen Vashti a voice
Scene from the Steven Spielberg film, *The Color Purple*	To encourage us to celebrate the sound of our own voice—the sound of the genuine
Calls the roll of prominent African American women	To show that these women retrieved their voice and freed themselves from dominant hegemonic power structures, patriarchy, and humiliatingly oppressive roles

Table created by Kimberly P. Johnson.

to save herself, but also gives her a voice. Verse 12 says, "Vashti refused to come. . . ." In other words, the scripture only records Queen Vashti's defiant behavior; it does not give her a voice. Queen Vashti's behavior is what tells us that she said, "No." Therefore, to insert Nez into the text to encourage the queen to respond in righteous indignation with an emphatic, "Hell no!" would match her human agency and her moral agency with a rhetorical agency that would reclaim her voice. Redemptive self-love calls one to make a proclamation to self and a proclamation to the dominant hegemonic powers at work.[46] This verbal proclamation would emphasize the queen's resistance to being objectified and humiliated by her husband.

At this point, the sermon begins to unfold the narrative of the text in order to provide the background information surrounding Queen Vashti's decision. Sampson discusses how the Book of Esther opens by describing a 180-day "shindig," or party, that King Ahasuerus holds to celebrate his recent conquests and then she reveals that he has an even more extravagant

7-day celebration for the citizens of Susa.[47] She explains that the king is "Drunk with wine and out of toys to display, [so] the king decided to go for the shock-and-awe factor. He summoned Queen Vashti to appear at the party immediately, adorned, as some would suggest, with only her royal crown."[48] Sampson is establishing the idea that the king, who has the highest authority in the royal provinces, is inebriated and has run out of items that show off his wealth. As a plan B, he requests that his wife come wearing only her royal crown. This type of display would flaunt his wealth, his power, and the seductiveness of the one who sexually pleases him. Having Queen Vashti stand naked, and more than likely dance as entertainment for the king and all of his inebriated male guests, would represent his wealth because the queen is his most prized possession and only the king can afford to place such a regal crown upon his wife's head. Displaying Queen Vashti would represent the king's power because it would show (1) that the king does not have to make a request in person to get what he wants, he can send his eunuchs to deliver a message for him; and (2) that even the most powerful woman in the province submits to the orders of her king, no matter the request. The nakedness of Queen Vashti dancing as entertainment would make the other men jealous as well as exploit her seductive qualities while revealing the contours and voluptuousness of her body. Therefore, to refuse the king's command would disrespect the king's wealth, power, and need to make others envious of his possessions.

Sampson notes that Queen Vashti's response is usually overlooked; "Yet to gloss over this monumental moment of liberation is to miss the making of a model of leadership in which following 'the sound of the genuine' within one's self is paramount." She explains to her audience, "The text reads, 'But Queen Vashti refused to come at the king's command conveyed by the eunuchs. At this the king was enraged and his anger burned within him.'"[49] "Such a model moves us from the sin of self-sacrifice and self-abnegation to the virtues of self-acceptance and self-development."[50] Here, Samson hints at her three main points, which she paraphrases and alludes to throughout the sermon. She claims, Vashti's metaphorical response of "Hell no!" became a "model for all the women in Susa," a threat to all of the men, and a reminder that we will sometimes have to pay a price to retrieve our voice, dignity, and self-worth—for the queen, the cost was banishment.[51] As Sampson unfolds the meaning of Queen Vashti's refusal and what it means to us, each revelation corresponds to one of the points she has just made. First, Sampson argues that "Vashti's insistence on taking care of herself reveals to us that we too will be faced with life-altering decisions when we decide to honor our own divinity."[52] The correlation between what Sampson says here and what Sampson said above in terms of the price Queen Vashti had to pay reiterates that we too may have to pay the price of banishment in order to retrieve our voice, dignity, and self-worth. Second, she contends that "Vashti's actions and the king's response are telltale signs that we too, will have to choose between revolution and apathy, between objectification and humanization, and between the inevitability of pain and the option of misery."[53] This statement corresponds to the fact that women are a threat because we have the power to choose between submitting to hegemonic powers and starting our own revolution that honors self. Third, she maintains, "We will all one day be summoned to the king and be forced to choose between a mealy-mouthed yes and an emphatic 'Hell no!'"[54] Redemptive self-love will always choose the emphatic "Hell no!" over the "mealy-mouthed yes" because this woman loves herself so much, she refuses to be oppressed by other people. This serves as a model for how women are to respond when the king, or even their own husband, summons them to fulfill a debasing request. All of these behavioral revelations are reiterated once again in Sampson's "three points to ponder."[55]

Sampson eventually arrives at the point in her sermon where she clearly identifies, through the use of signposts, the three main points that she wants her audience to understand and ponder: "First, we must beware of the invitations we entertain"; "Second, we must beware of the pride of the powerful"; "Third, we need to beware of false thrills; outward success is not equal to inner worth."[56] As she expounds on her first point, she warns women against "fall[ing] victim to a false sense of promotion that stems from our need to be recognized."[57] In a patriarchal society, men possess the power and are recognized as the authority figures. Therefore, to receive an invitation from a male authority figure does present an opportunity for recognition, but the type of recognition is not always a positive one. Sampson states, "Every invitation is not worth accepting and should be scrutinized thoroughly, or we too will be put in the position of appearing naked before the king's court."[58] Once again, this first point corresponds to Queen Vashti's metaphorical "Hell no!" serving as a model for all the women of Susa because it warns women how to respond when they are summoned.

The second point to ponder, "[W]e must beware of the pride of the powerful" also serves as a model for women, but more closely represents the notion that women are a threat to men.[59] Sampson explains that the king's pride was fueled by his perceived powerlessness of Queen Vashti.[60] She then takes us back to the song, "Hell No!" in the musical, *The Color Purple*, to point out, "When we respond to our voice, we threaten the pride of the powerful. We must learn how to fight back in ways that annihilate both the pride and the power of those who seek to enslave our bodies, minds, and souls."[61] Here, Sampson cautions women because she does not want the pride of the powerful to "thwart our inner ability to say, 'Hell no!,'" instead, she wants us to creatively figure out ways to destroy the pride and the power of those who seek to oppress us. By emphatically saying "Hell no!" or using other emphatic oral expressions, we not only threaten the pride of the powerful, we threaten their power as well.

The third point to ponder, "[W]e need to beware of false thrills; outward success is not equal to inner worth" corresponds to the price we pay to retrieve our voice, dignity, and self-worth.[62] When one is groomed to become the queen, one exudes the appearance of outward success, but once being chosen to be the queen, one is expected to submit to the king's every whim. Consequently, one becomes at risk of losing her inner self. Sampson cites Carol Lakey Hess in saying, ". . . had the queen disregarded her own feelings and submitted to the will of the king, she would have lost herself ever so quietly. . . . No one would have noticed; she would have simply colluded with quiet conspiracy."[63] I think the "quiet conspiracy" is a plot to, in the words of Sampson, "keep us beholden to weak-willed, fickle, and self-centered people."[64] This type of enslavement would inevitably seek to destroy our inner selves. Sampson finally proclaims, "The moral to Vashti's refusal is simple—outward success is not equal to inner worth. Material gain, position, and status are never worth giving one's soul away."[65]

After establishing the central idea of the sermon, Sampson moves her audience to a discussion about a particular scene in the movie, *The Color Purple*. By now, we have already transitioned from the song, "Hell No!" in the musical, *The Color Purple*, to a personal narrative/anecdote, to the biblical text, back to the musical, back to the biblical text, and now to the Steven Spielberg film, *The Color Purple*. Sampson highlights the scene where "Miss Millie, the mayor's wife, asks Sofia if she wants to come and be her maid. Sofia's response is classic: 'Hell no!' Astonished at her response, the mayor asks, 'What did you say, gal?' Sofia responds again, 'Hell no!'"[66] Unlike Queen Vashti's situation, Sofia ends up in a physical altercation and eventually gets sentenced to prison for many years. Upon her release, she is forced to do that which she so adamantly refused to do earlier—she has to go work for Miss Millie. Sampson points out that it is at the dinner table with her family that Sofia "reclaims her muted voice, recounts the reason for her response, and celebrates the sound of her own voice—the sound of the genuine."[67]

Sampson then shifts her audience to the last paragraph of her sermon by unveiling the profound question that the stories of Sofia, Queen Vashti, and all the women who gather around Nez's table reveal. She asks, "When is the last time you said, 'Hell no!'?" and then proceeds to list how several prominent African American women were able to acknowledge the sound of their own voices—the sound of the genuine.[68] She mentions Esther for the second time. Next, we hear about Fannie Lou Hamer, then Maya Angelou, followed by Sister Shange and Anna Julia Cooper. She says:

Esther resolved, "If I perish let me perish." Fannie Lou Hamer proclaimed, "I'm sick and tired of being sick and tired." Our great elder Maya Angelou penned, "And Still I Rise." Sister Shange shouted, "I found God in myself and I loved her/I loved her fiercely." Anna Julia Cooper said soundly, "When and where I enter, the whole race enters with me." God rejoices when we acknowledge the sound of our own voices. It is when we find our voices that we celebrate who God created us to be.[69]

In all five of the above examples that are given about these women, we never hear one of them utter the words, "Hell no!" We understand that they reclaimed their voice and are able to celebrate who God has called them to be but we do not hear the words that Sampson has trained us to say. On the surface, it does not appear as if the above examples of Esther, Hamer, Angelou, Shange, and Cooper represent "Hell no!" moments. But, once we dig deeper, or at least listen a little closer, we come to the understanding that our "Hell no!" moments represent the times when we "go for the shock-and-awe value and retrieve our voice, our power, and our bodies."[70] Sampson explains, "These women paid high prices for freeing themselves from male authority, patriarchal dominance, and humiliating roles. Yet their responses suggest that more times than not we need to say, 'Hell no!' Sometimes, a simple answer of 'No,' 'No thank you,' or 'I'm sorry, I'll pass' just doesn't get it. We need to go for the shock-and-awe value. . . ."[71]

In this sermon, Sampson has embodied the role of Nez to encourage all of us to go ahead and say the words, "Hell no!" when we find ourselves in a "Hell no!" moment. Consequently, she leaves us with the question, "What will you do when the king/queen comes for you?"[72] Her choice of words "king/queen" invites the men along with the women to come to terms with how they will respond when they are summoned—will they give a simple response or will they go for the shock-and-awe value by matching their actions and decisions with an emphatic "Hell no!"? Sampson's unconventional approach to the text allows her to re-envision Queen Vashti in a manner that takes away the shame, disgrace, dishonor, and condemnation that society has placed upon this queen. She transforms society's image of Queen Vashti, the villain, into an image of Queen Vashti, the heroine.

The Womanist Characteristics

Sampson, herself, has wrestled with putting her understanding of womanist preaching into words. She claims that she received clarity on how she was personally defining womanist preaching through a conversation with Katie Cannon.[73] She indicated, "Dr. Cannon says that what [she] is saying is that it [womanist preaching] really is an embodied mediated knowledge."[74]

Sampson suggests that "womanist preaching is about the hermeneutic and the delivery, but it is not necessarily a performance like a performing artist performance more than it is saying when one puts one's entire self into something, when one connects with something."[75] This definition reflects Sampson's embodiment of Nez throughout the sermon. Her "embodied mediated knowledge" was the knowledge of her grandmother. She took on the role of her grandmother to help others come to an understanding of the reverence for self—redemptive self-love. For Sampson, redemptive self-love is about "redeeming ourselves from who society has seen us as, redeeming ourselves from what we even see ourselves as to the point that we love ourselves unashamedly without apology."[76]

The most profound characteristic of womanist preaching is found in the audacity to say, "Hell no!" when we find ourselves in a "Hell no!" moment, which symbolizes an absolute reverence for self regardless of the cost or price one might have to pay for keeping her voice, dignity, and self-worth. Renita Weems claims that "Queen Vashti's integrity, before the company of women who looked up to her as a role model, depended on her courage to refuse to compromise."[77] The redemptive self-love quality of saying, "Hell no!" means going for the shock-and-awe factor to boldly stand in contradiction to stereotypes and what people say when oppressive forces of society seek to silence our voice. Or, as Shani Settles helps us to understand, it gives us the ability to reconstitute or construct self-identity by deconstructing Eurocentric patriarchal codes and structures.[78] We see this type of "righteous indignation" laced throughout the sermon. We see it in the song "Hell No!" from the musical, *The Color Purple*. We see it in Nez and in all the women who gathered around Nez's kitchen table "reclaiming, reviving, and revolutionizing black women's roles in church and society."[79] We understand the real-life application of it in Sampson's womanist dialogue that testifies about the times when her grandmother, her mother, and she herself have had to emphatically refuse what was being asked of them. She says:

> When [big momma] was asked if she would "honor and obey" her husband during one of her three wedding ceremonies, my big momma Nez, said, "Hell no!" When the pastor summoned my mother to ask her to consider staying with my father, even though he was physically and verbally abusive, my mother responded with a resounding, "Hell no!" When asked "if I would preach from the floor because the pulpit was reserved for male authority, I looked the deacon square in the eye and vehemently replied, "Hell no!"[80]

A number of us women stand in agreement with the emphatic "Hell no!" of big momma, Sampson's mother, and Sampson. For instance, a lot of us take issue with the "obey" part of the "honor and obey" clause in wedding ceremonies. Thinking about it even now takes me back to the "Hell No!" lyrics when Sofia sings, "Sick 'n tired how a woman still live like a slave."[81] Had Nez agreed to always obey her husband and submit to patriarchy, it would have put her back into the same role as her ancestors—she would have felt like a slave. Apparently, Nez loved herself enough to say, "Hell no!" Then, when we examine the situation of Sampson's mother, we see that a clergy person who has studied the Bible is asking her to submit to a life of physical and verbal abuse. The mother rightfully loved herself more than she loved her husband and was unwilling to submit to this type of male dominance, which meant a life filled with domestic violence. This internal love for self is what gave her the courage to say, "Hell no!" and walk away. Finally, when we look at the religious hypocrisy surrounding Sampson's experience, we see another authority figure of the church asking a woman to submit to religious patriarchy. The expectation was that Sampson would preach from the floor because the church believed that the sacredness of the pulpit was reserved for male preachers, not female preachers. It does not matter that the same God who calls men to preach is the same God who calls women to preach. Nor does it seem to matter that this particular church called Sampson to preach via an invitation. This church was set in its ways and wanted Sampson to submit to its authority. But, just like her mother and grandmother, Sampson loved herself enough and respected the calling that God placed on her life to the point where she would not allow herself to submit to religious patriarchy nor would she allow the church to degrade her anointing as a minister. Therefore, with righteous indignation, she too said, "Hell no!"

If we examine Sampson's anecdote that places Nez within the biblical text, we grow to understand that redemptive self-love is a knowledge that needs to be passed on to all generations. Sampson says, "When I read Vashti's story, I think of Nez, who, if she had been with Vashti after hearing the king's request, surely would have looked at the queen and given her the royal nod to repeat after her and say, "Hell no!"[82] Nez would have encouraged Queen Vashti to say, with righteous indignation, "Hell no!" to the king's request. She would have gotten the queen to go for the shock-and-awe factor. Instead, what we are left with is a metaphorical "Hell no!" The queen's refusal definitely got her point across and the price she paid was complete exile. But, the point that both Nez and Sampson seem to be communicating is that when a person tries to shock us with an outrageous request that silences us and dishonors who we are, we need to fight back with the "shock-and-awe value and retrieve our voice, our power, and our bodies."[83] Not only does this sermon re-envision Queen Vashti as a heroine who loved herself *regardless*—despite what other people said, thought, or tried to do to her—it also encourages us to match our actions and decisions with a forceful verbal response.

Although the sermon is mainly about a woman and uses examples of several women, it can still be considered an inclusive sermon. The target audience appears to consist of women, but the overall message, "Material gain, position, and status are never worth giving one's soul away," is so universal that the message becomes applicable to everyone. At the end of the sermon, Sampson asks, "What will you do when the king/queen comes for you?"[84] This "king/queen" signifies that she is directing the question to both women and men, and that all of us will one day have to choose between honoring our own divinity and honoring some humiliating request. Are we going to be courageous and audacious enough to say, "Hell no!" or are we going to opt for a more simple reply that shies away from countering a shocking request with a shocking response?

CONCLUSION: A COMPARISON AND CONTRAST OF RHETORICAL STRATEGIES BETWEEN REDEMPTIVE SELF-LOVE AND RADICAL SUBJECTIVITY

The two major rhetorical similarities between the two types of sermons—the redemptive self-love sermon by Melva Sampson and the radical subjectivity sermons by Elaine Flake and Gina Stewart—are that they name the oppression and they focus on self-love. Interestingly enough, their similarities also highlight their differences. Sampson names objectification and patriarchal dominance as the oppressive forces that Queen Vashti would have to decide if she was going to submit to. Flake and Stewart identify domestic violence and our male dominated social structures as the oppressive forces that women fall victim to that destroy their self-esteem. The difference between the oppression in a redemptive self-love sermon is that the oppression never comes to full fruition because the woman (i.e., Queen Vashti) adamantly refuses to submit to the request. This means that radical subjectivity sermons empower a woman to physically respond to her situation and redemptive self-love sermons empower a woman to match a verbal response to the decisions and actions she has already made. As I stated above, radical subjectivity sermons lend themselves toward moving the audience/self from victim to victor; however, redemptive self-love sermons lend themselves toward re-envisioning the audience's perception of a biblical character, a historical figure, or a more contemporary person from villain to heroine—one who has a "revolutionary love" for self.[85] These sermons restore the positive viewpoint of how society sees the person. Redemptive self-love sermons redeem the individual.[86] The more conventional way of preaching the Esther text vilifies Queen Vashti and exalts Queen Esther. Yet, Sampson's sermon takes the stain of shame off Queen Vashti and clothes her in a robe of heroism. Queen Vashti becomes a model for all people to consider when they have to make a life-changing decision.

Both radical subjectivity and redemptive self-love sermons focus on self-love, but they approach it from two different perspectives. Radical subjectivity sermons have to build up and affirm the individual because the woman is not secure in herself, she is on a journey toward identity formation, self love, and self-worth. Therefore, radical subjectivity sermons focus on getting the woman to love herself enough to change her situation. Redemptive self-love sermons focus on self-love, but they are lifting up the fact that the biblical character already loves herself enough to resist being silenced or losing her dignity or self-worth. Consequently, redemptive self-love sermons work at trying to get the woman to match her actions and strategies with an equally bold verbal response. In other words, the woman/character in redemptive self-love sermons has already exerted her own agency—she has already devised a plan to stand up for herself and taken the necessary actions. Redemptive self-love sermons, unlike radical subjectivity sermons, do not have to work on getting a woman to defend herself; they have to work at taking the socially perceived shame away from her actions. To further expound, radical subjectivity works at alleviating the shame a woman feels from being victimized. Redemptive self-love works at transforming the eyesight of society because it redeems the perception of a woman that society sees as shameful. A woman in a radical subjectivity sermon has to come to the understanding of self-love and self-worth, but a woman in a redemptive self-love sermon already loves herself *regardless*.

NOTES

1. Floyd-Thomas, *Deeper Shades of Purple*, 143.

2. Kelly Brown Douglas, "Twenty Years a Womanist: An Affirming Challenge," in *Deeper Shades of Purple: Womanism in Religion and Society*, ed. Stacey Floyd-Thomas (New York, NY: New York University Press, 2006), 146.

3. Ibid.

4. Ibid., 145.

5. Walker, *In Search of Our Mother's Gardens*, xi.

6. Douglas, "Twenty Years a Womanist,"147–149, 151–152.

7. Ibid., 147.

8. Ibid., 149.

9. Ibid., 152.

10. Ibid., 147–148, 150–152, 155.

11. Karen Baker-Fletcher, "A Womanist Journey" in *Deeper Shades of Purple: Womanism in Religion and Society*, ed. Stacey Floyd-Thomas (New York, NY: New York University Press, 2006), 161–162.

12. Ibid., 163.

13. Ibid., 166.

14. Ibid., 167.

15. Ibid.

16. Ibid.

17. Cheryl Kirk-Duggan, "Quilting Relations with Creation: Overcoming, Going Through, and Not Being Stuck," in *Deeper Shades of Purple: Womanism in Religion and Society*, ed. Stacey Floyd-Thomas (New York, NY: New York University Press, 2006), 178.

18. Ibid.

19. Ibid., 179.

20. Ibid.

21. Ibid., 179–180.

22. Ibid., 180.

23. Ibid.

24. Ibid., 181.

25. Matthew 22:37–40.

26. Kirk-Duggan, "Quilting Relations with Creation," 182.

27. Shani Settles, "The Sweet Fire of Honey: Womanist Visions of Osun as a Methodology of Emancipation," in *Deeper Shades of Purple: Womanism in Religion and Society*, ed. Stacey Floyd-Thomas (New York, NY: New York University Press, 2006), 192; see also Walker, xi–xii.

28. Floyd-Thomas, *Deeper Shades of Purple*, 195.

29. Ibid., 196.

30. Ibid.

31. Settles, "The Sweet Fire of Honey," 196–197.

32. Ibid., 198.

33. Ibid., 195, 198, 201.

34. Ibid., 198.

35. Walker, *In Search of Our Mother's Gardens*, xii.

36. Melva Sampson, email message to Kimberly P. Johnson, March 4, 2010.

37. Melva Sampson, phone interview by Kimberly P. Johnson, March 5, 2010.

38. Ibid.

39. Ibid.

40. Melva Sampson, "Hell No!" Reprinted from Ella Pearson Mitchell and Valerie Bridgeman Davis (eds.), *Those Preaching Women: A Multicultural Collection*, eds. (Valley Forge, PA: Judson Press, 2008), 27–31. Reproduced by permission of the publisher. (Appendix D)

41. Ibid., 27.

42. Ibid.

43. Ibid., 28.

44. Ibid.

45. Ibid.

46. Settles, "The Sweet Fire of Honey," 195.

47. Sampson, "Hell No!" 28.

48. Ibid.

49. Ibid., see also Esther 1:12, NRSV.

50. Sampson, "Hell No!" 28.

51. Ibid.

52. Ibid.

53. Ibid., 28 29.

54. Ibid., 29.

55. Ibid.

56. Ibid.

57. Ibid.

58. Ibid.

59. Ibid.

60. Ibid.

61. Ibid.

62. Ibid.

63. Ibid., 30.

64. Ibid., 29.

65. Ibid., 30.

66. Ibid.

67. Ibid.

68. Ibid.

69. Ibid.

70. Ibid.

71. Ibid.

72. Ibid.

73. Melva Sampson, phone interview by Kimberly P. Johnson, March 5, 2010.

74. Ibid.

75. Ibid.

76. Ibid.

77. Renita J. Weems, *Just a Sister Away: A Womanist Vision of Women's Relationships in the Bible* (Philadelphia: Innisfree Press Inc., 1988), 104.

78. Settles, "The Sweet Fire of Honey,"195, 201.

79. Sampson, "Hell No!" 27.

80. Ibid., 27–28.

81. Ibid. 27.

82. Ibid., 28.

83. Ibid., 30.

84. Ibid.

85. Settles, "The Sweet Fire of Honey,"198.

86. Stacey Floyd-Thomas, phone interview by Kimberly P. Johnson, February 15, 2010.

Chapter 5

Critical Engagement

> Critical engagement sermons seek to culturally critique society's
> oppressive forces by challenging the ways in which we view people's
> problems and by forcing us to confront our own internal system of
> beliefs, so that we can collectively combat external systems of belief.
> The preacher must offer a perspectival corrective that moves people
> toward partnership and inspires them to collectively change their
> thoughts and behavioral practices. The preacher must also devise a
> plan on how we can fix/eliminate the problem. Critical engagement
> reflects a cultural critique of society's cultural norms.

Critical engagement, the term that Stacey Floyd-Thomas uses to describe
the fourth tenet of the womanist definition emphasizes the need for womanist scholarship to continue to critically engage in discourses on religion and
society.[1] She defines it as "the epistemological privilege of Black women
borne of their totalistic experience with the forces of interlocking systems of
oppression and strategic options they devised to undermine them."[2] I understand critical engagement as a cultural critique of society's cultural norms.
In other words, any person using this particular critical lens is apt to analyze,
classify, and/or evaluate all aspects of culture—including, but not limited
to, religion, politics, visual arts, architecture, literature, the media, and tech-
nology. I believe that a womanist who utilizes critical engagement does so
for the sake of correcting society's normative view of "oppression." Floyd-
Thomas further explains it as "a hermeneutical suspicion, cognitive counterbalance, intellectual indictment, and perspectival corrective to those people,
ideologies, movements, and institutions that hold a one-dimensional analysis
of oppression; an unshakable belief that Black women's survival strategies
must entail more than what others have provided as an alternative."[3] Critical

79

engagement confronts what society sees as normative by asking the critical questions that challenge those norms. Central to this notion of challenging existing norms is the tension of the meaning of womanism and the identity politics of womanism in the field of religious studies.

Melanie L. Harris addresses the tension behind the religious identity politics of womanism and argues for religious pluralism. She challenges the exclusivity of womanism's Christian identity by introducing "womanist humanism" as a new hermeneutical lens that enables womanist theology to examine religious plurality.[4] Harris claims that womanist scholarship has overlooked Walker's pagan identity, which means that womanist theology has silenced the religious and ethical voice of the woman who coined the term, *womanist*. To date, there is limited research that considers both Walker's religious and ethical perspectives, which is why Harris proposes a womanist humanism.[5] Womanist humanism is derived from womanism and black humanism.

According to Harris, a womanist theological approach is situated within the lived experiences and acts of resistance that black women engage in as they fight against racism, classism, sexism, and heterosexism. This hermeneutical lens relies on the theological reflections and ethical worldviews of womanists in order to develop its theology of resistance and survival.[6] Likewise, a black humanist "nitty-gritty hermeneutic," a term that Harris borrows from Anthony B. Pinn, affirms human worth, agency, and responsibility as it focuses on the "problems of life" to move us closer toward black liberation. Black humanism questions the objectification of black bodies and dehumanization of black bodies.[7] The humanist aspect of womanist humanism helps womanist theology become more critical of its own religious categories and grow to be religiously inclusive. The womanist component pushes black humanism to examine how race, class, sexuality, and gender oppression impact the theological and religious reflections of black women.[8]

M. Shawn Copeland[9] argues that black women have been pushed to the margin in society and religion. As a result of being relegated to the outer edge, black women have learned to grasp and employ our own subjectivity in the quest for truth.[10] The phrase M. Shawn Copeland uses to describe the type of "serious thinking" that black women who are situated on the margins engage in is called *critical cognitive praxis*. This type of praxis questions patterns, tests and probes for answers, and weighs evidence against cultural codes and signs. In critical cognitive praxis, knowledge finds its authority in black women who are poor, despised, and outcast.[11]

According to M. Shawn Copeland, critical cognitive praxis yields a philosophical, theoretical, and concrete embodied relatedness to truth.[12] In a womanist cognitive praxis, the term critical denotes an intent to perform a radical critique of what is. This critique disrupts the status quo with its intellectual and practical aim of exposing the root of what is true.[13] M. Shawn Copeland claims that when black women engage in the critical cognitive praxis, they establish themselves as critical knowers (and doers).[14] For her, a womanist cognitive praxis, or as Floyd-Thomas calls it *critical engagement*, gives emphasis to the dialectic between oppression, a reflection on one's experience of that oppression, and a call to action that resists or eliminates the oppression.[15] Not only do their experiences become the texts, but their very bodies can become the rhetorical artifact as well.

In the article, "The Womanist Dancing Mind: Speaking to the Expansiveness of Womanist Discourse," Emilie M. Townes argues that the womanist dancing mind has the enormous intracommunal task of trying to understand the assortments of African American life along with the twists and turns of our communities.[16] One of the key questions for her revolves around *who* gets left out of conversations on liberation. Townes points out the fact that "Black women's experiences have been left out of the theoretical and material constructs of both Black and feminist theologies in the United States."[17] She also notes, that the existence of a liberation theology signals that someone or something gets left out of the "normative" theo-ethical discourses.[18] If the scope of feminist theology was deep and rigorous enough, there would be no need for womanist, African or Africana womanism, mujerista, or Asian theologies.[19] The womanist dancing mind exceeds our yearning to reshape the world in our own image and the need to even understand the different worlds around us because it invites others to come and participate in our new lived realities.[20]

For Townes, it appears that this fourth tenet of womanism, or as Floyd-Thomas calls it critical engagement, "challeng[es] the ways we know (epistemology) and the ways we think (orthodoxy) and the ways we act (orthopraxy). [And then proceeds to] make judgments on these."[21] The womanist dancing mind is an analytical tool that helps us to uncover the dynamics of oppression. The particularity of a womanist dancing mind allows her to rediscover the parts of herself that had gotten lost.[22] We are challenged to examine the places that the "isms" we project on others are turned back on us—through videos, magazines, television, radio, music, or the pulpit—and we are forced to see ourselves through the eyes of those whom we reject.[23] This type of critical engagement requires an intracultural inspection of African American life in order to uncover and deconstruct the hierarchies and the hegemonies that are both internal and external to African Americans. A womanist dancing mind helps blacks deal with our own internal "isms" so we can come together as a whole people and fight against the external "isms."

Alice Walker refers to this fourth tenet of her womanist definition as, "Womanist is to feminist as purple is to lavender."[24] What does this mean? For some it means that womanism is the darker hue of feminism. Since purple is a deeper shade of lavender, it also means that womanists have some deeper issues/forms of oppression that are unique to its own color/race. While Walker mentions this idea in her first tenet, "A black feminist or feminist of color," she takes the conversation of this fourth tenet in a different direction.[25] In her essay, "Only Justice Can Stop a Curse," she critiques the effects of the white man's crime against humanity and implies what affects one, affects everyone.[26] She notes this same earthly connection in another essay, "To the Editors of *Ms. Magazine*." It is here, she stresses the need for black women to be critical, not silent, and declares that women will never again consent to silent uncritical loyalty.[27] This continual thread of critically examining life runs throughout this fourth tenet. However, it also calls people to action. Walker poses the question, that Copeland asks, "What can we do?"[28] She urges us as individuals to get involved with saving Earth by talking with family, organizing friends, and educating people about the environmental threats that will inevitably affect humanity.[29] In short, what this fourth tenet tells us is that we need a global mindset, we must be critical in our thinking and brave enough to ask the critical questions, we must suggest call to action measures that will help resolve the problems affecting society, and we must then become involved by doing what we can.

RHETORICAL ANALYSIS OF CLAUDETTE COPELAND'S SERMON, "WHAT SHALL WE DO FOR OUR SISTER?"

"We have a little sister, and she hath no breasts: what shall we do for our sister in the day when she shall be spoken for?"

"Our little sister has no breasts. What shall we do for our little sister when men come along asking for her?"

"I urge you . . . sisters by our Lord Jesus Christ and by the love of the Spirit to join me in my struggle by praying for me." This is the Word of the Lord, the people said, thanks be to God.

Song of Solomon 8:8, KJV, MSG; Romans 15:30, MSG

Claudette Copeland's sermon, "What Shall We Do for Our Sister?" was delivered October 7, 2007, at Mississippi Boulevard Christian Church (The Blvd.), in Memphis, Tennessee, for their Breast Cancer Awareness Service.[30] The predominantly African American church, which seats just under three-thousand people, was filled to capacity for its ten o'clock Sunday morning service. Most of those in attendance were people who regularly attend church, but due to the marketing of this event, it is possible that some might have attended to hear Copeland preach and give her testimony about being a breast cancer survivor, while some might have attended to hear the musical guest gospel recording artist, Kurt Carr. However, a number might have been present to hear both.

Copeland, like many preachers, reuses her material, but she says, this was the first time that she preached this sermon with this content.[31] She thinks of herself as a sous chef who is able to pull together the right ingredients in order to make a good meal.[32] Likewise, she is able to pull narratives, anecdotes, imagery, metaphors, and exegetical work from the archives of her forty-plus years of preaching. For example, the part of her sermon that begins the discussion about breast is taken from chapter three of her book *Stories From Inner Space: Confessions of A Preacher Woman and Other Tales.*[33]

When asked, "What kind of difficulties or challenges do you experience in trying to make sure that your sermons reflect a womanist message?" Copeland admits, "I am fundamentally cut from a traditional Pentecostal mold— however that is interpreted. And the brand of traditional Pentecostalism from which I spring, there are certain things that are ingrained in my visceral way of worshipping and doing God. I think that is the thing that I continually have to step outside of, to reflect on, and to self-correct."[34] For her, the real challenge in preaching and forming sermons is that she must step out of what has been very comfortable and very nurturing for her.[35] It is in her attempt to model womanist concepts that she is able to step out of her traditional Pentecostal mold. Only through a close reading of her sermon will we be able to determine if she was successful or not.

ANALYSIS

"What Shall We Do for Our Sister?" is another racy sermon that challenges the ways in which we view other people's struggles and even challenges our own response to those struggles. The sermon divulges a number of experiences that Copeland encountered while fighting breast cancer. She incorporates plenty of humor in this one-hour-eleven-minute sermon to help her talk about the delicate subject of breast cancer and to assist her in relating to her audience. It is the longest out of all five sermons and it is packed with the most testimonies, personal narratives, anecdotes, and humor. Even prior to entering the pulpit, Copeland knew that her sermon would be lengthy, so she jokingly warned her audience before reading the scripture. She said, "Just kinda nudge your girlfriend, nudge the one next to you and just tell them, 'We gonna be here a minute' [laughing]."[36] Everyone laughed, but she was right, we were there for a nice while holding onto every word she said.

Copeland's preliminary sermonic moment begins with her prophetic singing. We usually see this in worship service when people yield themselves to the power of the Holy Spirit and sing words that the Spirit has placed on their heart. She sets up this moment of prophetic worship by saying to her audience, "Come on and clap your hands in this place if God has changed anything for you [clapping]. I said, clap your hands if God has changed anything for you [clapping]."[37] This is the point at which she begins to sing her words. As she sings, she testifies that God has changed her and made her stronger than what she was previously. Copeland's prophetic singing acts as a sermonic teaser, quite like a television teaser or preview that shows a highlight of what is to come in order to attract the audience's attention. She tells us that, "The devil thought he had me. He never thought I'd win. I know what ya'll heard about me; but, I'm stronger than I've ever, ever been."[38] She already knows that most of us are aware of her battle with cancer, so to say that she has changed, she is stronger, and she had the victory over Satan piques the curiosity of the audience.

Copeland incorporates a second teaser by commenting on the musical performance of the guest artist, Kurt Carr. She jokingly says, "Glory be to God forever. Kurt Carr is a terrorist [laughing]! The F.B.I. is outside now. They will be waiting to take you into custody."[39] While her comment claims that Carr's singing was so good, he terrorized the audience with his musical brilliance; it also implies that he has become a terrorist to Satan. I argue that this terrorist metaphor is Copeland's second teaser because it connects to a point that she later makes about people who pray becoming "Satan's greatest terror!"[40] Already, she is using her testimony as well as her comment about Carr's performance as windows into her sermon.

After the terrorist comment, we hear a formulaic introduction where the preacher greets the pastor, clergy, church people, and family members who came in support, which leads us into the sermon. The actual sermon begins with the reading of both scriptures, Song of Solomon 8:8 in two versions: the King James Version, "We have a little sister, and she hath no breasts: what shall we do for our sister in the day when she shall be spoken for?" as well as the Message Bible, "Our little sister has no breast. What shall we do with our little sister when men come along asking for her?" and Romans 15:30 in the New International Version, "I urge you . . . sisters, by our Lord, Jesus Christ and by the love of the Spirit, to join me in my struggle by praying to God for me"; then, the posed question/title of the sermon, followed by an anecdote of the Rat Trap in the Farmhouse. The placement of this anecdote is rather abrupt because we go from realizing that "Our little sister has no breasts" to hearing about a rat trap. However, Copeland's use of this anecdote is masterful because she describes a story that everyone can understand in order to demonstrate how what affects one really affects everyone. She says, "the moral of the story is: next time a rat tells you there's a rat trap in the farm house, you better understand that it affects the whole farm."[41] In the case of this sermon, the rat trap represents breast cancer, so she is really making the

Table 5.1 Claudette Copeland Rhetorical Tools

Rhetorical Tools	Purpose of Rhetorical Tools
Female and male biblical characters	To balance the gender conversation
Prophetic singing	To preview Copeland's victory over cancer (first sermonic teaser)
Terrorist metaphor	To preview the idea that people who pray become "Satan's greatest terror" (second sermonic teaser)
Anecdote of the "rat trap in the farmhouse"	To demonstrate how what affects one really affects everyone—breast cancer affects everyone
Statistical evidence	To identify the ratio of people who will never be affected by breast cancer
Imagery	To invoke a vicarious experience and passion in the hearts of the audience
Pastoral authority and moral authority	To confront any resistance to such a sensitive subject
Erotic/scenic language and medical terminology	To help the audience recognize their own hypocrisy, identify with the biblical character, and intellectually understand the affliction/oppression
Breast metaphor	To create enthymematic identification and to ease the comfort level
Critical cognitive praxis	To question the patterns and experiences by gathering and weighing evidence against cultural codes, signs, and hegemonic truths
Reversal	To shift from the positive side of being in love to discuss the negative side—wounds of the flesh wound the soul
Axiom	To establish the wounds of the body as the greatest wounds
Little sister metaphor	To symbolically reflect all our struggles/bodily wounds and that we are that sister
Personal testimony	To help the audience identify with Copeland's struggle with breast cancer
Multiple scriptures	To shift the focus toward the thematic text by using the second text to answer the question of the first text
Analogy of the incarnation of Christ	To demonstrate Jesus's partnership with us
Parallelisms	To establish the power of prayer/partnership and to demonstrate how a negative situation is transformed into a positive situation
Confession of "wanting to kill a negro"	To emphasize that prayer needs to be the weapon of choice
Anecdote of the sickly little "street doggie"	To remind us not to forget the refuge offered to us so we can extend it to others
Embodiment/embodied mediation	To challenge the way we view other people's struggles and the way we respond

Table created by Kimberly P. Johnson.

argument that breast cancer affects everyone, not just the one who has the disease. Her point is quite similar to the implied argument that we heard in the traditional communalism sermon—what affects one, affects everyone. Copeland's anecdote allows her audience to see what happens when we choose not to get involved in each other's struggles and she helps her audience envision what happens when we all choose to join in the struggle together as a community.

Like the rat who warns the farm animals, Copeland warns her audience, "there's a rat trap [clapping] in the farmhouse that affects all of us."[42] The rat trap she is talking about is called "breast cancer." She proceeds by identifying the ratio of people who will never be affected by breast cancer coupled with vivid descriptions of the discovery process. Her imagery allows the audience to vicariously experience what Copeland went through from the point when she found out that she had breast cancer to the point of her mastectomy. She says:

> Seven out of eight of you will never have to lay down on a surgical table and feel like you are laying down in your coffin only to come up from the surgical sleep altered forever. Seven out of eight of you will never have to search the face of your partner to find a comfort you cannot provide yourself—to hope your wounds will be kissed and caressed.[43]

Copeland's use of imagery is to invoke a vicarious experience and to invoke passion in the hearts of those seven out of eight people who will never personally battle against breast cancer. She has to invoke the passion in the beginning of her sermon because she calls them to some form of action at the end of her sermon. She notes, for most people, conversations about breast cancer and bodily affliction are just that—conversations where "you nod politely and you feel some intellectual curiosity and down in your being you say, 'Well thank God it ain't none of me!'"[44] Therefore, she has to strategically take her audience on a vicarious journey of what it is like to be forced to deal with breast cancer. So, she takes the time to satisfy their "intellectual curiosity" because if their curiosity is met, they will be more prone to sympathize with and walk alongside the next person who tells them that she/he has breast cancer.

Copeland recognizes that a sermon about breasts can be a touchy subject matter for a Sunday morning worship service, so she immediately confronts resistance with the use of pastoral authority and moral authority, which ultimately heightens her credibility. In an effort to calm the anxiety she subtly informs her audience that she has been invited by the pastor and women of the church to speak on this subject matter. Then, she explains, "If God can speak through a donkey[45] [laughing], if God can, c'mmon here God's gonna talk to you this morning through a breast [laughing]. Touch your friend and say, 'Relax.'"[46] She uses the pastoral authority of the church pastor and the moral authority of God to endorse the content of her sermon, which makes it extremely difficult for anyone to refute that she has the right to preach about breasts in a Sunday morning worship service.

Copeland shifts from preparing her audience for the conversation about breast to descriptively depicting the physicality, excitement, adoration, nicknames, and usage of our breasts. Here, she uses multiple metaphors to portray the physicality of women's breasts. She describes them as "a complex landscape of fifteen-to-twenty lobes within each one. Milk-holding receptacles exiting at a nipple—breasts. Highway system of complex ducts and thoroughfares—breasts. Struma, called fatty tissue and ligaments. Pectoral muscles, a waterway of lymphatic fluid—breasts," in order to show that they are "a miracle of creation."[47] Then, she reprimands her audience members who are sitting quietly as if they are mortified by the subject matter. Copeland says, "Don't you dare sit here this morning and act like you're embarrassed by the conversation because if I look at most of you closely, periodically, you try to show yours [shouting, laughing and clapping]. And, for those of you who have nothing to show, I don't mean no harm, but the others of ya'll trying to sneak-a-peak [laughing and clapping]."[48] Here, she points out their hypocrisy by identifying the type of uncanny behavior they engage in during worship service. If they are already trying to show their breasts or "sneak-a-peak," then there is no legitimate reason for the audience to act like they are embarrassed about the topic. This tactic of leveling the listening field puts all of her listeners at ease and they are able to finally relax enough to "go with [her] for a minute" as she preaches and tells her own story.[49]

Once the audience becomes relaxed enough to laugh again, Copeland reminisces on the excitement that little girls have as they await the arrival of their breasts and compare cup sizes. She even captures the dialogue that teenagers have when they ask, "What size you wear?"[50] She describes the adoration that young women have for their breasts and then contrasts that with how burdensome older women find them by saying, "Breasts, as young women, we display them like flags flown proudly in the wind. As older women, we kick them like burdens [laughter and clapping] scraping the ground [laughter]. Breasts, oh come on you can laugh!"[51] Next, she describes the common vernacular terms: "jugs, watermelons, mosquito bites [laughter], titties [laughter], boobs," and how we use our breasts.[52] She claims, "They are the intersection between the maternal and the erotic. They comfort our babies of any age [laughter and clapping]."[53] Shortly after she said this, an audience member yelled, "Preach Claudette!" Strategically, Copeland describes breast from a physiological standpoint all the way to a maternal/erotic standpoint. She helps her audience to become comfortable with the subject matter and to

understand the "lifelong friendly companionship" that develops with breasts
so they will realize the type of devastation women feel when we "find out that
our breast are out to kill us."[54]

After describing the intricacies of how one develops a friendly companionship with breast and then mentioning how that relationship can go bad, Copeland directs her attention to her first text, Song of Solomon 8:8. She explains
to her audience that the Song of Solomon "is a celebration of married love. It
is an allegory of praise between a man and a maiden. . . . It extols the beauty
of sensual love and the wonders of the human body."[55] Without delay, she
uses a reversal to shift the focus toward the negative side of being in love so
she can talk about how the wounds of the flesh wound the soul. She says:

> It is often said that "The greatest wounds are the wounds of the heart, the
> wounds of the emotions." But any woman who has undergone physical wound-
> ing, any woman that has undergone the wounds of the flesh . . . If you have ever
> been physically abused; if you've ever been slapped or hit; if you've ever been
> punched or had your hair pulled; if you've ever been kicked; if you've ever
> been raped or sexually violated; if you have ever suffered disfigurement in your
> body—the loss of a body part, the loss of your eyesight, the loss of a limb; then,
> that person, that woman knows viscerally, that the wounds of the body don't just
> wound the body, but they inscribe themselves as wounds on the soul.[56]

Remember, Copeland had just established that the Song of Solomon celebrates the beauty of love, so she needed to use the axiom as a transition into
what she believes are the greatest wounds—the wounds of the body because
"they inscribe themselves as wounds on the soul."[57] She starts off mentioning women, but then, in the middle of what she is saying, she drops the word
"women" and substitutes it with the word "you" as an inclusive strategy to
allow the women as well as the men to see themselves in the sermon because
"then, that person [man], that woman" can viscerally understand how bodily
wounds wound the spirit.[58]

Copeland refers to the scripture again, but this time, the audience is beginning to understand who the little sister is and what the question is really
asking. She says, "We have a little sister and she has no breasts. What shall
be done for our sister? What shall be done for her when men come to call?
What shall be done for those of you who sit outside the conversation of breast
cancer, but what shall be done for us?"[59] The little sister is all of us—those
with breast cancer and those without; those who are HIV positive, those
whose child has been killed by a drive-by shooting, those who have had a
heart attack, those suffering with lung problems due to smoking, those who
have spouses that decide they do not want to be married anymore, and those
who have business partners or friends that betray them.[60] Here, the focus
becomes what Townes calls "intracommunal" because Copeland images the

struggle of the little sister who has no breasts to symbolically reflect all of our struggles. The little sister represents all of us who have some form of bodily wound that has somehow wounded our spirit. The real question being asked is what shall people do for us that will help our spirit heal when we are wounded ourselves?

Copeland begins to describe her own wounding experience with breast cancer. She tells her audience that she was "at the top of [her] game" at the age of thirty-eight, "preaching at all the right doors on all the best platforms" when the doctor informed her that she had "Infiltrating ductal adenocarcinoma, a kind of cancer that arises quickly, spreads quickly, and kills quickly."[61] She then proceeds to ask her litany of questions:

> What shall be done for me? There comes a time when a Mercedes Benz don't help [clapping and shouting]. . . . What shall be done for our little sister when men come to call? . . . I wasn't cute . . . but I had hair. Come on Survivors! . . . I could swing it like the best of the girls. What shall be done for me when I sit in the bathroom and wipe the last strand of hair off my head? What shall be done when I walk up in church hyper-pigmented looking like a dead woman with my head rag on watching all of the daughters in the church beginning to audition for my job? [shouting] "Pastor David, how are you? Do you need a pie? Do you need somebody to cook for you?" I'm over there sick and dying, but "Pastor David." Parenthetically, letting him know that she still had two breasts [shouting, Tell the story! Tell the story!]. What shall be done for our little sister?[62]

In all of these examples, Copeland's question is paired with her relationship toward a material object, a bodily part, or other women. First, she lets her audience know that material possessions, such as a Mercedes Benz, a diamond, or a Rolex will not help them when they have a disease that kills quickly. Second, she talks about her relationship with her long hair and how it was one of her defining characteristics. Third, she reveals that the medicines made her hair fall out. So, the part of her body that she seemed most proud of was no longer there to give her comfort either. Fourth, she reveals that the daughters of the church were more concerned with becoming Pastor David's next leading lady than they were about helping their own Pastor Copeland. She watched them as they were "Parenthetically, letting him know that [they] still had two breasts [Tell the story! Tell the story!]."[63] Here, a person is yelling, "Tell the story!" probably because it just seems so outrageous that, as a co-pastor, Copeland would have to witness all of the daughters of the church trying to go after her husband. The normal expectation is that the daughters would try to assist Copeland, but they did not.

Up to this point, Copeland has identified two problems: (1) losing a breast due to breast cancer and (2) having a support system failure. I believe the latter problem is why she repetitively asks, "What shall be done for me?"

and "What shall be done for our little sister?"[64] In her effort to call people to some form of action, she shifts the sermonic focus toward the second scripture (theme scripture), Romans 15:30, "That I urge you by the Lord, Jesus Christ, and by the love of the Spirit, join me in my struggle by praying to God for me!"[65] Copeland uses this second text to answer the question of the first text. She says, "Couple of things I want to leave with you today, I don't know if you're going to be happy or not. But there's a rat trap in the farm house. What shall we do for our little sis? The first thing that I pick up in my experience both in life and in the text, is that if you want to do anything for your little sister, the first thing that we need from you is your partnership."[66] Copeland's first response to the question, "What shall we do for our little sis?" is one of partnership, "Join me, when people are suffering and when they're struggling."[67] She informs them that sick people become invisible and that the church prays for you when you are sick for about three weeks, which implies that that the church stops praying after a while and may even forget that the individual is sick. Then, she reminds her audience, "Cancer is not contagious, you can't catch it."[68] What happens when people are contagious is that others stop going around them. So she is telling her audience that it is okay to go visit and be in the presence of those battling cancer. Next, she shifts back into her testimony, but this time she shares it by thanking God for the men who are not afraid to partner with their woman/wife, who do not run off to the comforts of another woman, and who know how to "hold you 'til it gets better."[69] I refer to this as a testimony because in her words of praise, she is implicitly thanking God for her own husband and how courageous he was in partnering with her. Following this moment of praise, Copeland offers concrete examples to help her audience understand exactly how they can partner with her in the struggle against breast cancer, "wear the pink ribbon, give, run, walk, march, do what you've gotta do, but don't leave me out here by myself."[70] This is her first call to action and she compares it to the incarnation of Jesus. She says, "That is the whole story of the incarnation when Jesus did not stand back, but he said, 'Look-a-here, prepare me a body and I'll go down and I'll be touched and tempted at all points, just like you! I'll show you how to overcome in a body! Partnership.'"[71] Her analogy makes the point that Jesus did not leave us out here by ourselves, so we should not leave each other alone.

Copeland immediately transitions into her second call to action. She explains to her audience, "The second thing that I raise up today has already been said. What can you do for me? Acknowledge that it's a painful struggle and that even though yours may not be like mine, validate me and tell me that you understand what pain is like."[72] Whereas the first remedy sought partnership, the second one seeks acknowledgment, validation, and understanding. Here, Copeland takes her audience back to the scriptures by reminding them of the text where Paul says, "Join me in my *painful* struggle."[73] She emphasizes *painful* because she is asking the audience to acknowledge that the struggle is painful. Her emphasis allows her to critique modern-day Christianity by making the argument that "Modern theology is a painless Christianity [Come on now!]. Modern theology is devoid of a cross, it is absent of a struggle."[74] She is critiquing the myth that Christians do not have to go through a struggle or experience hardships. As she reminds her audience of the cross, which is central to Christianity, she identifies the various environmental, physical, financial, psychological, parental, sexual, and spiritual struggles. Copeland explains:

> Life is marinated in pain. It was Haiti yesterday, Darfur last night, Jena, Louisiana this morning. Every Christian in this society has a struggle. Yours might not be a disease, yours might be that you're broke [laughing] up in here today looking good on credit [laughing and clapping]. Yours might be mental instability. If we catch you one day when you miss your medicine, we'd all be in trouble [laughing and clapping]. Somebody say, "painful struggles." Yours might be raising children without resources or respite. Aging parents that you're trying to care for, a loveless marriage. Struggles with sexuality, sexual choices, no sex [laughing]. Struggles: moral failure and spiritual dryness; breast cancer; chemotherapy; disfigurement; radiation; reconstruction; fear of metastasis. Life for none of us has been no crystal stair [clapping].[75]

Copeland's critical lens widens the reach of her target audience far beyond those who have fought against breast cancer or experienced physical wounds and emotional wounds due to relationships. Here, the struggles move beyond disease and relationships to include environmental disasters, financial insecurity, mental instability, fatigue, being a caregiver, and sexual lifestyle. A sermon that started off talking about breasts and breast cancer has now been able to reach those who might have felt marginalized by the conversation about breasts. By now, it has become extremely clear that the entire audience— male and female—represents the little girl who has no breasts and that the breasts serve as a metaphor for our own struggles. So, it does not matter the type of struggle we experience, Copeland is telling the audience to join each other in their struggles.

At this point, Copeland revisits the notion that she is stronger than she has ever been, a phrase that we heard from her prophetic song prior to the sermon. She testifies as to how her struggle has made her stronger and helped her to lean on God's Everlasting Arms. According to Copeland, she had to lay down her own arrogance and leave her ego at the altar before she could completely lean on God.[76] She wants God to do a new work in the lives of the people, so she dares them not to run from their struggles and explains that God regenerates us through our struggle by changing us, saving us, and delivering us.[77]

Copeland encourages her audience to be thankful for the struggles because struggles keep pushing us. She says, "It pushed you beyond your reach, pushed you beyond, come on here, your lovers [clapping]. It pushed you beyond the alcohol bottle and pushed you all the way to the cross of Jesus Christ! [shouting and clapping]"[78] She acknowledges that pain pushes people to the cross because it forces us to lean on God.

After discussing the need for partnership along with acknowledgment, validation, and understanding, Copeland discloses the third remedy in her plan of action. She says, "The third thing I want to raise up today is prayer. In the midst of all that's going on, Paul says, "Join me in my struggle by your *prayers* to God for me.""[79] This ending clause contains the third step, which is prayer. Copeland creates a litany of parallelisms to establish the power of prayer in a manner that will demonstrate how a negative situation is able to transform into a positive situation and how a bad reality gets transformed into a good reality. She explains, "[T]here is a conduit called prayer [Yeah!]. It is the privilege of the believer. It is the sanctuary of the saint. It is the refuge of the righteous. It is the comfort of the Christian, if you will pray."[80] In other words, prayer is a special benefit, a sacred space, a protective covering, and a place where believers find solace.

Copeland tells another personal narrative, but this time she is at a women's conference with "big name evangelists" and amid people praising her for her books and her ministry, somebody yells out, "Hey Clyde!" which is a name she was known by in high school and college when she did not always do what was right. Clyde represents the "flesh" woman, "personal" woman and not the public persona of Claudette Copeland. Then, she weaves in the story where Jesus yells out, "Simon!" which is Peter's "flesh man, personal man" and not the public persona of Peter.[81] She says,

I heard Jesus say, "Look-a-here Simon, I have prayed for you! When people forget you, when people are embarrassed by your suffering, when people walk a wide circle around you, this is your comfort, Simon! With all of your disfigurements, with all of your failures, with all of your weaknesses," I'm talking to somebody in here today, "with all of your confusion about what is right, I have prayed for you!"[82]

Copeland uses this story to tie back to her first point about partnership. "When people forget you, when people are embarrassed by your suffering" is parallel to the comment "sick folk become invisible."[83] The phrase, about people walking a wide circle around other people is the reason she had to make the statement, "Cancer is not contagious, you can't catch it."[84] Then, she locates the struggles of her audience members in their disfigurements, failures, weaknesses, and confusion to communicate that Jesus has prayed for them, which means that Jesus is partnering with them.

Copeland decides to continue her testimony by telling her audience, "I'm so glad I found Christ before I found cancer! I'm so glad I have an organizing principle in the midst of my life and it is founded upon the prayers of the Great High Priest, who sits at the right hand of the Father praying for me."[85] Here, we see that she has assigned a masculine pronoun to God. However, in all fairness, my initial conversation with Copeland on the day that she preached this sermon is what sparked the research question to this project: Do sermons preached by womanists reflect and or reinforce womanist thought? In that exchange, she told me that "[she] considers [herself] a womanist, but [she] doesn't think it comes across clearly in [her] preaching."[86] Her use of a masculine pronoun represents one of those instances where her preaching does not clearly communicate womanist thought. In an interview, Copeland explained that she is "fundamentally cut from a traditional Pentecostal mold" and that she "must self-correct [her] fundamental formation which was very much male nurtured."[87] She says, "The male nurturing has written itself very indelibly in the way [she] sees the church and the way [she] sees God, from a very elementary place."[88] So, she thinks "[her] real challenge, always in preaching and in forming sermons, is the challenge to [herself] that [she] must step out of what has always been very comfortable for [her] and very nurturing to [her]."[89] We see this same instance of assigning a masculine pronoun to God in her sermon. Copeland applies pronouns four times and uses the word "father" once. We first see this when she quotes the old saints by saying, "*He's* kept you from dangers seen and unseen." Then, when she describes being angry with God and wanting to put her "fists in *his* face. And say to *him*, if this is how you treat your friends, I see why you have so few!... Woe is me, I'm unclean and undone, but *he* touches the coal on my lips...." And finally, when she says, "... the Great High Priest, who sits at the right hand of the Father."[90]

Immediately following her first masculine pronoun slip, Copeland jumps back into her third call to action—prayer. She says, "Prayer, prayer, prayer, if you want to do something for me, let's join together in prayer 'cause first of all, a saint who prays is Satan's greatest terror!"[91] Her comment ties back to what she said about Kurt Carr being a "terrorist" prior to preaching this sermon. The reason people should want to be this type of terrorist or "Satan's greatest terror" is because "[Satan] is afraid of saints who will pray!"[92] Copeland explains to her audience, "I need you in my life. This is what I need you to do for me. I need you to have my back in the realm and domain where principalities still want to take my life!"[93] Similar to how we want certain people to have our backs when we get into a brawl or fight, Copeland differentiates between the type of person she wants to have her back. She does not call upon someone who is still saying beginner prayers; she wants someone whose prayers are more advanced. She describes the power of prayer and how prayer makes us "become Satan's greatest nightmare!"[94] She declares:

> For when you pray . . . demons begin to get discombobulated [shouting and clapping]. When you have been in the thrown room with God, oh . . . you can walk in and ain't got to say a word, you just change the atmosphere. . . . [W]hen you pray, you can see some things. Ah . . . I can discern spirits, I know whether it's an angel or a demon, I know whether it's human or Divine, I know whether it's going to be healing or death. When I pray I can see some things. Not only can I see some things when I pray, but my God, I can stop some things![95]

Copeland wants her audience to realize that prayer gives them power and that prayer is the weapon of choice in the warfare against demons, sickness, and disease.

Continuing in this same notion, Copeland makes her second point about prayer by testifying that "prayer is self's greatest refiner."[96] Here, she tells the funniest personal narrative in the entire sermon. She begins the testimony by confessing her thoughts and actions from the time when she was sick, her body was deteriorating, and she saw the women of the church going after her husband. Copeland admits to her audience:

> I didn't know I could still cuss [laughing and clapping] like I could cuss [laughing and clapping]. . . . I did not know that I could actually go down to the state of Texas and apply for a license for a pistol permit to carry, put it in my pocketbook, bring it to church, and sit it right down by my pew [laughing]. Somebody say, lift your hands and say, "Refine me Lord." [Yes He will!] 'Til I got sick and afflicted and had to fight with the enemy, I did not know I still had the capability on the inside to make up my mind, excuse me, I'mma kill a negro [laughing]. Oh yes I am, I'mma kill a negro and I'm just gonna go sit in prison and have a prison ministry [laughing, shouting and clapping]. I didn't know it was still in me![97]

Copeland's confession reveals that a Christian, more or less a minister, can have impure thoughts as well as behaviors and still be a Christian. Her testimony comes in when she states, "I've learned how to pray. . . . [A] life of prayer becomes . . . sufferings' greatest reward. It takes me into an intimacy with God. . . . And, I found out when I learn in the midst of my suffering to pray, something called serendipity happens."[98] Copeland goes into another narrative, but this time about a poor mountaineer, named Jed, who eventually strikes oil. She professes, "[N]o matter what life means for evil, God's got a way of turning that thing around and around and around!"[99] This story of

Jed helps Copeland make the point that prayer "becomes suffering's highest reward."[100]

Copeland recaps for her audience the three points she has mentioned about prayer and then introduces a fourth point. She poses the question, "What can you do for us? Learn to pray because not only do you become a terror to the devil and does your spiritual life become refined, not only do you find a great reward for all the suffering that you've been through. But prayer, survivors, we can testify, is the saint's surest refuge [clapping and shouting]." By telling the story about the characters in Gunsmoke, The Rifleman, and Paladin, Copeland is able to compare prayer to being a refuge that will hide her and that she can duck under in times of trouble.[101] To further expound on this idea of prayer as a refuge for the saints, Copeland tells her final anecdote about a sickly little "street doggie" that was rescued from an alley by a veterinarian. The veterinarian washed her, stitched her up, de-wormed her, "de-flead" her, gave her medicine, fed her, and gave her shelter and refuge.[102] The little doggie and the veterinarian develop a wonderful relationship. He tells the doggie, "All I want you to do little girl is just stay!"[103] However, one day the veterinarian could not find the doggie anywhere so he resolved that the streets had reclaimed his doggie. Then, sometime later, there is a commotion in his front yard. Copeland says:

> Oh, as far as the eye could see, nothing in his front yard but yards and acres of doggies! And then, bless the Lord, right down the middle aisle, here came his little doggie [laughing and clapping]. Came up to him with her tongue hanging out. He said, "Where you been? I thought I told you to stay!" She said, "I know you told me to stay, but all the while that I was up here in the shelter and the refuge of your house, I kept on thinking about my sister doggies that still live down in the alley and I had to go and tell them that I found a man that likes doggies, that gives doggies a refuge, that heals doggies, that restores doggies to life again!

Copeland ends the story and the sermon with the following words, "What can you do for your sister? Don't forget where you came from! Don't forget the refuge that has been offered to your life."[104] She presents this idea of refuge as a fourth reason why saints should pray. However, the refuge, according to the story, acts as its own entity, a fourth call to action or remedy that serves to answer the question, "What can you do for your sister?"[105] While Copeland argues that she has three things that she picks up from the text, I argue that she really has four calls to action: a call for partnership; acknowledgment, validation, and understanding; prayer; and for us not to forget the refuge offered to us so that we can extend it to others. Copeland talked about refuge under the guise of prayer; however, her last anecdote communicated the need for us to "not forget the refuge that has been offered to [our] lives" and it was divorced from a conversation about prayer.[106] Therefore, this plea for us to remember from whence we came and the refuge we have received stands alone as a fourth step that the audience members can take in answering the question, "What shall we do for our sister?" by extending what has been given to us, to others.[107]

In this sermon, Copeland has embodied the role of the little sister who has no breasts through the storytelling of her own experience with breast cancer in order to challenge the ways in which we view other people's struggles and the ways we respond to those struggles. Copeland also helps her audience to understand that they too represent the little sister in the way she re-envisions what struggle symbolizes in the text. According to Copeland, the little sister signifies everyone—the sisters and the brothers—those with breast cancer and those without, those who are HIV positive, those whose child has been killed by a drive-by shooting, those who have had a heart attack, those suffering with lung problems due to smoking, those who have spouses that decide they do not want to be married anymore, and those who have business partners or friends that betray them.[108] Copeland presents an "intellectual indictment" to the myth, that "breast cancer only affects the one who has it." Her sermon offers the "perspectival corrective" that what affects one, affects everyone and so we need to join each other in each other's struggles. She transforms her audience's perception about sickness and struggle in order to collectively call them to action to help others.

The Womanist Characteristics

According to Copeland, womanist preaching is an "embodied mediation." She argues:

> There is something about the body, the physicality of woman presence in the pulpit. In the way that I handle myself, my body, just the physicality of my presentation mediates for the listener, the brothers, for the women who watch my life. It says more than I can say. It affirms the feminine. I think I'm always conscious, when I come to the pulpit, of the way the visual speaks volumes to reinforce the auditory. Womanist preaching is more than just what we say; it is the presentation of our voice and our movement and in the best sense of the word, the drama of the feminine presence in the pulpit.[109]

This "embodied mediation" that Copeland describes is a performative characteristic that allows the preacher to embody her argument. Robert Hariman's discussion about performative expectation helps us understand this dramatistic element in the pulpit. Hariman argues that performative "expectations involve both specific compositional details of the pertinent communicative art, and a general, dramatistic sense of how to move in the realm of appearances."[110] Throughout the sermon, we witness Copeland's negotiation of how she takes on the role of the characters in the sermon and how she uses her own personal experience to embody her argument. These "embodied mediations," which I also discuss in my examination of the "Hell No!" sermon from the previous chapter, are visually and audibly present in the embodiment of her argument through testimony, personal narratives, and anecdotes.

In addition to this "embodied mediation" characteristic, Copeland also demonstrates what M. Shawn Copeland calls a "critical cognitive praxis." In short, this type of praxis entails the questioning of patterns and experiences, testing and probing, gathering and weighing evidence against cultural codes, signs, and hegemonic truths.[111] We see this type of questioning in Claudette Copeland's sermon when she asks the question, "What shall we do for our little sister?"[112] This sermon allows her to create what Stacey Floyd-Thomas calls a "cognitive counterbalance, intellectual indictment, and perspectival corrective" to our understanding of struggle, our thoughts about who it affects, and our behavioral practices.[113] Her sermon counterbalances the initial idea that God is incapable of speaking through a breast—a female body part in a Sunday morning service, along with the notion that breast cancer only affects women—the women who have it. Copeland utilizes the breast cancer theme as a "perspectival corrective" to aid her audience in recognizing that what affects one, affects everyone. The person who is going through the sickness or struggle is obviously affected, but then Copeland advocates for everyone else to join the person in that struggle: to develop compassion and understanding, as well as to acknowledge and pray for the individual. The conversation about breast cancer becomes a "dialectic between oppression, a reflection on one's experience of that oppression, and a call to action that resists or eliminates the oppression.[114] Copeland's sermon calls everyone to a collective form of action by helping the audience comprehend that we all have important roles to play in each other's lives as we endure the pains of life.

Additionally, Copeland demonstrates a womanist characteristic that appears to be exclusive to this sermon, she balances her texts. The first text has a young lady as its focal character, while the second text has Apostle Paul as the focal character. So even though she comes to talk about breasts and breast cancer, she balances the genders by using biblical texts that equally focus on both sexes. This balancing act furthers the scope of her target audience because it causes the sermon to be more inclusive of genders.

However, the point at which Copeland fails to reiterate womanist thought is when she assigns a masculine pronoun to God a total of four times and the word "father" once. Do the five verbal slips discredit her sermon from being a womanist sermon? My response is "No" for two reasons. First, I believe the multiple characteristics of womanist thought exemplified within this sermon far outweigh these four masculine pronoun slips. Second, for a sermon that is one hour and eleven minutes in length to have just four verbal blunders when God is mentioned at least thirty-five times tells me that Copeland did not intentionally mean to image God as a male to her audience. If I were to penalize her efforts by discrediting this sermon as a womanist sermon, then I would have to discredit other sermons from other forms of preaching that fail to adhere to their rhetorical conventions.

CONCLUSION: A COMPARISON AND CONTRAST OF RHETORICAL STRATEGIES BETWEEN CRITICAL ENGAGEMENT AND TRADITIONAL COMMUNALISM

The two major rhetorical similarities between the two types of sermons—the critical engagement sermon by Claudette Copeland and the traditional communalism sermon by Cheryl Kirk-Duggan—are that they both perform cultural critiques from a both/and vantage point of self and community, plus they call their audience members to a form of action. These similarities also illuminate their differences. Copeland presents a cultural critique of society's one-dimensional view toward breast cancer and she approaches the topic through the subjectivity of her own experience with breast cancer. Copeland's aim is to put forth a "perspectival corrective" to ways in which people view and react toward breast cancer, breasts, sickness, and struggle. Kirk-Duggan offers a cultural critique of what I consider an internalized oppression—a crippling spirit. Kirk-Duggan's aim is to enhance the community by first enhancing self, which is why she requires introspection.

While both sermons contain the notion, what affects one, affects everyone, with their both/and vantage point, they take different approaches. A critical engagement sermon shares the dual focus of self/community, but the difference is that these sermons are mainly concerned with targeting the community to change the community's behaviors and thought processes. Copeland mainly targets the women of the community, but she also demonstrates concern for those who sit outside the conversation of breast cancer and have no personal connection to breast cancer when she re-images, for her audience, what struggle looks like. Her goal is to change their view toward other people's struggles and even change their behavioral response. Then, in a roundabout manner, she targets self when she invites her audience into the biblical text as the little sister who has no breasts. Throughout the sermon, she poses the question, "What shall we do for our little sister?"[115] So, when she answers this question, she is also informing self on how the community is to treat self.

On the other hand, the both/and vantage point of traditional communalism sermons primarily targets self in order to improve self so that self can be a more effective member of the community. The way Kirk-Duggan accomplishes this is by holding self accountable. She poses questions such as: "[A]re you willing to be free so that you can help others to be free?" and "What are we willing to do to be free from our 'bent overness?'" "What will each of you do today . . . ?"[116] Additionally, Kirk-Duggan also targets the community by targeting Presbyterian women ministers, and her communal lens also shows concern for those outside of the community. She says to her Presbyterian audience, "if you're in a very wealthy Presbytery . . . and you're doing good work there, well continue, but don't forget that there's a world out there dying!"[117] She cautions her audience to not forget about those who sit outside their community. Therefore, she is not only concerned about improving self so that self can be of a greater service within the community, but she wants self to also benefit those outside the community.

Similarly, the call to action of critical engagement sermons and traditional communalism sermons targets the same primary focus as their both/and vantage point. Critical engagement sermons offer a collective call to action that outlines what the community can do together to help fix/eliminate the problem. This communal target is important because Copeland has to answer the question, "What shall we do for our little sister?"[118] She suggests partnership; acknowledgment, validation, understanding; prayer; and for us to not forget the refuge that has been offered to us—we are to offer the refuge that has been extended, to us, to others just as the little doggie did for all her doggie friends. In contrast, traditional communalism sermons put forth an individual call to action that will improve self and ultimately through self-improvement, enhance the community. Kirk-Duggan provides three challenges that will help us recognize if we are spiritually crippled. First, "[T]o look in the mirror and take a risk and get to see, do you really know who you are?"[119] Second, "[T]o take some Sabbath time to rethink the vows you took. And, to take another look at, "Who is God in my life? Who am I?" Not what you do, but, "Who are you? Who am I? And, what is God calling you to do today?"[120] Third, "[T]o look and see, what is your call and are you still interested? If you're not interested, then maybe it's time for you to do something different."[121] Although this call to action is very much self-oriented, it still has a communal slant because of the concern that "God's people ought not suffer because we're bent over, busted up, and burned out."[122] In the final analysis, traditional communalism sermons lend themselves toward devising a plan of accountability that will help individuals become more effective members of their community, whereas, critical engagement sermons critique the social forms of oppression in a manner that challenges the ways we know, think, and act, as well as pose the question, "What can we do?"

NOTES

1. Floyd-Thomas, *Deeper Shades of Purple*, 10.
2. Ibid., 208.
3. Ibid., 208.
4. Melanie L. Harris, "Womanist Humanism: A New Hermeneutic," in *Deeper Shades of Purple: Womanism in Religion and Society*, ed. Stacey Floyd-Thomas (New York, NY: New York University Press, 2006), 212.
5. Ibid., 211.
6. Ibid., 212.
7. Ibid., 213.
8. Ibid.
9. I will distinguish M. Shawn Copeland from Claudette Copeland by referring to her by her full name from this point forward.
10. M. Shawn Copeland, "A Thinking Margin: The Womanist Movement as Critical Cognitive Praxis," in *Deeper Shades of Purple: Womanism in Religion and Society*, ed. Stacey Floyd-Thomas (New York, NY: New York University Press, 2006), 227.
11. Ibid. See also Bernard Lonergan, "Cognitional Structure," in *Collection: Papers by Bernard Lonergan*, ed. Frederick E. Crowe (Montreal: Palm Publishers, 1967), 221–239.
12. M. Shawn Copeland, "A Thinking Margin," 227.
13. Ibid., 228.
14. Ibid.
15. Ibid., 229.
16. Emilie M. Townes, "The Womanist Dancing Mind: Speaking to the Expansiveness of Womanist Discourse," in *Deeper Shades of Purple: Womanism in Religion and Society*, ed. Stacey Floyd-Thomas (New York, NY: New York University Press, 2006), 237.
17. Ibid., 238.
18. Ibid., 246.
19. Ibid., 240.
20. Ibid., 237.
21. Ibid., 247.
22. Ibid., 244.
23. Ibid., 242–244.
24. Walker, *In Search of Our Mother's Gardens*, xii.
25. Ibid., xi.
26. Ibid., 340–341.
27. Ibid., 353.

28. Ibid., 345; see also Appendix E.

29. Ibid.

30. This sermon was not published, but I personally attended the service, so I have included a transcript of the sermon in Appendix E. A complete DVD of the sermon is available at Mississippi Boulevard Christian Church, Memphis, Tennessee.

31. Claudette Copeland, phone interview by Kimberly P. Johnson, March 16, 2010.

32. Ibid.

33. Ibid. See also, Claudette Copeland, "Stories From Inner Space: Confessions of a Preacher Woman and Other Tales" (San Antonio: Red Nail Press, 2003).

34. Claudette Copeland, phone interview by Kimberly P. Johnson, March 16, 2010.

35. Ibid.

36. Claudette Copeland, "What Shall We Do for Our Sister?" October 7, 2007, Mississippi Boulevard Christian Church, Memphis, Tennessee (transcribed by Kimberly P. Johnson, see Appendix E).

37. Ibid.

38. Ibid.

39. Ibid.

40. Ibid.

41. Ibid.

42. Ibid.

43. Ibid.

44. Ibid.

45. See numbers 22:28.

46. Appendix E.

47. Ibid.

48. Ibid.

49. Ibid.

50. Ibid.

51. Ibid.

52. Ibid.

53. Ibid.

54. Ibid.

55. Ibid.

56. Ibid.

57. Ibid.

58. Ibid.

59. Ibid.; see also Song of Solomon 8:8, KJV.

60. Appendix E.

61. Ibid.

62. Ibid.

63. Ibid.

64. Ibid.

65. Ibid.

66. Ibid.

67. Ibid.

68. Ibid.

69. Ibid.

70. Ibid.

71. Ibid.

72. Ibid.

73. Ibid.

74. Ibid.

75. Ibid.

76. Ibid.

77. Ibid.

78. Ibid.

79. Ibid.

80. Ibid.

81. Ibid.

82. Ibid.

83. Ibid.

84. Ibid.

85. Ibid.

86. A personal conversation with Claudette Copeland on October 7, 2007 at the Madison Hotel, Memphis, Tennessee.

87. Claudette Copeland, phone interview by Kimberly P. Johnson, March 16, 2010.

88. Ibid.

89. Ibid.

90. Appendix E.

91. Ibid.

92. Ibid.

93. Ibid.

94. Ibid.

95. Ibid.

96. Ibid.

97. Ibid.

98. Ibid.

99. Ibid.

100. Ibid.

101. Ibid.

102. Ibid.

103. Ibid.

104. Ibid.

105. Ibid.

106. Ibid.

107. Ibid.

108. Ibid.

109. Claudette Copeland, phone interview by Kimberly P. Johnson, March 16, 2010.

110. Robert Hariman, "Prudence/Performance," in *Rhetoric Society Quarterly* 22: 27.

111. M. Shawn Copeland, "A Thinking Margin," 227.

112. Appendix E.

113. M. Shawn Copeland, "A Thinking Margin," 227.

114. Ibid., 229.

115. Appendix E.

116. Appendix C.

117. Ibid.

118. Appendix E.

119. Appendix C.

120. Ibid.

121. Appendix C.

122. Ibid.

Chapter 6

Conclusions about Womanist Preaching and Womanist Rhetoric

The five sermons by five different self-proclaimed womanist preachers—Elaine Flake, Gina Stewart, Cheryl Kirk-Duggan, Melva Sampson, and Claudette Copeland—help us to understand (1) what womanist preaching looks like when it is executed well and (2) that womanist preaching is a clarion call for social justice and liberation. Womanist preaching has a boldness which mandates that systems of oppression be named in the preaching moment. We have learned that the preacher must use imagery that will "invite the congregation to share in dismantling patriarchy by artfully and deftly guiding the congregation through the rigors of resisting the abjection and marginalization of women."[1] Therefore, womanist preaching must not only inspire people to action but also carry the burden of helping people to recognize their participation in their own oppression, in their own unhealthy relationships, attitudes, and behaviors, in how they have strayed away from true authenticity, and in how to reclaim their own voice.

WHAT WE LEARN ABOUT WOMANIST PREACHING

Who Can Be a Womanist? Essentialism versus Particularity

As I draw this discussion back to the essentialism *versus* particularity debate, let us examine the narratives and scriptures that the five preachers employed in their sermons. Flake uses *Enough* as her movie narrative, which has a Latina, not an African American as the main character. Stewart uses *What's Love Got to Do with It?* as her movie narrative, featuring an African American woman as the lead character. Both preachers utilize Genesis 29 as their sermonic text, which focuses on the story of Leah. Kirk-Duggan uses her own experience of being a poor seminary student struggling in exegesis class as her narrative along with Luke 13:10–13, the story about the woman with the crippling spirit. Sampson uses a song from the musical, *The Color Purple*, a scene from the movie, *The Color Purple*, and personal stories about her and the women in her family as narratives. The sermon is based on the story of Queen Vashti, in Esther 1:1–12. From the scripture to the movie to the song to the personal narratives, the focus is on women and when Sampson talks about the women sitting around Nez's table, those women are African American. Copeland uses her own experience as a breast cancer survivor to serve as her main narrative in conjunction with two pericopes—Song of Solomon 8:8, the little sister with not breasts; and Romans 15:30, the Apostle Paul urging the sisters (and brothers) to join him in his struggle by praying for him. Copeland is attempting to balance the sexes by using both female and male biblical characters in her sermon. As we already know, womanist sermons do not have to always focus on female biblical characters, but they must incorporate a universal message of hope, redemption, communal beliefs and values, or empowerment.

Out of all five primary narratives, Flake's sermon is the only one that steps outside of the boundaries of discussing an African American woman's experience. The movie, *Enough*, is about the struggles of a Latina woman named Slim, played by Jennifer Lopez. Does the narrative persona of a Latina woman negate the sermon from being classified as a womanist sermon? My answer is no for two reasons: (1) If a preacher does not want to enact or embody an argument herself, the preacher can create a narrative in which the narrative persona embodies the position being argued and then the womanist preacher can speak to liberate, redeem, heal, or even call that person back to her(/his) cultural beliefs, and the preacher can critique the dominant normative views of society to figure out how we can collectively help that individual and others in the same situation. (2) Although the narrative persona of Slim does not communicate the message of a particular African American woman, it speaks to the human condition of abuse and neglect that so many women experience after they say, "I do."

To some, it may seem as if the narrative persona of Slim almost dictates that a womanist does not have to be African American. I am an "Alice Walker Womanist," therefore, I fall on the side of essentialism. Walker created womanism because second-wave feminism was not speaking to her needs, in terms of race, class, and gender, as an African American woman living in the United States. Second-wave feminism was more focused on the needs of middle-class white women, which is why many African American women decided to (re-)identify as womanists. Black women wanted to be fully represented and they wanted to finally speak for themselves without having someone who does not share in their struggles to serve as the spokesperson for African American women. For this reason alone, I think that a womanist should be an African American woman. We should not have to go through the same sick cycle of others speaking for us (i.e., white women, white men, black males . . .) telling us what we should think, how we should feel, how we should express ourselves, who we should love, how we should behave, and what we should advocate for when fighting for social justice. If women and men from other races self-identify as womanists and become the spokes person for black women, then womanism will no longer be situated in the African American female experience because the stories about the lived experiences of African American women will inevitably be replaced by another agenda. However, I am not against other individuals who want to join in the womanist struggle, but fall outside of the essential social conditions of being a "black female" and "Christian," from borrowing the "womanist" term only if they qualify womanist with an adjective that communicates their essential social conditions for membership. This does not give in to the particularity argument because only individuals who share in the same essential requirements for membership and the same "lived experiences" are able to speak for that group of people. This prevents non-African American females who may or may not be Christian from speaking for (black) womanists.

Once womanism flourished and made its way into the academy, womanist theology came along. When Katie Geneva Cannon, Jacquelyn Grant, and Delores Williams developed this new type of theology, it was formed through a womanist theological Christian lens. By this time, to self-identify as a womanist carried the assumption that the person possessed Christian beliefs. But this was problematic for black women who did not subscribe to the Christian experience. Hence, other forms of womanism emerged, which also dictated "essential" social conditions for membership. Debra Mubashir Majeed talks about converting from Christianity to Islam and says, "Once a Muslim, I discovered something I had not realized as a Christian—the womanist agenda often made normative the Christian experience of African American women."[2] The Muslim Womanist Philosophy is situated in the racist and patriarchal hegemonic power structures of the United States, in the variations of black struggles, in pursuits of Islamic legitimacy, the adaptability of the Qu'ran, justice, equity, and the social activism of African American Muslim women.[3] Diana L. Hayes, who claims to be a Catholic womanist, identifies with womanists in terms of having experiences that are uniquely African. Similar to Majeed's argument, Hayes claims, that black Catholic women are oppressed by race, class, gender, and religious faith.[4] Her goal as a Roman Catholic womanist is to examine the intersectionality of race, class, gender, sexuality, and religion to see how it perpetuates an ethos of subordination of women and other persons of color.[5]

Not only did black women in the United States question the ability of feminism to fully represent them, so did African and Afro-American women in the African diaspora. In 1985, Chikwenye Okonjo Ogunyemi coined the term African womanism. This perspective "is situated in the African experience and it applies to the traditional African religions in addition to the African-derived religions in the global African diaspora."[6] This type of womanism seeks to combat racism as its main focus because it "understands black sexism as a microcosmic replica of Euro-American racism—a racist hegemonic power structure exercised over African and Afro-American women by Western culture.[7] Clenora Hudson-Weems coined the term Africana womanism in 1987. "Africana womanism is situated within the Africana culture and it examines womanism through the lenses of African studies, black nationalism, and pan-Africanism. Africana womanism recognizes racism and classism, on both national and global levels, as their most prominent obstacles in their collective struggle toward survival."[8]

While I do side with the "essentialism" argument in determining who can be a womanist and who can speak for African American women, I see nothing wrong with other ethnicities and/or religious groups qualifying what type of womanist they claim to be by putting Muslim, Catholic, African, or Africana in front of the word "womanist." This lets people know what "essential" social conditions are necessary for membership. This also dictates who can speak on the lived experiences of those members and prevents others who do not share in those experiences from speaking for them because womanists need to be able to tell their own stories.

Who is God in Womanist Preaching?

Womanist preachers try to avoid verbalizing masculine pronouns by using inclusive language when describing God. If masculine pronouns or masculine metaphors are used, womanist preachers try to balance the gendered pronouns or imagery by incorporating feminine pronouns or feminine metaphors. Mitchem describes the Triune God as "the three persons of Parent, Son Jesus, and Holy Spirit."[9] Kirk-Duggan describes God by saying:

> God is a personal, powerful, compassionate, liberating God who encompasses masculine and feminine qualities and cares about individuals and communities. This God of Black folk combines a "making a way out of no-way God" with a God who is a "mother to the motherless and father to the fatherless." Relationship with this God allows one to accept the gifts of creativity and substance, to survive and transcend, and to celebrate the gifts grounded in that creation. The Womanist view of God celebrates a relationship with persons that produces intimacy, mercy, love, compassion, and solidarity. This God is real and present. Persons created by this God are created in Imago Dei, created in a life experience of diversity, mutuality, and wholeness.[10]

Whenever I preach, I am very intentional about avoiding masculine pronouns when mentioning God. I do this because too many young girls and women have been raped by men who were supposed to be protective of them, yet those men chose to take advantage of them. I remember, back when I was a student, I was walking to the classroom with my teacher and a fellow class-mate and we were engaged in a deep conversation on the topic of sexual assault. To our surprise, my teacher told us that she did not know a black woman who had not been sexually harassed or sexually assaulted in some form, and she, herself, was not excluded from that comment. I have never forgotten that. Therefore, when I step into a pulpit to attempt to proclaim the Word of God, I am intentional about the words that I use because I never want to prevent someone from connecting to God during the sermon, which is why I typically reference God as "God." If a scripture, such as Isaiah 40:28, uses the "he" pronoun, then I take the creative liberty to rewrite the text—"Do you not know? Have you not heard? The Lord is the everlasting God, the Creator of the ends of the earth. *God* will not grow tired or weary, and *God's* under-standing no one can fathom." This gives people the freedom and opportunity to image God for themselves in a way that will nurture their relationship with the Creator.

Cultural Artifacts and Personal Narratives Become Sacred Texts

Womanist preaching pushes the boundaries on what can be considered a sacred text. Usually, the Bible is considered the sacred text of the preaching moment, but these womanist preachers seem to transform the idea of what can be considered sacred by their use of movies, lyrics, personal narratives, anecdotes, and testimony to develop the main arguments of the sermon. Flake uses the movie *Enough* as the sacred text to establish three points: (1) Slim was physically, mentally, emotionally, and verbally abused—domestic violence; (2) Slim needed to decide she had enough in order to get out of her situation—moment of epiphany; and (3) Slim's change of self-perception moved her from being a victim of her current state to being victorious over the situation. Likewise, Stewart uses the movie *What's Love Got to Do with It?* as her sacred text to establish her three points: (1) the night Tina left Ike was a defining moment in Tina's life—alludes to the idea that Tina had to run from her abuse; (2) Tina needed to decide that she had enough of unpro-ductive, unhealthy relationships that were physically, emotionally, and men-tally abusive—moment of epiphany require action; and (3) Tina's defining moment opened a new chapter in her life—moments of epiphany will open a new chapter in our lives. Kirk-Duggan re-images the woman with a crippling spirit in the Luke 10:13 text into a "lived experience" from her own life—the woman with the crippling spirit became a poor seminary student struggling in exegesis class while trying to figure out what it meant to be a Presbyterian. At the end of her personal narrative, she re-casted the image of the bent over woman with the crippling spirit to include church people and seminary professors—she casts her younger self and her older self in the sacred text along with everybody else in the room. Kirk-Duggan's narrative helped to establish that: (1) many of us are bent over by circumstance, fear, and family pathologies; (2) sexism, heterosexism, racism, classism, faux churchism, and skewed traditions cripple and stop the manifestation of God in our lives; and (3) we all need to choose to be set free in Christ Jesus as we work for justice through the power of the Holy Spirit. Sampson uses an excerpt from the song, "Hell No!" in the musical, *The Color Purple* and anecdotes of all the women in her family who would sit around Nez's kitchen table saying, "Hell no!" to whatever sought to silence their voices as her sacred texts, including her own "Hell no!" moment. The lyrics tell us three lessons: (1) that girls are not safe in a house full of men, (2) women must fight against their oppressive situation(s), and (3) it is okay to be our own person, sometimes we just need to tell people "Hell no!" The anecdotes of her family sitting around big momma's kitchen table and her own "Hell no!" testimony help to make three points as well: (1) "Hell no!" signaled an emphatic refusal used to express discontent toward a person, (2) "Hell no!" is a saying of righteous indignation, an acknowledgment of reverence for ourselves, and (3) we need to revolutionize our roles in church and society by saying, "Hell no!" when people try to silence or oppress us. Copeland's sermon is embedded with so many stories that I will focus on what four lessons her personal testimony of surviving cancer and the anecdote of the rat trap in the farm house along with the anecdote of the sickly little "street doggie" teach us. Together, the testimony and anecdotes explain that (1) what affects one affects everyone, (2) we need *partnership* because when a person gets sick, the church only prays for that person for about three weeks—the church needs to join in partnership when people are struggling and suffering, (3) people need to join in prayer—a praying saint is Satan's greatest terror, and (4) do not forget where you came from—do not forget the refuge that has been given to you. What we learn from womanist preaching is that what is sacred can become secular and what is secular can become sacred.

Who are these Sermons Addressing?

All five sermons address the needs of African American women, but they also have a universal reach. Flake and Stewart's liberation aim speaks to self-love, self-affirmation, and self-worth by speaking against the oppressive forces of domestic abuse, infidelity, rejection, bondage, subordination, patriarchal domination, insecurity, wounded self-esteem, and emotional dependence.

Kirk-Duggan's healing/liberation/Jeremiad aim speaks to freedom, salvation, the ability to discern "bent overness," and being the people of God by coming against the oppressive forces/crippling spirits of racism, sexism, heterosexism, patriarchy, misogyny, classism, and faux churchism. Sampson's redemptive aim speaks to self-love, self-acceptance, self-development, revolution, reverence for one's self, and righteous indignation by speaking against the oppressive forces of objectification, silence, exile, the pride of the powerful, and patriarchal dominance. Copeland's aim of performing a cultural critique of society's oppressive forces offers a perspectival corrective along with a plan on how to fix/eliminate the problem by speaking to the importance of prayer, participation, acknowledgment, understanding, compassion, and sharing our refuge as we combat the oppressive forces of breast cancer, wounds of the flesh, wounds of the spirit, invisibility, and other types of struggles that may come as we travel this journey called life.

Womanist preaching is supposed to serve as a perspectival corrective to the problem with black preaching, which tends to limit discussions about racism and sexism to topics on economic exploitation, equal employment opportunities, political injustices, stereotyping, and social stratification.[11] Flake claims that "pulpits have been largely occupied with preachers who deny the existence of misogyny and the patriarchal underpinnings of violence against women."[12] Flake says, "If preaching is to truly reach the hearts, minds, and souls of African American women, preachers must employ an analysis of Scripture that reconstructs the Word of God in ways that are liberating to women as well as men and that reflect the totality of the African American experience."[13] Therefore, the target audience for any womanist sermon should always be African American women, but the content must lift up some universal message in order for the sermon to be transformative enough to liberate all oppressed people.

What is Gained or Lost in Womanist Preaching?

What is gained or lost in transforming/adapting Alice Walker's four tenets? I believe we gain a lens that not only allows us to see into the life of the biblical character, but helps us to see into the life of the preacher as well. Womanist preaching gives women a license to embody their argument so that their audience will be able to identify with them or the biblical character in their sermon. However, while I am able to recognize this strength of womanist preaching, I also think that we lose two important attributes. When we examine the radical subjectivity sermons, we see the "outrageous, audacious, courageous or willful behavior of a woman," but we lose seeing the woman who is "Wanting to know more and in greater depth than is considered 'good' for one."[14] We lose seeing the sassy side of women. Instead, we see the women who are courageous enough to fight for their life—physical, spiritual, psychological, or emotional well-being. In terms of traditional communalism, we hear Kirk-Duggan challenge heterosexism by saying, "Heterosexism is a crippling spirit that fears God's gift of sensuality and sexualities."[15] But, she never comes back to this discussion on sexuality, which makes me wonder how much attention womanist preachers really give to the topic of sexuality? Although she, like Walker, acknowledges a mutual respect for different sexualities, I am still left asking, does womanist preaching direct enough attention toward liberating those who are sexually oppressed by fighting against heterosexism and homophobia? My sense from examining these five sermons is that sexuality takes a back seat in the fight against oppression, and thus gets lost.

The closest I have come to witnessing "sexuality" get addressed in a sermon was at my former home church in Memphis, Tennessee, and at my current home church in Nashville, Tennessee. The first time was when I heard Copeland preach her sermon, "What Shall We Do for Our Sister?" She discussed the sexual character of a woman's breasts by taking us on a long scenic route of human anatomy to describe:

> a complex landscape of fifteen-to-twenty lobes within each one. Milk-holding receptacles exiting at a nipple—breasts. Highway system of complex ducts and thoroughfares—breasts. Struma, called fatty tissue and ligaments. Pectoral muscles, a waterway of lymphatic fluid—breasts. Don't you dare sit here this morning and act like you're embarrassed by the conversation because if I look at most of you closely, periodically, you try to show yours [Shouting, Laughing & Clapping]. . . . We admire them in bathroom moments assessing their usefulness and attractiveness to the latest man in our lives. They are fondled, caressed, they are kissed and suckled [Laughter]. They are breasts. . . . They are the intersection between the maternal and the erotic. They comfort our babies of any age [Laughter & Clapping].[16]

At various points, Copeland had to ease the tension in the room because we were not accustomed to hearing about breasts as the focal point of a sermon. It did not even matter that it was breast cancer awareness month, as I explained in chapter five, she had to invoke pastoral authority and moral authority as evidence in support of her talking about breasts during a Sunday morning church service. If the congregation was that uneasy over a conversation about breasts, imagine the level of anxiety we would have wrestled with if the sermon had been about sex.

Since then, I have witnessed my current pastor, Judy D. Cummings, senior pastor of New Covenant Christian Church, in Nashville, Tennessee, address sexuality or counter heterosexism on several occasions during our Sunday morning worship services. Cummings has told us that she is not naïve to the fact that single men and women are engaged in sexual relationships. She explained her position that sex is okay only if the two people are in a committed relationship and the sex is consensual. Cummings has even been candid about how she approaches her own marriage. She says that she is faithful to her husband, Charles, but just because she has had the same sexual partner for over forty years, that does not prevent her from getting tested for HIV/AIDS on a regular basis. She claims that she still needs to know her status for her sake and for the sake of her relationship with her husband.

New Covenant is an "Open and Affirming" church, we support the views of our denomination, Christian Church (Disciples of Christ). As a result, we have same-sex loving couples (both married and non-married) in our church. When my pastor invites people to join the church, she is constantly reminding the congregation and reassuring our guests that this is a "judgment free zone" and that we are an "open and affirming" church. Last year, Cummings had the honor of officiating her first same-sex marriage ceremony. Again, the Christian Church (Disciples of Christ) is an "open and affirming" denomination, which means that the Christian Church performs same-sex marriages. My pastor was so excited to talk about her experience in helping the couple attain their civil right to be legally bound together in marriage. I think the fact that topics of sexuality, heterosexism, and homophobia often get omitted from Sunday morning sermons is probably indicative of the unfortunate reality that the African American community does not have a lot of "open and affirming" congregations. I compare being a member of an "open and affirming" church to my parents telling me, when I was a kid, that I could talk to them about anything, including sex. Being able to talk about sex communicated to me that I really could talk to them about anything and they would share their perspective with me. Likewise, being a member of an "open and affirming" church tells me that my pastor will freely talk to us about any subject matter—no subject is off limits—and she will give us her pastoral opinion. I believe, when a congregation chooses to no longer be bound to the constructs of heterosexism, a sense of freedom emerges that tends to ease every anxiety and cast away every fear.

How Does Womanist Preaching Go Unnoticed?

Although womanist preaching is unique, it goes unnoticed because it is a genre. "A genre is a group of acts [or a fusion of elements] unified by a constellation of forms that recurs in each of its members. These forms, in isolation, appear in other discourses. What is distinctive about the acts in a genre is the recurrence of the forms together in constellation."[17] Said another way, womanist preaching is fused with elements that are intrinsic to African American preaching, prophetic/liberation preaching, thematic preaching, narrative preaching, expository/textual preaching, and postcolonial preaching to name a few. Frank A. Thomas defines African American preaching as being "fundamentally both a rhetorical and theological enterprise" because the preachers employ the oral traditions of West Africa and the oppressive experience of American slavery to shape their verbal and nonverbal communication during the sermonic moment.[18] Marvin A. McMickle defines prophetic preaching as a perspectival corrective that shifts the focus of a congregation away from what is happening to them in their local church and centers their vision on what is happening to them as members of a larger society. He argues that prophetic preaching asks, "What is the role or the appropriate response of our congregation, our association, and our denomination to the events that are occurring within our society and throughout the world?"[19] Thematic preaching means that the minister is preaching from themes and topics rather than a specific scripture. When it comes to narrative preaching, Eugene Lowery suggests that "a sermon is a plot (predicated by the preacher) which has as its key ingredient a sensed discrepancy, a homiletical bind. Something is 'up in the air'—an issue not resolved. Like any good storyteller, the preacher's task is to 'bring the folks home'—that is resolve matters in light of the gospel and in the presence of the people."[20] James Earl Massey argues that textual and expository preaching are one and the same as long as the sermon expounds on the text in which it is based.[21] Sarah Travis maintains that "the term 'Postcolonial' recognizes that we exist in a state of continuity and discontinuity with colonial/imperial projects," which means that we are living with the consequences of our colonial history and facing contemporary forms of colonialism all at the same time.[22] She posits that this type of preaching must "contribute to a process of repairing, reconciling, and renewing a global community that has been torn and bruised by the ongoing tug of war."[23]

It is my belief that when we hear a sermon preached by a black minister and all of our personal prerequisites that we have for the sermon get checked off, we simply chalk it up as good African American preaching. For example, if a sermon can do the following—provide a theologically sound message, show traces of the oral tradition through its imagery and the use of action words, expound on a scripture, give us a story, resolve a problem with a social justice message that tells us what we can do locally and globally, and if the preacher can sprinkle on a little call and response, sing a chorus or two, and whoop and shout while taking us to Calvary, and if we are lucky, stir us up to the point where we catch the Holy Ghost—then that sermon will probably be considered as one of the black preaching "Hall of Famers" on our personal list of favorite sermons. This is why womanist preaching needs to be codified and taught more readily in both academic and religious institutions. If students, professor, clergy, and congregants would learn the tenets, typology, and the rhetorical/theological aim of radical subjectivity sermons, traditional communalism sermons, redemptive self-love sermons, and critical engagement sermons, listeners would be able to recognize when they are hearing a womanist sermon and this style of preaching would cease to go unnoticed.

General Womanist Preaching Characteristics

Several womanist characteristics seem to crossover into the different types of womanist preaching. For example, Kirk-Duggan's sermon, "Women of the Cloth," culturally critiques the various "isms" that cripple people: sexism, heterosexism, racism, classism, and faux churchism. Although her sermon demonstrates a sense of critical engagement, the primary aim of her sermon is for the communal healing of those in ministry so that they can be free from their oppression and she does this by calling them back to their fundamental religious beliefs. Hence her subject, "Weaving New Cloth: Confronting the Chorus of Bent Over Women."[24] Since sermons tend to weave in and out of the various forms of womanist preaching, I have derived my own typology of womanist preaching that reflects the crossover, or general womanist traits, found in three or more of the five sermons which includes, but is not limited to, the influences of Cannon, Allen, and Flake discussed in chapter one.

GENERAL WOMANIST PREACHING TYPOLOGY

1. Eliminates destructive female images and linguistic violence
2. Challenges patriarchy and androcentric language within the biblical text and our contemporary socio-context
3. Addresses the marginalization of women in the Bible
4. Uses non-gendered or inclusive language when discussing the Trinity
5. Makes use of identification to help the audience see themselves in the sermon and/or to develop their own value judgments
6. Explores the liberating values within the Old and New Testament that affirm the humanity of women
7. Honors tradition and/or African ancestry
8. Identifies and resists all forms of oppression including linguistic sexism, heterosexism and homophobia
9. Culturally critiques the black church, the black community, and the oppressive aspects of this nation that continue to restrict women
10. Verbally and metaphorically avoids male-bashing through its use of imagery
11. Addresses violence on systematic levels
12. Employs methodologies that identify abusive, unhealthy toxic relationships

13. Empowers people to operate out of their own human agency to resist systems of domination and oppression
14. Conveys a message of hope and wholeness for self and/or the larger community
15. Historically reconstructs the biblical text and re-images biblical characters
16. Embodies the argument by privileging personal experience or embodies the biblical character by taking on the role of a woman in the Bible
17. Uses the artistic proofs of logos, ethos, and pathos to engage listeners critically
18. Shares performative attributes that are characteristics of both the oral tradition and traditional black preaching such as call and response, repetition, storytelling, enactment and embodiment, role-playing, rhythm, and African American colloquialisms
19. Has a rhetorical agency or power within the message itself that guides its listeners to a particular end
20. Engages in pedagogical strategies of empowerment and critical thinking.

This list is limited to twenty items for the simple reason that I wanted to base my findings on the sermons that this project has analyzed. However, if I were to include two more characteristics, I would add:

21. Presents Jesus/God as a Friend and Advocate for women; and
22. Does not need to always address issues related to women, but it must convey a universal message that gives us hope, redeems, calls us back toward communal values, or empowers us to some form of action that will fix or help eliminate oppression

These additional traits are rooted in womanist thought, and Flake discusses certain aspects of them in her book. The reason number 21 is important is that by imaging Jesus and God as "Friends to women and Advocates of women," preachers are able to ground their redemptive argument in the moral authority of the Godhead. I believe number 22 is vital to womanist preaching because it informs people as well as reminds preachers that womanist preaching does not always have to focus on "women." The same rhetorical strategies can be used to identify and combat the oppressive forces in a text that focuses on a male biblical character.

What we learn from the above typology about womanist preaching is that it really is a social justice rhetoric that has been birthed out of and grounded in the authority of the African American female experience to critique and confront the oppressive nature of the community at large and, more particularly, the black church. The rhetoric "interrogate[s] the social construction of black womanhood in relation to the African American community," the black church, and the Bible.[25] Cannon claims:

In each preaching event, the religious practices and deep seated theoethical beliefs of the Black church are reinvented in and through specific scriptural interpretation. Investigation of the integral connection between the preacher who creates the sermon, the sermon's internal design, the world that the sermon reveals, and the religious sensibilities of the congregation that are affected by the sermon invites us to a higher degree of critical consciousness about the invisible milieu in which we worship.[26]

Consequently, womanist rhetoric is used as a tool by which to reconstruct knowledge through its epistemological privilege of lived experiences. Thus, womanist rhetoric becomes a discourse of experience that "situates rhetoric as a site of struggle for inclusion and survival."[27] Womanist rhetoric addresses and identifies the marginalized and then it produces a rhetoric of resistance that defies those oppressive forces that have assigned people to the fringes of mainstream society. Furthermore, it possesses a rhetorical agency or transformative aspect that empowers women to operate out of their own human agency to act on behalf of self and/or community.

The majority of each minister's sermon reflects the above womanist characteristics. We have witnessed how the preachers address the marginalization of women by challenging patriarchy, naming oppression, deconstructing negative images of women, affirming women, re-imaging the text/biblical character, embodying the argument/biblical character, empowering women to operate out of their own human agency to change their situation, and by using non-gendered language to reference God. These traits appear to be the staple characteristics of womanist preaching not only because they emerge in the majority of the sermons I examined but some of them also surface in the typologies of Cannon, Allen, and Flake.

FOUR RHETORICAL MODELS OF WOMANIST PREACHING

Since womanist characteristics do in fact crossover into the different forms or categories of womanist preaching, how can the preacher or listener tell if s/he is delivering or hearing a particular womanist sermon? Through my close textual analysis, I have discovered rhetorical strategies that are specific to the four categories of womanist preaching. Radical subjectivity sermons lend themselves toward moving the individual audience members from victim to victor. Its focus is on self rather than the community at large. These sermons document one's journey toward identity formation, self-love, and self-worth. Plus, they detail the moment of epiphany, all in an effort to authorize and encourage the audience to act on behalf of self as well. Traditional communalism sermons lend themselves toward some form of communal healing and communal remembrance to live out the Christian faith. In other words, it functions as a Jeremiad because it calls us back to our communal values. The focus is simultaneously on self and community because to successfully work at community, one must first start with self—one must improve self in order to improve one's relationships with others. Similar, to radical subjectivity, there is a newfound self-awareness that takes place. Redemptive self-love sermons lend themselves toward transforming the eyesight of society because it redeems the perception of a woman that society sees as shameful, whereas radical subjectivity sermons work at alleviating the shame that self feels from being victimized. Critical engagement sermons lend themselves toward culturally critiquing society's cultural norms in a manner that challenges the ways we know, think, and act, and poses the question, "What can we do?" These sermons always focus on self and community, primarily community, because their goal is to devise a plan that outlines what the community can do to help fix/eliminate the problem, and they explain what self can expect from the community.

I have constructed four models that reflect the rhetorical attributes of womanist preaching which coincide with the radical subjectivity, traditional communalism, redemptive self-love and critical engagement sermons. I created these rhetorical models in an effort to benefit rhetoricians, public speakers, listeners, womanist theologians, ethicists, preachers, and students. My fellow communication colleagues will benefit from having a framework that charts the rhetorical attributes of womanist preaching, which can also be used as a methodological approach to analyze other forms of womanist rhetoric and to determine which tenet the rhetoric they are examining mirrors. Listeners will benefit by finally having a framework that they can reference which will help them recognize whether or not they are hearing a womanist sermon, and if they are, this framework will help them in differentiating between the various facets of womanist preaching. Womanist theologians and ethicists will greatly benefit because of the mere fact that womanist preaching has been intuitive thus far, but now they will have a framework that details the rhetorical strategies and attributes of womanist preaching which will help them engage in pedagogical strategies of teaching and passing down the tradition of womanist preaching. Furthermore, this study gives them a framework that will help them to make sure that their own preaching reflects and reinforces womanist thought. I believe these charts will help students and preachers understand how to deliver a womanist sermon that reflects a particular model, what the goals are of that particular facet of womanist preaching, and what the rhetoric sounds like.

The following models are structured by three columns that outline the rhetorical strategies, explain the purpose of each strategy, and offer a rhetorical example of each strategy. Each model identifies the sermonic focus on self and/or community, the overall goal/aim of the sermonic form, the oppression, the type of language used, specifies what type of agency the sermon encourages, names what the sermonic form values, and uncovers some of the oppressive forces that are named within that facet of womanist preaching.

I should note that the rhetorical tools used by Flake in table 2.1, Stewart in table 2.2, Kirk-Duggan in table 3.1, Sampson in table 4.1, and Copeland in table 5.1 are not all included in the four rhetorical models mainly because anyone who wants to create a womanist sermon should not feel boxed into using every tool that the preachers used in their sermons. Another reason why the models neglect to list all of the rhetorical tools that each preacher has pulled out of her rhetorical toolbox to support the aim of her sermon is because I have already discussed them in the analysis section of chapters 2 through 5 and I do not want anyone who is developing a womanist sermon to feel trapped or confined to using certain rhetorical tools over others. I have simply identified within each model the primary rhetorical tool that seems to advance the aim of the sermon. For example, while several of the preachers embodied the biblical character in their sermon, I do not want to mislead people into thinking that a particular type of womanist preaching requires the preacher to embody the biblical character. One does not have to embody a biblical character in order to deliver a womanist sermon. Embodiment comes into play automatically because preaching is performative in itself—the preacher speaks as the presumed mouthpiece of God, which means that during the preaching moment, the preacher embodies the Word of God. Then, when it comes to a preacher's homiletical creativity, otherwise known as invention in the communication field, the orator employs whatever rhetorical tools that work best at leading the speech to a particular end. Frank Thomas argues, "no performer or agent is an independent actor or isolated performer. . . . Invention is a social/spiritual process, and words, ideas, concepts, movements, inflection, and so on are already part of the tradition in which the preacher is situated and from which the preacher draws. The preacher orchestrates or performs out of the tradition and is responsible to the Holy Spirit and the tradition."[28] I want preachers to understand that they have the freedom to use any rhetorical tools that will ensure the aim of the sermon is reached.

While all public speakers, including preachers, use Aristotelian proofs (logos, ethos, and pathos) as their three forms of influence to effectively persuade their audience, I believe the determining factor that makes womanist preaching "womanist preaching" is found in the logical arguments—logos. Any preacher can use ethos to establish her credibility as one who personally identifies with the struggles of the biblical character in the sermon, but that alone does not make the sermon a womanist sermon. Likewise, any preacher can use anecdotes, imagery, or even whooping to create emotional appeals

Table 6.1   Rhetorical Model 1. Radical Subjectivity Sermons (Victim to Victor)

Rhetorical Strategy	Purpose of Strategy	Example of Strategy
Focuses on self	To heighten maturity level—increase identity formation, self-love and self-worth	"God is calling for brave and determined women to adopt an attitude of intolerance for those things in their lives that abuse, confuse, and restrict"
Aim: Liberation	Moves a woman from being a victim to being a victor	"When she has a change of self-perception, she is able to move from a place of victimization to victory"
Identifies inner weakness and unhealthy relationships that consist of physical, emotional, and mental abuse. Then, pinpoints a woman's moment of epiphany	To affirm the power that exists in choosing to get out of destructive relationships	"Leah's emotional dependence upon Jacob robbed her of security and self-worth." "Leah had a reality check. She finally realized that she couldn't make Jacob love Leah, but she could love Leah . . ."
Rhetorical tool: Uses fight/war language and imagery*	To show the extremes of the abuse and the perversion of the abuser	". . . she wages a deliberate and systematic attack on him," "bludgeon her to death," "crush or be crushed"
Encourages a human agency and a rhetorical agency	So that women will change their oppressive situation and realize and proclaim to themselves that they do not have to live in an oppressive situation	"I do not have to settle for less. I do not have to participate in my own oppression." . . . "This time I will praise the Lord"
Sermonic values: Self-love, self-affirmation, self-worth	To affirm a woman's humanity in the midst of her oppression so she will stop looking for validation from others	"My value is not determined by anybody else. . . . My worth and my value come from God"
Names oppressive forces: Domestic abuse, infidelity, rejection, bondage, subordination, patriarchal domination, insecurity, wounded self-esteem, emotional dependence	To lead people to a type of self-transformation: physically, spiritually, mentally and/or emotionally	"He cheats on her but makes her feel that his cheating, like his beatings, is what she deserves." "She is clear that her husband is not going to give up or change, so the only way she is going to be free requires her to change"

*Rhetorical tools are not limited to what is reflected by the asterisk. Please refer to tables 2.1 and 2.2. Table created by Kimberly P. Johnson.

Table 6.2 Rhetorical Model 2. Traditional Communalism Sermons.
(Jeremiad – A calling back to original values)

Rhetorical Strategy	Purpose of Strategy	Example of Strategy
Focuses on self and community—has a both/and vantage point	To push people toward improving self so they can improve their relationships with others	"I challenge you to look and see, what is your call and are you still interested?" "God's people ought not suffer because we're bent over, busted up, and burned out."
Aim: Calling back to cultural beliefs and values, healing, and liberation	Moves a woman toward an individual healing, a communal healing, and calls us back to our original values	"Are you willing to be free so that you can help others to be free?"
Identifies our spiritual, pathological, and ideological infirmities along with our pathological behavior—performs a cultural critique	To encourage self-introspection and inspire women to free themselves from their illness by no longer practicing their sickness	"Racism mocks and violates God's precious, magnificent color and cultural palate of peoples;" "Faux churchism limits our experience of God and condemns the experiences of others"
Rhetorical tool: Uses a language of sickness and a Rhetorical Jeremiad*	To identify our current condition and what cripples self/community. Plus, it calls individuals/communities back to their original values	"For you see, with all the 'isms,' each 'ism' cripples us in a very dynamic way;" "So the question is, are you living the message of the gospel before them?"
Encourages a human agency	Encourages individuals to make sure they are living the gospel message, so that the community as a whole can be the people God has called them to be	"To be church means discerning all the 'bent overness' and deal with them. Starting first with ourselves"
Sermonic values: Being the people of God, discerning "bent overness," freedom, salvation	To affirm a woman's humanity in the midst of her oppression so she will stop looking for validation from others	"We can't talk about being the people of God if we don't live the people of God"
Names oppressive forces: Crippling spirits, racism, sexism, heterosexism, patriarchy, misogyny, classism, faux churchism	To lead people to a type of self-transformation: physically, spiritually, and/or emotionally	"How can we transform our passive aggressive behavior born out of patriarchy and misogyny? We must expose our internal societal oppressions if we want to be well"

Table created by Kimberly P. Johnson.

Table 6.3   Rhetorical Model 3. Redemptive Self-Love Sermons. (Villain to Heroine)

Rhetorical Strategy	Purpose of Strategy	Example of Strategy
Focuses on one's ability to love herself regardless and the community's perception of her actions	To praise women who love themselves enough to resist being silenced or losing their dignity or self-worth so that it can begin to change society's negative perception of those women	"But Queen Vashti refused to come at the king's command . . . Queen Vashti's response often is overlooked for the more palatable story of Esther"
Aim: Redemption	Removes the socially perceived shame of a woman away from her actions to take her from being a villain to being a heroine	"Vashti's metaphorical response . . . became a model for all the women in Susa and a threat to those who would have found pleasure in her debasing display"
Identifies heroine qualities in women who are regarded as shameful, wicked, and/ or evil	To reveal the integrity that the woman has and the morals by which she lives	"Yet to gloss over this monumental moment of liberation is to miss the making of a model of leadership . . . following the sound of the genuine within one's self is paramount"
Rhetorical tool: Uses provocative language along with a metaphorical "Hell No!"*	To encourage women to go for the shock-and-awe value to help us retrieve our voice, our power, and our bodies	"Hell no!""I'm sick and tired of being sick and tired;" "If I perish let me perish"
Encourages a rhetorical agency	Empowers a woman to match her human agency and moral agency with a rhetorical agency—an emphatic verbal response	"I think of Nez, who, if she had been with Vashti . . . surely would have looked at the queen and given her the royal nod to repeat after her and say, 'Hell no!'"
Sermonic values: Self-love, self-acceptance, self-development, revolution, reverence for one's self, righteous indignation	To affirm women in listening to their own voices in order to be true to self	". . . the sound of the genuine within one's self is paramount" "Outward success is not equal to inner worth"
Names oppressive forces: Objectification, silence, exile, pride of the powerful, patriarchal dominance	To encourage a woman not to submit to quiet conspiracy and lead them to actually start a revolution that reverences self by honoring the divinity that is inside of her	"A simple answer of 'No thank you,' or 'I'm sorry, I'll pass' just doesn't get it. We need to go for the shock-and-awe value and retrieve our voice, our power, and our bodies"

Table created by Kimberly P. Johnson.

Table 6.4   Rhetorical Model 4. Critical Engagement Sermons. (Cultural Critique)

Rhetorical Strategy	Purpose of Strategy	Example of Strategy
Focuses on self and community with a both/ and vantage point—but, primarily focuses on community	To push people to confront their internal system of beliefs in order to build community so they can collectively combat the external system of beliefs	"Cancer is not contagious, you can't catch it. I need partnership while I go through"
Aim: A cultural critique of society's oppressive forces	Offers a perspectival corrective that moves people toward partnership on devising a plan on how WE can fix/eliminate the problem	Asks: What shall/can we do?
Identifies society's normative view of oppression via its own cultural critique of a particular situation	To challenge the ways in which we view other people's struggles	"There's a rat trap in the farm house and if affects the whole farm" (What affects one, affects everyone)
Rhetorical tool: Uses a critical cognitive praxis*	To question the patterns and experiences by gathering and weighing evidence against cultural codes, signs, and hegemonic truths	"What shall we do for our little sister?" "What shall be done for her when men come to call?" "If God can speak through a donkey . . . God's gonna talk to you this morning through a breast"
Encourages a human/ rhetorical agency	Inspires people to collectively change their thoughts and behavioral practices so they can help fix/eliminate the problem	"What shall we do for our little sis? . . . if you want to do anything for your little sister": Partnership, acknowledgment, validation, understanding, prayer
Sermonic values: Prayer, joining others in their struggle, acknowledgment, understanding, compassion, doing for others, sharing our refuge	To affirm the power one has and the need for us to come together in support of each other	"I need somebody who can . . . say, 'I bind the power of sickness and disease. You gonna live and not die." "A saint who will pray is Satan's greatest nightmare"
Names oppressive forces: Breast cancer, struggle, wounds of the flesh, wounds of the spirit, becoming invisible	To reassure people who are struggling that Jesus has prayed for them and is with them, and to lead people to emulate that same type of behavior toward each other	"I heard Jesus say . . . 'I have prayed for you!' When people forget you, . . . are embarrassed by your suffering, . . . walk a wide circle around you, this is your comfort"

Table created by Kimberly P. Johnson.

(pathos), but that alone does not categorize the sermon as a womanist sermon. Instead, I believe the logical appeals, which support the overall aim of the sermon, are what classify a sermon as a womanist sermon. The logical arguments are what help us to differentiate these sermons between typical black preaching and womanist preaching.

WHAT WE LEARN ABOUT WOMANIST RHETORIC

What does womanist preaching say about womanist rhetoric? After examining the five case studies, I think it is easy to conclude that womanist preaching appears to do an excellent job in liberating African American women from their physical, mental, and emotional abuse by re-imaging a woman from being a victim of circumstance to being victorious over her current situation in radical subjectivity sermons; in calling women back to their communal beliefs and values which bring about an individual and communal healing through the use of a rhetorical Jeremiad in traditional communalism sermons; in removing the socially perceived shame of a woman away from her action, to take her from being a villain to being a heroine in redemptive self-love sermons, and offering a perspectival corrective to society's normative oppressive views that inevitably moves people toward partnership in devising a plan that fix/eliminate the problem through critical engagement sermons. But, it is also apparent that certain topics tend to get sidelined in a religious setting—sexuality, heterosexism, and homophobia. For this reason, I argue that when we pull womanist discourse outside of our sacred institutions and begin to proclaim womanist rhetoric in the public sphere on a local, regional, national, and global level without the restrictions of religious doctrine, we will begin to see more fully its transformative ability to truly fight for the wholeness and liberation of all oppressed people. We will start to hear more speeches that advocate policies and legislation regarding women's rights, human rights, worker's rights, disability rights, LGBTQ rights, religious freedom, immigration reform, healthcare reform, and equal pay.

Are There Topics or Forms of Oppression Yet to be Explored?

The introduction of this book begins with a quote from Maria Stewart, "How long shall the fair daughters of Africa be compelled to bury their minds and talents beneath a load of iron pots and kettles?,"[29] because she was the first woman in America who taught us to speak up for what we believe in and to fight for our political rights. Maria Stewart had no formal education, yet she was the first woman to ever speak publicly to a mixed audience of men and women. She proved that we not only can be taken seriously but also need to be taken seriously. Maria Stewart dedicated her life to religious and political activism after she was cheated out of her husband's estate when he died.[30] I am not identifying Maria Stewart as a womanist, but she was definitely a proto-womanist—one who came before the womanist term existed to demonstrate to black women everywhere how to liberate oppressed people through a social justice discourse.

As I think about what proclamations of womanist rhetoric in the public sphere would sound like (separate from sacred womanist rhetoric), I imagine more discourses that will combat racism, classism, sexism, heterosexism, homophobia, ageism, colorism, the effects of colonialism, and the contemporary forms of postcolonialism, police brutality, racial profiling, wrongful incarceration, gentrification, social inequality in public schools, hate crimes, gun violence, and gang violence. I also expect womanist rhetoric to advocate more profoundly for policies and legislation concerning women's rights, including the right for us to make decisions about our own bodies without government interference; healthcare reform; equal pay for equal work; worker's rights, veteran's rights for those who served on active duty and received an honorable discharge or general discharge; the support of government funding to improve the infrastructure and bring back jobs to the poorest cities in the United States; social justice for the LGBTQ community and for persons who are disabled; religious freedom both in the United States and globally, and immigration reform.

My hope is that womanist rhetoric will expand the target audience to include people with disabilities because I think womanist preaching has a tendency to forget about this part of the population. I think we do a wonderful job preaching about the woman with the issue of blood (Luke 8:43–48) who touched the hem of Jesus' garment and was healed. But, what about the woman who still has an issue of blood because her blood has never stopped flowing? We can teach and preach about the man who was blinded from birth (John 9:1–6), Jesus spat on the ground to create mud from his saliva and put it on the man's eyes. Jesus told him that he needed to go and wash in the pool of Siloam. The blind man did exactly what he was told and immediately, he was healed. But, what about the disabled female or male who wakes up every morning after having been touched by the breath of new life that the Lord chose to breathe into her or his body, who has to come to terms with the fact that she or he will never see, hear, move, walk, or talk? Preachers can stir up a crowd with the story about Jesus healing a man with leprosy (Matthew 8:1–4), who knelt before Jesus and asked the Lord to make him clean. The Lord told him to be healed and he was healed. But, what about the person whose body is ravaged with disease and no matter how many times people pray over that person and say, "be healed," she or he has to reconcile the fact that their physical healing will not come on this side of heaven? Granted, out of the five case studies, two out of five sermons dealt with some form of disability or physical deformity. However, in both cases, someone was healed. In the Kirk-Duggan sermon, the biblical character was healed from the crippling spirits. In Copeland's sermon, Copeland was healed from her breast cancer. Will we ever hear sermons that do not have happy endings—sermons that actually cause us to wrestle with what we deeply believe about God?

The reason I must imagine what womanist rhetoric *would* sound like is because womanism is still quite new to the field of communication. We have yet to archive womanist speeches and identify the names of all the womanist rhetoricians. Womanist rhetorical scholarship is gravely missing from the oratorical tradition. Marsha Houston and Olga Idriss Davis argue that "Out of our specific situations of multiple oppression, African American Women have developed traditions of thought, discourse, and activism intended to create not simply our own liberation, but a truly humane social order."[31] Therefore, it is imperative that African American's women's public and private discourse that is both sacred and secular be explored.

Ultimately, the existence of womanist preaching, womanist theology, womanist ethics, and womanist literature demands further exploration into womanist rhetoric. Like womanist preachers, womanist rhetoricians must speak against the domination and marginalization of all oppressed people, regardless of race, ethnicity, sexuality, or gender. Although womanist preaching brings theology and Christology to the center of its message, the overall *aim* of womanist rhetoric and womanist preaching are one and the same. A womanist rhetorician must work at re-imaging victims to victors, calling us back to our communal beliefs and values using a rhetorical Jeremiad, re-imaging villains to heroines, and offering a cultural critique of the oppressive power structures that continue to marginalize people. Both womanist preaching and womanist rhetoric have the moral responsibility to fight for the social justice and liberation of all people.

We have stories to tell and to teach. Those stories are our experience.
That experience is our knowing. That knowing is our struggle.
That struggle is our survival. That survival is our strength.
That strength is our center.

—Olga Idriss Davis[32]

NOTES

1. Cannon, *Katie's Canon*, 120.

2. Debra Mubashir Majeed, "Womanism Encounters Islam: A Muslim Scholar Considers the Efficacy of a Method Rooted in the Academy and the Church," in *Deeper Shades of Purple: Womanism in Religion and Society*, ed., Stacey M. Floyd-Thomas (New York: New York University Press, 2006), 42–43.

3. Ibid., 45–46.

4. Diana L. Hayes, "Standing in the Shoes My Mother Made: The Making of a Catholic Womanist Theologian," in *Deeper Shades of Purple: Womanism in Religion and Society*, ed., Stacey M. Floyd-Thomas (New York: New York University Press, 2006), 54–76.

5. Ibid., 64.

6. Kimberly P. Johnson, "Womanism," in *The Wiley Blackwell Encyclopedia of Gender and Sexuality Studies*, ed. Nancy A. Naples (Oxford: John Wiley & Sons, Ltd., 2016), 2.

7. Ibid. See also Chikwenye Okonjo Ogunyemi, "Chikwenye Okonjo Ogunyemi's African Womanism," in *Deeper Shades of Purple: Womanism in Religion and Society*, ed., Stacey M. Floyd-Thomas (New York: New York University Press, 2006), 26.

8. Johnson, "Womanism," 2. See also Clenora Hudson-Weems, "Clenora Hudson-Weems's Africana Womanism" in *Deeper Shades of Purple: Womanism in Religion and Society*, ed., Stacey M. Floyd-Thomas (New York: New York University Press, 2006).

9. Mitchem, *Introducing Womanist Theology*, 118.

10. Kirk-Dugan, *Exorcizing Evil: A Womanist Perspective on the Spirituals* (Maryknoll: Orbis Books, 1997), 140.

11. Flake, *God in Her Midst*, 3–4.

12. Ibid., 4.

13. Ibid., xiv.

14. Walker, *In Search of Our Mother's Garden*, xi.

15. Appendix A.

16. Appendix E.

17. Karlyn Kohrs Capmbell and Kathleen Hall Jamieson, "Form and Genre in Rhetorical Criticism: An Introduction," in *Readings in Rhetorical Criticism.* 3rd ed. (State College: Strata Publishing, 2005), 408–409.

18. Frank A. Thomas, *Introduction to the Practice of African American Preaching* (Nashville: Abingdon Press 2016), 55.

19. Marvin A. McMickle, *Where Have All the Prophets Gone?: Reclaiming Prophetic Preaching in America?* (Cleveland: Pilgrim Press, 2006), 2.

20. Eugene L. Lowery, *The Homiletical Plot, Expanded Edition: The Sermon as Narrative Art Form* (Louisville: Westminister John Knox Press, 2001), 11.

21. James Earl Massey, *Designing the Sermon: Order and Movement in Preaching* (Nashville: Abingdon Press, 1980), 50.

22. Sarah Travis, *Decolonizing Preaching: The Pulpit as Postcolonial Space* (Eugene: Cascade Books, 2014), 1.

23. Ibid.

24. Kirk-Duggan, "Women of the Cloth," March 23, 2006, Austin Presbyterian Theological Seminary, Austin, Texas, (transcribed by Kimberly P. Johnson, see Appendix A).

25. Linda Thomas, "Womanist Theology, Epistemology, and a New Anthropological Paradigm," in *CrossCurrents* 48, (Winter 1998), 488.

26. Cannon, *Katie's Canon*, 116.

27. Olga Idriss Davis, "Theorizing African American Women's Discourse: The Public and Private Spheres of Experience" in *Centering Ourselves: African American Feminist and Womanist Studies of Discourse*, eds., Marsha Houston and Olga Idriss Davis (Cresskill: Hampton Press, Inc, 2002), 38.

28. Frank A. Thomas, *They Like To Never Quit Praisin' God: The Role of Celebration in Preaching* (Cleveland: Pilgrim Press, 2013), 7.

29. Patricia Hill Collins, *Black Feminist Thought*, 1.

30. Shirley Wilson Logan, *With Pen and Voice: A Critical Anthology of Nineteenth-Century African-American Women* (Carbondale: Southern Illinois University Press, 1995), 1.

31. Marsha Houston and Olga Idriss Davis (eds.), *Centering Ourselves: African American Feminist and Womanist Studies of Discourse* (Cresskill: Hampton Press, Inc, 2002), 6.

32. Davis, "Theorizing African American Women's Discourse," 49.

Appendix A

"The Power of 'Enough'"[1]

Elaine M. Flake

Genesis 29: 31–35

> She conceived again and bore a son, and said, "This time I will praise the Lord."

—Genesis 29:35

Enough, starring Jennifer Lopez, is one of my favorite movies. In it Lopez plays a character named Slim who is married to an unfaithful and abusive man. Their relationship begins wonderfully with a storybook courtship, wedding, and honeymoon. But the honeymoon soon ends with the husband's adultery and selfish behavior. After the birth of their daughter, Slim is forced to contend with the angry blows and cruel behavior of her mentally disturbed but wealthy husband. It is a nightmare

He beats her, then says that he loves her. He cheats on her but makes her feel that his cheating, like his beatings, is what she deserves. As is typical, his abuse is followed by repentance and declarations of love. The cycle continues with each beating more brutal than the preceding one. When Slim tries to break free, her husband prevents her departure, only to inflict more perverted displays of temper and contempt. She is a prisoner in her marriage and her home.

Not only is this woman abused physically, but she is also abused verbally. Emotionally and mentally manipulated, she is constantly told: "It's your fault. You deserve it. You make me have to hit you." And of course, her husband uses the famous line "I will kill you if you try to get away from me." Slim becomes a woman who is sadly frightened, timid, and living in the emotional prison of low self-esteem.

She eventually attempts to get away with her daughter; however, when she changes her identity, either he or one of his violent friends finds her, and she has to flee again. She remains his prisoner.

One day, in the midst of her depression and despair, Slim has a change of attitude. Everything that has happened *to* her finally causes something to happen *within* her. As a result, her life begins to change. She is afraid and feels absolutely helpless, and she would have resigned herself to the seeming ubiquitous influence and power of her husband for the rest of her life. But one day she experiences the inner power that comes with saying, "Enough!" For it is when Slim makes up her mind that she has had enough that everything in her life begins to fall into place.

It is when she decides that she has run enough, hidden enough, cried enough, and lost enough that her life takes on new direction. It is when she understands that she has begged enough, apologized enough, kept quiet enough, and blamed herself enough that she finds the strength to take charge of her circumstances. When she finally understands that she has to find a way to take charge of her life and all of its madness in order to live the life she wants to live, and when she has a change of self-perception, she is able to move from a place of victimization to victory.

What happens to make the difference? Well, it seems that one day something jolts Slim's spirit, pushing her toward the woman she had never had the nerve to become. She starts to have confidence in herself. Her desire for deliverance and self-improvement motivate her to move to a better place. Life and its abuses have trampled her self-esteem, self-love, and hope for personal growth. One day she has an "ah-ha" moment.

Something inside Slim makes her realize that if she does not overcome some inner weaknesses, she will never move out of her place of oppression. She is clear that her husband is not going to give up or change, so the only way she is going to be free requires her to change. She develops a plan. She gets some financial assistance from her long-lost father, sends her little girl away with a friend, and enrolls in a self-defense class. She trains for many weeks. Her teacher and mentor instructs her how to kick, punch, and duck. She develops courage and speed. With each day her confidence increases, her self-esteem is raised, and her determination is intensified.

She finally reaches the point where she is ready to work her plan. She travels back to the city where they had lived and breaks into his home, and while he is away at work, she sets the stage for her attack. She removes all of the guns in his arsenal. She familiarizes herself with the layout of his apartment and waits for his return. And when he gets home, she wages a deliberate and systematic attack on him. To his amazement and indignation, she who had always backed down is backing down no more. They fight back and forth. When an opportunity presents itself for him to kill her, he tries to bludgeon her to death. Then it hits her: it is either crush or be crushed. She gets a surge of power, jumps up, and shoves him with all of her might. He crashes into the rail, breaking it and falling to his death. She is finally free of her tormentor. It is an accident that sets her free.

To be clear, I am *not* celebrating the death of the abuser; however, I do celebrate this woman's realization that she has to take charge of her messy and miserable life and find a better way to live. I celebrate the fact that when she decides that she has lived with violence, weakness, and unhappiness long enough, she reaches down into her untapped inner resources and finds a power that has been hidden from her by her circumstances. As a result, she lifts herself out of a mental and emotional rut and frees herself of long-standing bondage. We must remember that we are not so weak or so oppressed by sin and sorrow that we cannot turn our situation around.

The word of the Lord to every woman who has spent too much time settling for relationships, jobs, and situations that are not fulfilling, nurturing, or true to your potential is that there is power in deciding you have had enough. Today is the day for women to realize that we can create a better life for ourselves by clearing our space of emotional clutter and the people who create a toxic internal reality. How much better our lives will be when we stop subjecting ourselves to environments and personalities that take away our freedom and self-esteem.

God is calling for brave and determined women to adopt an attitude of intolerance for those things in their lives that abuse, confuse, and restrict. Our divine Provider is just waiting for some of us to say, "I am not going to go on like this. I am ready to walk in my privilege and break though [*sic*] to a new way of being." God is just waiting to work in us and with us to replace fear with self-confidence, guilt and shame with the determination to be better, and low expectation for self to a conviction that says, "I am better than this, so I can do better than this."

Let's examine the text. Genesis 29 tells the story of a homely and mistreated woman named Leah. Leah was Jacob's first wife and Rachel's sister. From the very beginning, Jacob did not love Leah; he loved her younger sister, Rachel. But Laban, Leah and Rachel's father, felt that his older daughter should get married first, so he tricked Jacob into marrying Leah. While Jacob was married to Leah, it was Rachel who had his heart. Jacob pursued Rachel until she was his wife, too. Rachel was his woman of choice, while Leah was a woman of convenience, for although he did not love her, he did sleep with her.

The writer of this biblical story implies that Leah spent a lot of her mental and emotional energy trying to find love in this love-impoverished situation. Rejection is never easy to take. It is especially devastating in your own home or spiritual community. Leah did everything she could to live up to Jacob's standards so that she could find a place in his heart. Since Leah was not very pretty, I imagine she spent a lot of time trying to make herself attractive to Jacob. In her mind, Rachel was the competition. Yet in reality, she would never be able to compete with the beautiful sister for Jacob's love.

Day after day, Leah concentrated on Jacob, Rachel, and her personal misery. The Bible says that when God saw that Leah was not loved, God opened her womb. Perhaps the blessing of reproduction was designed to make her see that sometimes you have to create new life for yourself apart from the one that cannot give you what you need.

When Leah gave birth to her first son, her thoughts were only of Jacob and her misery. She named him Reuben, which means "surely my husband will love me now." Her son's name is an indication of her desperation. She had another son, but his birth gave Leah no joy or self-appreciation. All she could see in the midst of divine creation was "because the Lord saw that I am hated, God gave me Simeon." She had a third son, but still she was controlled by fear, poor judgment, and emotional dysfunction, and she was never able to celebrate the creative process that was God's gift to her to motivate her to emotionally connect to herself. Instead, her response to God's blessing upon the birth of Levi was "Now my husband will become attached to me because I have given him three sons."

Somewhere between the third and the fourth pregnancy, it appears that Leah experienced a spiritually motivated personal transformation. One day a defining moment gave birth to a change of attitude. This change of attitude changed her focus and reshaped her inner reality. For the first time, she was able to get in touch with who she was. She realized that her life had to be bigger than Jacob. She had enough of trying to deny who she was and trying to be who Jacob wanted her to be.

The text reveals that by the time Leah gave birth to her fourth son, her thoughts were not about Jacob first. She had finally had enough of feeling sorry for herself, enough of being depressed because she was not desirable to a man who never loved her to begin with, enough of feeling guilty and ashamed. This time she was in touch with reality. This time she was clear that she could not make Jacob love her, but she could make Leah love Leah. The new Leah vowed with the birth of Judah, "This time I will praise the Lord."

So many women have some "Jacobs" in their lives that they need to put in proper perspective. Jacob is that person, experience, or memory that prevents you from appreciating the woman that you are and discovering the purpose that is yours. Like Leah, you need to decide that your life is bigger than that one sexual encounter, that experience of date rape, or that job promotion you didn't get. You are not defined by another person's opinion of you, your divorce, or your husband's numerous seasons of infidelity. Your relationship with God will empower you to see who you really are.

With this change of attitude, in addition to giving birth to Judah, Leah gave birth to a new Leah. When she found the courage to declare "Enough!" and when she saw the self-destructive nature of her thinking and decided to change her attitude, she was empowered to find her best self and worship the Lord. She walked away from a desperate, insecure, and needy Leah and found the Lord, and when she found the Lord, she found a new Leah.

Every woman who is ready to walk away from situations that are abusive and dead, who is ready to dream big, think judiciously, and live out of the box, and who is committed to not apologizing for her gifts must understand her responsibility to realistically and spiritually access her life and see how much better it can be when she identifies the sources of her bondage and decides that "enough is enough." For every Leah who is ready to be free of bad habits, negative attitudes, and ungodly behaviors that keep her in bondage, things can change when she draws the line and begins to walk in godly strength.

You have lived underneath the weight of oppression and suppression long enough, and you will experience life anew when you begin to stand up for yourself and stand up in God. Become a real fighter and force with which to contend in this spiritual war for your life. If you want to grow and get out of life's ruts, you must battle daily with negative thoughts about yourself and forgive yourself for past mistakes. Know that God is going to give you the strength that you need to get the job done. God is committed to your growth, liberation, and moral well-being.

To be weak, self-debasing, and insecure is to be carnally minded. To let men lie to you and women deceive you is to be carnally minded. To say that I cannot go to school, I cannot leave him, and I am not able to improve is to be carnally minded—and a carnal mind is enmity against God. When you are truly seeking God, you cannot settle for anything that is inferior or substandard. When your mind is being transformed, you will be renewed and will no longer be imprisoned by your attitude and thoughts. You will begin to tell yourself you have worried enough, agonized enough, taken enough, justified enough, and begged enough.

Although you may have dealt with a lot and been through a lot, you are stronger than everybody says you are. You will only live life at its best when you decide that you are at a place of enough. It is only when we learn and accept the truth about ourselves and the circumstances that surround us that we make progress. It is only when we get fed up with the unproductive, abusive, negative, and oppressive behaviors that lead to failure that we can forge ahead. We can break away from the stuff that ushers us into dangerous territory so that we can thrive and find help for a brighter future. Sometimes we cannot wait for deliverance; we have to fight for it. We have to break free of some relationships, some friendships, some guilt, and some shame to get to the next level. Being women of God requires that we recognize our own oppression and our own destructive and ungodly behavior. When you are really walking with the Lord, you will eventually get to the place that you know that your survival and growth depend on your ability to say, "No more!"

To the Leahs and Slims who are fed up with being abused by life and determined to find a more excellent way, this is the time for something wonderful to happen. Make a vow to God today, declaring, "I am giving myself over to an internal makeover, and it is my change on the inside that is going to help me work on some stuff that is going down on the outside. I am appropriating the God-essence that is in me so that I might defeat oppressive forces that seek to mess up my life." Reject the spirits of apathy, failure, and lies that have hidden God's truth in your life. Denounce the spirits of fear and defeat. Know that God has enough love, joy, peace, and unmerited favor to turn your life around. And this time, release God's power within. And like Leah, this time praise the Lord. God is enough. You are enough. Enough is enough!

NOTE

1. Elaine M. Flake, "The Power of Enough!" Reprinted from Elaine M. Flake, God in Her Midst: Preaching Healing to Wounded Women (Valley Forge, PA: Judson Press, 2008) 41–47. Reproduced by permission of the publisher.

Appendix B

"Enough Is Enough!"[1]

Gina M. Stewart

Genesis 29

> She conceived again, and when she gave birth to a son, she said,
> "This time I will praise the Lord." So she named him Judah. Then she
> stopped having children.

—Genesis 29:35, NIV

One of my favorite scenes in the movie *What's Love Got to Do with It?*
Is when Tina Turner runs to a motel after an out-and-out brawl with Ike.
Her lips are swollen and bleeding, her hair is disheveled, and she's semi-
barefooted. She runs across the parking lot to a motel and says to the desk
clerk, "I've got 36 cents and a Mobil card, but if you give me a room for the
night, as soon as I am able, I will repay you." That night, according to the
movie, was a defining moment in Tina's life. She walked away from a life
of physical, emotional, and mental abuse. That night, she walked away from
an emotional and psychological prison. When Tina decided she had had
enough and decided to say no to an unproductive, unhealthy relationship,
she opened the door to a new and exciting chapter in her life. And those of
us familiar with Tina's career know that from that night forward, the rest is
music history.

When I think about Tina's story, I am reminded of the character in the
text, Leah, whose name means "wearied" or "afflicted one." She was the oldest daughter of Laban, the older sister of Rachel, and the first wife of Jacob.
Biblical historians imply that Leah was not a pretty sight. The Bible describes
her as having delicate or weak eyes. As far as Jacob was concerned, Leah
was inferior in attractiveness and personality. But her younger sister, Rachel,
whose name means "ewe," female sheep, was Jacob's beloved. Jacob did not
keep his love for Rachel a secret; in fact, even though Jacob was married to

Leah first, it was Rachel who captured his heart, and Jacob was willing to work for seven years to have her hand in marriage. But at the end of seven years, Laban gave Leah to Jacob as a substitute for Rachel. But Jacob was sprung. He loved Rachel so much that he was willing to work another seven years to get the woman of his choice.

Now the text doesn't tell us whether Leah loved Jacob, but it does imply that Jacob didn't love Leah. The tragedy about Leah's relationship with Jacob was not just that Jacob loved someone else. Jacob should have been free to marry whomever he wanted to marry, and Laban shouldn't have deceived him, but the fact that Laban had to trick Jacob into marrying Leah speaks volumes about Laban's opinion of his oldest daughter. After all, Leah never made the short list for Jacob. She wasn't even on Jacob's radar screen for marriage; it was Laban who orchestrated the marriage. It was customary for the oldest daughter to marry first. But the fact that Laban had to trick Jacob into marrying Leah says a lot. From reading the text, we get the impression that Leah invested a lot of time and mental and emotional energy trying to gain Jacob's affection. And Leah had something that Rachel didn't have. Leah could produce.

The text says that when the Lord saw that Leah was unloved—the King James Version says hated—he opened her womb. And Leah produced sons. Now the fact that God opened Leah's womb is significant. Leah lived in a culture that was unapologetically patriarchal, where the individual value of a woman was shaped by a social structure that sustained and perpetuated male dominance over females. In a culture where the relationship between women and men was one of subjugation, subordination, and domination, women were subordinate to men in power and economically dependent upon them for survival. A woman's redemption was in childbearing, and her worth was attached to whether she could produce. Childbearing was so important that institutions were established, like polygamy and adoption, to preserve a father's name on earth. Brothers married their deceased brother's widow if no sons were born prior to his death to leave an heir for the dead.

But despite the fact that Leah was fertile, Jacob didn't change. Each time she gave birth to a son, the names of her sons were an indication of the cry of her heart toward Jacob. The depth of her pain and expectation is illustrated by the names that Leah gave each of her sons. When Leah gave birth to her first son, she named him Reuben, meaning "Lord has seen" my misery. She thought, *surely Jacob will love me now*. She had another son and named him Simeon, which means "because the Lord heard" that I am unloved. She had a third son and named him Levi and said, "Now this time my husband will become attached to me, because I have borne him three sons." But in spite of her hope and expectation, Jacob never heard, never saw, and never connected. Consequently, Leah's emotional dependence upon Jacob robbed her of security and self-worth. Although Leah could produce, Jacob did not appreciate her strengths, because she was not Rachel. Leah suffered a wounded self-esteem. She relied too much on Jacob's estimation and evaluation.

Like Leah, so many of us suffer from wounded self-esteem because of someone else's evaluation of us. Although self-esteem refers to our estimation of our own worth, many of us inherited our initial perception of ourselves from other sources: from the Jacobs and Labans in our lives. We never consulted God about our worth. So we suffer from impaired vision, holes in our soul, insecurity, and mistaken identities. Throughout our lives, other people affected our identity by the way they treated us or spoke to us. Some of us have been coddled and cheered all of our lives; some of us have been berated for imperfections over which we had no control. Some of us were always being compared with someone else and never learned to appreciate our own strengths. We have been tolerated rather than celebrated. We feel we are not good enough because we experienced rejection in primary relationships. Consequently, many of us are not just emotionally fatigued, emotionally empty, and emotionally numb, but we are emotionally dependent, believing that the ongoing presence and nurture of another person is necessary for one's security and self-worth. And Leah was emotionally dependent upon Jacob.

But one day, Leah experienced a defining moment that changed her attitude. One day, Leah decided that enough is enough. The change of attitude changed her focus and reshaped her perspective and inner reality. She realized that she could no longer live her life dependent upon the ongoing nurture and approval of Jacob. By the time Leah gave birth to her fourth son, Jacob no longer consumed her thoughts. Leah had a reality check. She finally realized that she couldn't make Jacob love Leah, but she could love Leah, and most of all, God loved Leah! Somewhere between verse 30 and verse 35, Leah experienced a transformation. She gave birth to another son and a new Leah. With the birth of Judah, her fourth son, she said, "This time I will praise the Lord."

I believe Leah must have said to herself, "I had Reuben, and he didn't see me. I had Simeon, and he didn't hear me. I had Levi, and he wouldn't become attached to me. But I can't worry about Jacob any more. I can't live my life or see myself through Jacob's eyes; I can't be my best self, dependent on Jacob's approval and acceptance. I can't grow as long as I am obsessed with what someone else thinks about me. I cannot experience my potential as long as I keep investing my emotional and mental energy in love-deficient relationships. I can't give myself away trying to measure up to somebody else's idea of what acceptable is." Because sometimes, Jacob does not change. And if Jacob's transformation does not take place, I must experience my own transformation. I believe that Leah must have said to herself, "Jacob may not change, but I can change. He may not see me, he may not hear me, and he won't even try to get to know me. But thank God, God sees me, God hears me, and God has blessed me. And this time I will praise the Lord. I am not going to wait until Jacob accepts me. I am not even going to worry that I am not Rachel. I am going to praise the Lord. Because being loved by God is greater than being loved by Jacob."

Like Leah, many of us have Jacobs in our lives. Jacob doesn't necessarily have to be a husband or a lover or a significant other. Jacob could be any primary person in our life we looked to for affirmation and approval. Jacob is the person whose ongoing presence and nurture we believe is essential for our sense of security and self-worth. But at some point, we have to do what Leah did—and say enough is enough. My value is not determined by anybody else. My worth is not based on what I look like, where I live, or the kind of clothes I wear. My worth and my value come from God. And because my value comes from God, I can praise the Lord. Because God is enough, I am enough, and enough is enough.

There comes a time when we have to decide that enough is enough. There is a freedom that accompanies the reality that I was designed and created for more. I do not have to settle for less. I do not have to participate in my own oppression. I was created to live a life of excellence. I was created for good works that God ordained from the beginning. I am better than this situation, and I can do better. We have to decide that our lives are bigger than our pasts. No matter what my mistakes or my shortcomings, the God I serve will empower me to see not only who I am but also what I am capable of becoming. The God I serve will empower me to get to the point where I can say enough is enough. Enough really is enough! We are more than the clothes we wear, the car we drive, the letters behind our name, the titles that we wear, our dress size, or the status we have achieved. God does not love us because of these things; God loves us in spite of these things. In fact, God demonstrated the high value of our lives by giving the life of his Son to die in our place. And that is enough!

A version of this sermon has been preached, with variations, in several places over a number of years, but "Enough Is Enough" was first preached at Berean Baptist Church, in Memphis Tennessee, for their 2006 Women's Revival.

For more prophetic preaching on this and other biblical texts that speak to wounded and abused women, see Elaine Flake, *God in Her Midst: Preaching Healing to Wounded Women*, Ed. Kathryn V. Stanley (Valley Forge, PA: Judson Press, 2007).

NOTE

1. Gina M. Stewart, "Enough is Enough!" Reprinted from Ella Pearson Mitchell and Valerie Bridgeman Davis (eds.), *Those Preaching Women: A Multicultural Collection* (Valley Forge, PA: Judson Press, 2008) 9–13. Reproduced by permission of the publisher.

Appendix C

"Women of the Cloth"[1]

Cheryl Kirk-Duggan

Luke 13:10–13

Now Jesus was teaching in one of the synagogues on the Sabbath. And just then, there appeared a woman with a spirit that had crippled her for eighteen years. She was bent over and quite unable to stand up straight. When Jesus saw her, he called her over and said, "Woman, you are set free from your ailment." When he laid his hands on her, immediately she stood up straight and began praising God.

When we look at this text, it's clear that the woman is bent over. Perhaps she was physically bent over. But the text says, that she was bent over by a spirit. *Point one*: Sexism, heterosexism, racism, classism, faux churchism, and skewed traditions cripple and bust the joy, an image of God, in God's people.

The woman had a crippling spirit. It was stopping the manifestation of God in her life. We can imagine that she knew no joy, that she was tired. We can imagine that she was a poor seminary student who was confused and…and had difficulty in exegesis [Laughing] and wasn't too clear about what it meant to be a Presbyterian in 2006 [Laughing]. She might have been a Presbyterian woman on the journey for 20 or 30 years and still trying to figure out, "God, was this your joke on me? [Laughter] What's going on? I don't quite get it." "In many respects, the church has gone backwards from where it was when I first said that I had a call, accepted it, when I had to go before the session and had to take ordination exams, what's going on?"

Well you see, most people in the world, including church people and seminary professors, are bent over. For it is sometimes that we think because we have accepted Jesus as Lord, because we've been blessed to have communion and study and learn, that we don't have issues. Beloved, we all have issues

[Amen]. Some of us are better at hiding them than others [Laughter]. Some of us are less bent over than others. Some of us are quite delusional [Clapping & Laughter]. And we think that we are really cool, and we've gotten over, and people don't really see us, see who we are. So I challenge you, to look in the mirror and take a risk and get to see, do you really know who you are?

For you see, with all the "isms," each "ism" cripples us in a very dynamic way. Sexism is a crippling spirit that violates and needs to control gender. Heterosexism is a crippling spirit that fears God's gift of sensuality and sexualities. Racism mocks and violates God's precious, magnificent color and cultural palate of peoples. How dare we not like someone because of the color of their skin. When you think about it, it must really grieve God and it really makes us quite stupid [Laughter]. Classism violates and has disdain for the poor and those with less status. And let us be really clear, we don't really want the poor people from the wrong side of the track, who may be a little smelly, sitting on those pews that my mama, or the group from the session, bought for this church. After all, this is First Presbyterian Church; we have our standards [Laughter]. And I tell you, because of that attitude, not only in Presbyterian, but Catholic, and Baptist, and Methodist, and all kinds of churches, Jesus would not be welcomed if he showed up on Sunday. Because faux churchism limits our experience of God and condemns the experience of others.

You know, it makes me laugh and cry at the same time when I think about all the folk who say, "It's my way or the highway!" What makes a person so arrogant that he or she thinks, and they have the audacity and the gall to say, "My way or the highway?" They're very big hypocrites and they're not really clear about the theology, often times, that they espouse because if God is so great, as many of these folk claim, then why couldn't God choose to anoint various persons with various visions of ways to do church?

In some of this faux churchism and faux, you mean like faux fur—false church—we are hurting more than we are helping. It would benefit and behoove many of us to hang up our Bibles and stoles and perhaps go out in the desert or go to a retreat center and get clarity. And so I invite, this is my second challenge, all my preacher friends and teacher friends to take some Sabbath time to rethink the vows you took. And, to take another look at, "Who is God in my life? Who am I?" Not what you do, but, "Who are you? Who am I? And, what is God calling you to do today?" For, if you knew that today was the last day of your life on this planet, what would you be doing and what kind of minister would you be?

Point two: Many of us are bent over by circumstances, fear, and family pathologies.

In many instances, women are where we are today and our churches are where we are . . . where they are today because of the other women—it's not so much the men keeping us down. For, if there are churches where women cannot be ordained or have leadership capacity, as I often tell my good Baptist and Catholic women friends, I would dare them, two Sundays in a row, just two, to not show up and to not spend a dime, to not send that tithe, and you want . . . you think Joseph Smith had a revelation, it would be no kind of revelation [Clapping, Laughing, and Shouting]. It would be no kind of revelation compared to what would happen in the American Baptist, Southern Baptist, and the Roman Catholic Church. Pope Benedict would have to make a new encyclical in a heartbeat [Laughter]. Because without women in the church, we do not have church.

But the problem is, because of patriarchy and misogyny, we as women have been so bent over for so long that we've learned how to play the game of being passive aggressive. You know, we tell our brothers, our fathers, our husbands, over pillow talk, "Well, honey, I think you know. What do you think about having a new youth program? Well, don't you think that it would be really great for our Presbytery?" We tell them in a way to make them think that they thought it up [Laughter]. And then, they'll bring it to the church, the Presbytery, and the next thing you know, we have this wonderful new ministry and it was her idea. Well, now that we have more women in leadership places, what happens is that we haven't learned how not to do the passive aggressive thing. And since we haven't learned how to do that, we are often very catty among women.

Many of us, as women, are closer friends with men than women because men, often times not all the time, but men often times will listen. They will help you decide what you need to do and if you have a fight, you have a fight, and then you go on. But many times, we women, we have a fight and we wanna hold on to it. "Well, twenty years ago, they didn't let me preach at Austin Seminary and I haven't been happy since and I'm not gonna send any money for alumni fund and they can ask me all they want [Laughter]." Or, "So-and-so didn't show up for my ordination. So-and-so is talking to Sally and she didn't talk to me at the Women in Cloth Conference. And you better, huh, you'll be surprised the next time she asks me to do something and I will just conveniently not be available." That is the games that women play. I'm just telling the truth. I'm just telling what I've seen. Doesn't matter race, doesn't matter age, I've watched little girls, I've watched older women play the same ridiculous games. We cut each other's throat. We backbite. We humiliate. That is not what Jesus would do. And the church cannot move forward until we name, what I call patriarchal sexism. And it's in the Academy too.

I've had some of my most difficult times with women who were already in the Academy and should have known better. But, they didn't 'cause they were so bent over from the pain that they went through as students during their doctoral programs that they didn't know how to relate to me, so I proved a threat. I didn't look like them. I didn't sound like them. And that was intimidating, so they had to try to cut my throat. But, what they didn't realize is I have a cloud of witnesses in glory and a cloud of witnesses here. And so do you! [Shouting] And therefore, I fear no one!

I'm up here because of the invitation, but the invitation was given because God called me to preach and teach, I really wasn't interested [Laughter]. And I challenge you [Laughter continues], I challenge you to look and see, what is your call and are you still interested? If you're not interested, then maybe it's time for you to do something different. God's people ought not suffer because we're bent over, busted up, and burned out.

For you see, Jesus did not condemn the bent over woman, but he saw her and he named her freedom. How many times have we seen people bent over due to depression, drugs, alcohol, sex, gambling, and we refuse to acknowledge them? How many times do you go to the grocery store and act like the cashier is an extension of the cash register? Have you ever thanked the garbage men for picking up your garbage faithfully? God's church cannot be the church until we name the bent overness and help to set people free.

Many women remain bent over because of their patriarchal and misogynistic conditioning. They've never gotten over the fact that they're not the son that their dads wanted. They've not got the healing and therapy that they needed because they were molested or raped. They've become bitter and so bent over like . . . when they stand up straight, it's still like they're bent over touching their toes. And, when you're bent over and touch your toes, you cannot see what's before you. You can only see what's beneath and behind.

To set people free is the fundamental key of salvation. I think many of us Christians get it wrong when we have people worrying about what's going to happen when they die. Well, we don't know what's going to happen when we die. Scripture gives us about 3 or 4 iterations about what might happen. But you know, there's not a lot we can do about it. Are we helping set people free today? And it's not enough to teach and preach Jesus is Lord because if their stomachs are growling too loud, if they're hurting too bad, the noise of their pain will drown out any message of the gospel that you preach. So, the question is, are you living the message of the gospel before them? If we do not live the message of the gospel, they will not, cannot, be able to hear the message of the gospel.

Isn't it interesting, Jesus did not sit down and write a ten-volume set of dogmatics [Laughing]. Jesus said, they're hungry, let me kind of multiply some of this fish and bread. They can't see, let me slap some mud on their eyes so they can. What are you doing to feed the hungry—spiritually hungry, physically, mentally, emotionally hungry?

Freedom is more than eschatology, it is lived reality. So, are you willing to be free so that you can help others to be free? Are we willing to allow everyone have a voice? Or, do they only need to be Presbyterians with a lot of money with the right kind of clothes, driving the right kind of car? Or, are we willing to set others free? Or, do we have a need to control them?

Point three: as friends, faculty, staff, and students of Austin Presbyterian Theological Seminary, let us press on to embrace the legacy of women who hear the call of God and experience ordination to a variety of ministries. As we choose to be set free in Christ Jesus, as we name the pathologies, and work for justice through the power of the Holy Spirit.

To be church means discerning all the "bent overness" and deal with them. Starting first with ourselves. Some of us are running so hard, we can't see straight, get enough sleep. Some of us are eating things we ought not to eat, drinking things we ought not to drink, and buying stuff we cannot afford. Stop it! [Laughter] 'Cause, when you do that you are practicing your illness, your sickness. That is pathological, that is not salvation. So, your ordination certificate may be framed and gilded in gold. You may have put aside a nice retirement plan, but if you are in prison to drugs, alcohol, to people, to people's opinion of you, to getting a big church, to having a big car, all that stuff, you aren't really saved, 'cause you're not really free. How bent over are we? How bent over are the women in our lives, the children in our lives? When was the last time that your Presbytery really dealt with the fact that they are building jails, right now, based upon the third grade population across the United States. When was the last time you had a Native person or a Hispanic or an African American person preach at your church? Teach at your church? How many of you all have Black neighbors or Brown neighbors or Asian neighbors that you really talk to? We can't talk about being the people of God if we don't live the people of God! I'm just saying, let's get real.

Now, you know, if you're in a very wealthy Presbytery, very wealthy parish, and you're doing good work there, well continue. But, don't forget that there's a world out there dying! And seminary students, don't forget, this is a privilege you have being here. So stop all the moaning and groaning! Nobody has an oozy or AK-47 at your head saying you got to be here! [Shouting] So, if you're going to be here, choose to be here, choose to learn. You'll get over your stuff! Faculty, if you're not reading new books, learning to teach in new ways, using blackboard, traveling, making things problematic for yourself, get over it, wake up! It's a privilege to teach. It is a gift to teach and if you're a smart professor, you recognize that. You are a teacher/learner, you don't know everything. You can't know everything, even if you had ten PhDs because you still have not mastered every language in the known world. Therefore, you don't know everything [Laughing]. And smart professors know that. Now, I mean . . . I know that all the professor here at Austin Seminary, Sally, are smart [Laughing]. I'm just saying what I'm saying [Laughing]. And I'm just passing that on so you all can share with some of your friends who are bent over [Laughing continues].

But, what about your session? Your Presbytery? How can we transform passive-aggressive behavior born out of patriarchy and misogyny? We must expose our internal societal oppressions if we want to be well. We cannot afford to engage in intellectual masturbation about the reality of what's going on in the world when people are dying. Now, I love to wax eloquently with theory, but if my theory cannot somehow be converted to praxis, I'm in trouble and I'm not helping anybody. I might feel good about myself, but you can only naval gaze for so long before it gets boring. And, I know that's not what God called me or us to do. So what are we willing to do to be free from our "bent overness?" What will each of you do today, not tomorrow because you may be dead tonight? And this is not about fear, this is about wake up! So, what are you willing to do today to speak truth to power? In the words that Dr. Cynthia Campbell mentioned this morning, she said, "We are bent over when others are silenced around us and when we do not pay attention to race and class and culture." Beloved, this is our day—tomorrow, standing up straight, tomorrow grace, tomorrow freedom, tomorrow love. What are you willing to do for there is a balm in Gilead? God bless you (Amen).

This sermon was preached at delivered on March 23, 2006, at Austin Presbyterian Theological Seminary, 100 E. 27th Street, Austin, TX 78705.

NOTE

1. Cheryl Kirk-Duggan, "Women of the Cloth." Reproduced by permission of the author.

Appendix D

"Hell No!"[1]

Melva L. Sampson

ESTER 1:1–12

But Queen Vashti refused to come at the king's command conveyed by the eunuchs.

—Esther 1:12, NRSV

Girl child ain't safe in a family o' mens.
Sick 'n tired how a woman still live like a slave.
You better learn how to fight back while you still alive . . .
But he try to make me mind and I just ain't that kind . . .

—From "Hell No!" *The Color Purple*, the musical

Around my big momma's kitchen table, where green beans were snapped and the daily rumor mill was spun, the phrase, "Hell no!" signaled an emphatic refusal used to express discontent toward a person, place, or thing. While the saved, sanctified, and filled with the Holy Ghost folk considered the phrase profane and not fit for Christians, especially women, in Nez's kitchen, as we affectionately called it, "Hell no!" was a saying of righteous indignation, the opposite of blasphemy but an acknowledgment of the reverence for ourselves as wholly holy and without restraint to resist whatever sought to silence our voices. "Hell no!" was sho' nuff grown woman's talk. When uttered, one could visualize the exclamation point that followed in the form of cutting eyes, between hissed teeth, and spewing from pursed lips. Women in my family sat around the kitchen table reclaiming, reviving, and revolutionizing black women's roles in church and society. When asked if she would "honor and obey" during one of her three wedding ceremonies, my big momma, Nez, said, "Hell no!" When the pastor summoned my mother to ask her to consider staying with my father, even though he was physically and verbally abusive, my mother responded with a resounding, "Hell no!" When asked if I would preach from the floor because the pulpit was reserved for male authority, I looked the deacon square in the eye and vehemently replied, "Hell no!"

When I read Vashti's story, I think of Nez, who, if she had been with Vashti after hearing the king's request, surely would have looked at the queen and given her the royal nod to repeat after her and say, "Hell no!"

The story recorded in Esther opens by describing a lavish party sponsored by King Ahasureus. The 180-day shindig celebrated the king's recent conquests. To top off his excessive display of wealth, the king sponsored an even more extravagant 7-day affair for all of the citizens of Susa. Drunk with wine and out of toys to display, the king decided to go for the shock-and-awe factor. He summoned Queen Vashti to appear at the party immediately, adorned, as some would suggest, with only her royal crown. The text reads, "But Queen Vashti refused to come at the king's command conveyed by the eunuchs. At this the king was enraged and his anger burned within him." Vashti was banished from the kingdom and ordered never to come before the king again. Her crown would be given to another who would be better than she.

Queen Vashti's response often is overlooked for the more palatable story of Esther. Yet to gloss over the monumental moment of liberation is to miss the making of a model of leadership in which following the sound of the genuine[2] within one's self is paramount. Such a model moves us from the sin of self-sacrifice and self-abnegation to the virtues of self-acceptance and self-development. Vashti's metaphorical response of "hell no!" became a model for all the women in Susa and a threat to those who would have found pleasure in her debasing display. The price she paid for dissing the king was dear—banishment. Yet, I imagine it was only a small price to pay for retrieving her voice, dignity, and worth. Vashti's insistence on taking care of herself reveals to us that we too will be faced with life-altering decisions when we decide to honor our own divinity. Vashti's actions and the king's response are telltale signs that we, too, will have to choose between revolution and apathy, between objectification and humanization, and between the inevitability of pain and the option of misery. We will all one day be summoned to the king and be forced to choose between a mealy-mouthed yes and an emphatic "Hell no!" The cost of living within the empire had become too great. Exile was yet a light affliction in exchange for her ability to answer the call to her own integrity and freedom. Her story provides us with three points to ponder.

First, Vashti's response reveals that we should beware of the invitations we entertain. As in the queen's case, we can rest assured that at some point in time we will be summoned to come before the king and in some cases bearing only our royal crown. We will be called to stand before the intellectually impotent and the spiritually bankrupt. We must beware of the invitations we entertain so as not to fall victim to a false sense of promotion that stems from our need to be recognized. Every invitation is not worth accepting and should be scrutinized thoroughly, or we too will be put in the position of appearing naked before the king's court.

Second, we must beware of the pride of the powerful. The pride of the king was fueled on the perceived powerlessness of Vashti. In the musical *The Color Purple*, adapted from the Pulitzer Prize-winning novel by Alice Walker and the film by Steven Spielberg, the character Sofia and her sisters sing and dance their way into a spiritual frenzy as they respond to Harpo's pride, the alleged powerful, with a loud "Hell no!" When we respond to our voice, we threaten the pride of the powerful. We must learn how to fight back in ways that annihilate both the pride and the power of those who seek to enslave our bodies, minds, and souls. The pride of the powerful is fueled by our silence. It desires to keep us beholden to weak-willed, fickle, and self-centered people. The pride of the powerful thrives on complete control and seeks to conquer our inner psyche, which if successful can ultimately thwart our inner ability to say, "Hell no!"

Third, we need to beware of false thrills; outward success is not equal to inner worth. Vashti was groomed to give the appearance of outward success. Being chosen as queen was a sign of successful training. Vashti's story is symbolic of struggles we face as we seek to assert ourselves in contexts where we are expected to submit and care only about others. Carol Lakey Hess cautions that had the queen disregarded her own feelings and submitted to the will of the king, she would have lost herself ever so quietly. She notes, "No one would have noticed; she would have simply colluded with quiet conspiracy."[3] The moral to Vashti's refusal is simple—outward success is not equal to inner worth. Material gain, position, and status are never worth giving one's soul away.

In a scene in the movie *The Color Purple*, the mayor and his wife approach Sofia. The couple is portrayed as somewhat liberal in a time when racism was excessive and flagrant. Miss Millie, the mayor's wife, asks Sofia is she wants to come and be her maid. Sofia's response is classic: "Hell no!" Astonished at her response, the mayor asks, "What did you say, gal?" Sofia responds again, "Hell no!" A verbal argument ensues and then a physical altercation. The crowd violently subdues Sofia in front of her children and takes her off to jail, where she spends many years. When she is released, she is sent to work for Miss Millie after all. After she completes her time with Miss Millie, she dines with her family. At the dinner table she reclaims her muted voice, recounts the reason for her response, and celebrates the sound of her own voice—the sound of the genuine. The stories of Sofia, Vashti, and women around Nez's table reveal a profound question.

When is the last time you said, "Hell no"? Esther resolved, "If I perish let me perish." Fannie Lou Hammer proclaimed, "I'm sick and tired of being sick and tired." Our great elder Maya Angelou penned, "And Still I Rise." Sister Shange shouted, "I found God in myself and I loved her/I loved her fiercely." Anna Julia Cooper said soundly, "When and where I enter, the whole race enters with me." God rejoices when we acknowledge the sound of our own voices. It is when we find our voices that we celebrate who God created us to be. These women paid high prices for freeing themselves from male authority, patriarchal dominance, and humiliating roles. Yet their responses suggest that more times than not we need to say, "Hell no!" Sometimes, a simple answer of "No," "No thank you," or "I'm sorry, I'll pass" just doesn't get it. We need to go for the shock-and-awe value and retrieve our voice, our power, and our bodies. As the song in the musical urges, "We have to learn how to respond while we're still alive." What will you do when the king/queen comes for you?

A version of this sermon was preached at First African Presbyterian Church, June 2007.

NOTES

1. Melva L. Sampson, "Hell No!" Reprinted from Ella Pearson Mitchell and Valerie Bridgeman Davis (eds.), *Those Preaching Women: A Multicultural Collection* (Valley Forge, PA: Judson Press, 2008) 27–31. Reproduced by permission of the publisher.
2. Howard Thurman, "The Sound of the Genuine," 1980 baccalaureate address, Spelman College, Sisters Chapel. Thurman explains this sound as the authentic voice within everyone, the voice that beckons us to be true to the divinity within.
3. Carol Lakey Hess, *Caretakers of Our Common House: Women's Development in Communities of Faith* (Nashville: Abingdon, 1997), 44.

Appendix E

"What Shall We Do For Our Sister?"[1]
Claudette A. Copeland

Song of Solomon 8:8

> We have a little sister, and she hath no breasts: what shall we do for
> our sister in the day when she shall be spoken for? Our little sister has
> no breasts. What shall we do for our little sister when men come along
> asking for her? (The Message Bible)

Romans 15:30

> I urge you sisters by our Lord Jesus Christ and by the love of the
> Spirit to join me in my struggle by praying for me.

The Song of Solomon. I will look this morning at chapter eight. Just kinda
nudge your girlfriend, nudge the one next to you and just tell them, "We
gonna be here a minute" [Laughing]. The door is not locked, if you've gotta
leave, we understand. Song of Solomon 8 and then we will notice for your
theme scripture, Romans 15:30. Song of Solomon the eighth chapter and I
will read from the eighth verse. Listen for the Word. The King James Version says:

> *We have a little sister, and she hath no breasts: what shall we do for our sister
> in the day when she shall be spoken for?* The Message Bible says, *"Our little
> sister has no breasts. What shall we do for our little sister when men come along
> asking for her?"*
>
> Romans 15:30 says this, *"I urge you sisters by our Lord Jesus Christ and by
> the love of the Spirit to join me in my struggle by praying for me."* This is the
> Word of the Lord, the people said, thanks be to God.

What shall we do for our sister? (Give me just a little less up here, I'm
getting an echo in the monitor) A Rat went around the barn yard frantically.

Yes, I said a rat [Laughing] went around the barn yard frantically exclaiming to everyone that she met, "There is a rat trap in the farm house." Well, she went up to the chicken and told the chicken, "Have you heard? I said, there's a rat trap in the farm house." Where upon the chicken said, "That does not concern me in the least," and went on about her way. The rat kept on frantically around the barn yard and met a pig and said, "Have you heard? There's a rat trap in the farm house." The pig said, "Well uh, I'm sorry, I'm not a rat; that does not concern me." Frantically, the rat kept on proclaiming and exclaiming to everyone she met. She met a cow and said, "Lord have mercy, did you know there's a rat trap in the farm house?" The cow said, "that is none of my concern." Well, just a few days later, a snake got caught in the rat trap. When the farmer's wife went to investigate, the snake bit her and she got sick. Well, everybody knows what's good for you when you don't feel good, chicken soup [Laughing & Clapping]. Where upon the farmer rang the chicken's neck and proceeded to prepare chicken soup. Well, she lingered a good long time. The illness would not abate and neighbors from far and near came to sit with the farmer's wife and everybody knows that you got to feed visitors [Laughing & Clapping]. Where upon, he slaughtered the pig so he could have some barbeque [Laughing]. And bless God when the prayers of the saints did not avail, the woman finally died. And, when the out of town folks came and stayed a good long time and the food ran out. Well, you know when there's a funeral, you've gotta have something to eat for them and he butchered the cow. And the moral of the story is: next time a rat tells you there's a rat trap in the farm house, you better understand that it affects the whole farm. [Clapping & Shouting].

Seven out of eight of you who sit here this morning will never be affected by breast cancer. You'll never be forced to experience the gripping fear when your fingers explore the terrain of your chest only to make the heart stopping discovery of that thing, that hard pea, that marble, that walnut size, that Robbin's egg mass that you had never discovered before. Seven out of eight of you will never make that dreaded trip to the physician's office to have the skinny needle biopsy, to have the wire inserted, to have the surgical cut-down. You will never have to wait for the pathology reports to confirm or deny your worst fear. The old saints used to say, "He's kept you from dangers seen and unseen." Seven out of eight of you will never have to lay down on a surgical table and feel like you are laying down in your coffin only to come up from the surgical sleep altered forever. Seven out of eight of you will never have to search the face of your partner to find a comfort you cannot provide yourself—to hope your wounds will be kissed and caressed. And I pray that you will not be among the women who search only to find in their lover's face revulsion and rejection, or simply the stunned helplessness when he sees an empty chest, a snaking scar in the place that he used to lay his head. Seven out of eight of you will never have to have this conversation with yourself. Most of us this morning, we engage in the conversation about cancer and bodily affliction and it's a, it's a *conversation*. And you nod politely and you feel some intellectual curiosity and down in your being you say, "Well thank God it ain't none of me!" But this morning, thanks to this man of God and these women of God in this great church, we came to tell you that there's a rat trap in the farm house [Shouting & Clapping] and it affects the whole farm. We have a little sister and she has no breasts? What shall we do for our little sister? One out of eight of us this morning is the little sister. And I came by this morning to have a conversation with you to tell you, I ain't going away, I'm telling you there's a rat trap [Clapping] in the farm house that affects all of us.

What a subject for a Sunday morning—breasts [Laughing]. What a conversation to have in a holy pulpit on a Sunday morning when I know half of you came in here, my God, to be encouraged, to hear that God's gonna pay your bills, God's gonna give you a husband, God gonna bring you out all right, oh. . . I know what you came for [Laughing]. This morning, we gonna talk about breasts [Laughing & Clapping]. If God can speak through a donkey [Laughing], if God can, c'mon here God's gonna talk to you this morning through a breast [Laughing]. Touch your friend and say, "Relax."

Breasts, a complex landscape of fifteen-to-twenty lobes within each one. Milk-holding receptacles exiting at a nipple—breasts. Highway system of complex ducts and thoroughfares—breasts. Struma, called fatty tissue and ligaments. Pectoral muscles, a waterway of lymphatic fluid—breasts. Don't you dare sit here this morning and act like you're embarrassed by the conversation because if I look at most of you closely, periodically, you try to show yours [Shouting, Laughing & Clapping]. And, for those of you who have nothing to show, I don't mean no harm, but the others of ya'll trying to sneak-a-peak [Laughing & Clapping]. Breasts, what a miracle of creation.

Breasts, we impatiently await their arrival when we're little girls. We proudly compare them when the buds begin to appear. Covered up in training bras [Laughter] sometimes when there ain't nothing in training [Laughter]. We compare them in adolescent bathroom moments—"What size you wear?" [Laughter] Come on ladies and go with me for a minute. Breasts, as young women, we display them like flags flown proudly in the wind. As older women, we kick them like burdens [Laughter & Clapping] scraping the ground [Laughter]. Breasts, oh come on you can laugh! We augment them when there're too little and we reduce them when they become too burdensome.

Breasts, in the common vernacular known by many names [Laughter]: jugs, watermelons, mosquito bites [Laughter], titties [Laughter], boobs. They get us attention. They interfere with us buttoning our clothes. They cut groves in our shoulders. They are the intersection between the maternal and the erotic. They comfort our babies of any age [Laughter & Clapping]. Breasts, they . . . [Preach Claudette] oh this is God, they literally sustain life. They satisfy the longings. Come on sisters, we wash them, we oil them, we powder them, we lace them, we liberate them. We harness them or we let them hang [Laughter]. We admire them in bathroom moments assessing their usefulness and attractiveness to the latest man in our lives. They are fondled, caressed, they are kissed and suckled [Laughter]. They are breasts. I can't get no help in here [Laughter]. They are, they are, they are lain upon for comfort. But mostly, after a while, we just settle in with them for a lifelong friendly companionship. That is unless one day we find out that our breasts are out to kill us.

The Song of Solomon is a celebration. It is a celebration of married love. It is an allegory of praise between a man and a maiden. For those of you who can't get with me, just remember here, just remember. It extols the beauty of sensual love and the wonders of the human body—The Song of Solomon. It is often said that "The greatest wounds are the wounds of the heart, the wounds of the emotions." But any woman who has undergone physical wounding, any woman that has undergone the wounds of the flesh, c'mmon just nod at me if you can't admit it. If you have ever been physically abused; if you've ever been slapped or hit; if you've ever been punched or had your hair pulled; if you've ever been kicked; if you've ever been raped or sexually violated; if you have ever suffered disfigurement in your body—the loss of a body part, the loss of your eyesight, the loss of a limb; then, that person, that woman knows viscerally, that the wounds of the body don't just wound the body, but they inscribe themselves as wounds on the soul. The wounds of the body are inextricably bound up with the woundings of my spirit.

"We have a little sister and she has no breasts." What shall be done for our sister? *"What shall be done for her when men come to call?"* What shall be done for those of you who sit outside the conversation of breast cancer, but what shall be done for us? On the day when your blood test comes back HIV positive, what shall be done for us? Your family on the day that your child is killed by a drive-by shooting, what shall be done for us? You better touch somebody and say, "us, us, us, us." When your heart attacks you because you refuse to get delivered from the hog maws and the pig feet [Clapping]. What shall be done for us when years of cigarette smoking and reefer smoking come to call [Clapping]. What shall be done for us on the day that you hit fifty and your husband comes home and says, "I'm trading you in for two twenty-fives [Laughing], I just don't want to be married no more." What shall be done for us? What shall be done when your business partner betrays you and runs off with the money? What shall be done when the best friend, your covenant sister that you thought you would grow old with betrays you?

What would anyone do for me on that day when I was thirty-eight years old at the top of my game? Preaching at all the right doors on all the best platforms. Living in the neighborhood that I wanted to live in and driving what I wanted to drive. When I walked in the doctor's office that day and he said, "Rev. Copeland, there is no good way to give you bad news. You have Infiltrating ductal adenocarcinoma, a kind of cancer that arises quickly, spreads quickly, and will kill you quickly." What shall be done for me? There comes a time when a Mercedes Benz don't help [Clapping & Shouting]. There comes a time when I don't need another diamond or a Rolex watch. What shall be done for our little sister when men come to call? What shall be done for you when you ah... you were, you were, I was never cute. I wasn't cute. I wasn't cute. I didn't have no shape, I didn't have pretty legs, but I had hair. Come on Survivors! I hadn't bought the hair, I hadn't weaved the hair, it was my hair [Clapping]! I could swing it like the best of the girls. When a catheter is threaded down my superior vena cava comes out my chest and for the next ten months I am pumped full of Adriamycin, 5-FU, and Cytoxan. What shall be done for me when I sit in the bathroom and wipe the last strand of hair off my head? What shall be done when I walk up in church hyper-pigmented looking like a dead woman with my head rag on watching all of the daughters in the church beginning to audition for my job? [Shouting] "Pastor David, how are you, do you need a pie? Do you need somebody to cook for you?" I'm over there sick and dying, but "Pastor David." Parenthetically, letting him know that she still had two breasts [Tell the story! Tell the story!]. What shall be done for our little sister?

Well, I know that we've got to go to lunch and I've got to get a plane. The Romans text that you all chose for your background scripture today says, Romans 15:30, "That I urge you by the Lord, Jesus Christ, and by the love of the Spirit, join me in my struggle by praying to God for me!" Couple of things I want to leave with you today, I don't know if you're going to be happy or not. But there's a rat trap in the farm house. What shall we do for our little sis? The first thing that I pick up in my experience both in life and in the text, is that if you want to do anything for your little sister, the first thing that we need from you is your partnership. Join me, when people are suffering and when they're struggling. How many of you know that sick folk become invisible [Yeah]? Ah, you don't know it, you on the sick list today, we gonna pray for you for about three weeks, but don't you stay sick too long [Clapping]. Cancer is not contagious, you can't catch it. I need partnership while I go through. Brothers, brothers, thank God for those of you who are not afraid of suffering [Clapping]. Thank God for a man who knows how to just take a woman in his arms and just rock her [Clapping]. Thank God for a man who doesn't run to the comforts of somebody else's breasts when his own wife is losing hers [Clapping & Shouting]. Ain't nobody gonna help me in here [Clapping]. Thank God for courageous brothers who know how to go with you to the chemotherapy [Clapping] and hold you 'til it gets better.

What shall we do for our sister? Join with me in my partnership: wear the pink ribbon; give; run; walk; march; do what you've gotta do, but don't leave me out here by myself. That is the whole story of the incarnation when Jesus did not stand back, but he said, "Look-a-here, prepare me a body and I'll go down and I'll be touched and tempted at all points, just like you! I'll show you how to overcome in a body?" Partnership."

The second thing that I raise up today has already been said. What can you do for me? Acknowledge that it's a painful struggle and that even though yours may not be like mine, validate me and tell me that you understand what pain is like. I know you're saved and Spirit-filled and been a part of the Mississippi Boulevard Christian Church for fifteen long years and you have your Bible on your knees and you've marked all the correct passages, and uhh you're prominent in the things of God. But, behind your persona [Clapping], behind your title, behind your vestments and your preacher robes, somebody has got to tell the truth that pain has touched us all and kissed every one of us in the mouth [Shouting & Clapping]. You don't get so deep, you don't get so holy, you don't get so full of the Word where you cannot acknowledge that all of us got something [Clapping]. I can't look down on you and yours 'cause you don't know mine. It is a painful struggle. The text that Paul says, "Join me in my *painful* struggle." Modern theology is a painless Christianity [Come on now!]. Modern theology is devoid of a cross, it is absent of a struggle. The media version of Christianity is what most of us have bought and you're in the church now on sound bites. You're in the church now, chasing celebrity clergy [Clapping]. You're in the church now, my God, because you saw a picture in a slick magazine in a glossy photo and you said, "I'm gonna go up in that church and see can I get next to them." Modern theology offers us a painless Christianity. But, I came by this morning unashamed, stronger than I've ever been, to tell you that every life has a struggle—every celebrity, every society is bathed in struggle. Life is marinated in pain. It was Haiti yesterday, Darfur last night, Jena, Louisiana this morning. Every Christian in this society has a struggle. Yours might not be a disease, yours might be that you're broke [Laughing] up in here today looking good on credit [Laughing & Clapping]. Yours might be mental instability. If we catch you one day when you miss your medicine, we'd all be in trouble [Laughing & Clapping]. Somebody say, "painful struggles." Yours might be raising children without resources or respite. Aging parents that you're trying to care for, a loveless marriage. Struggles with sexuality, sexual choices, no sex [Laughing]. Struggles: moral failure and spiritual dryness; breast cancer; chemotherapy; disfigurement; radiation; reconstruction; fear of metastasis.

Life for none of us has been no crystal stair [Clapping]. And, I came this morning to tell you, that I would take nothing for the struggle. I wouldn't take nothing for my journey right now because my struggle, my God, has made me stronger! [Clapping] It has been in the midst of my struggle that I have been stripped of my own self-sufficiency [Shouting]. It has been in the midst of my struggle; you don't wanna have to talk to me, but I'm talking to you; that I have had to lay down my own arrogance [Yeah!]. I've had to give my ego and leave it at the altar [Shouting]. It has been in the midst of my own struggle where God has had to break my legs and leave me limping, but I'm leaning now on an Everlasting Arm [Clapping & Shouting]. I said, there's a struggle going on for each of us, but I dare you not to run from the struggle! For it is in the midst of my struggle that God has done a new work in my life! [Shouting] Yes, if it were not for the struggle for some of us, struggle ran you into the church [Yeah]. You came into the church for relief from your struggle. Ah, but when you came looking for relief, God, by the Holy Ghost, gave you regeneration [Yeah!]—changed you, saved you, and delivered you! The struggle kept pushing you. It pushed you beyond your reach, pushed you beyond, come on here, your lovers [Clapping]. It pushed you beyond the alcohol bottle and pushed you all the way to the cross of Jesus Christ! [Shouting & Clapping] You better thank God for your struggle! [Clapping] Glory to God forevermore!

What can you do for your sister? Stop fronting and acting like you're immune and that I'm in this thing by myself! We have a little sister, I'm trying to hurry on. What shall be done for her? The third thing I want to raise up today is prayer. In the midst of all that's going on, Paul says, "Join me in my struggle by your prayers to God for me." How does a reality that begins with affliction end up with ability? [Clapping] How, how does a life situation that begins with, "I can't make it!" end up over here with, "I can do all things [Shouting & Clapping] through Christ that gives me strength"? [Shouting & Clapping] How does a reality bathed in despair and aborted hope and the tendency toward suicide, how does it transform itself over here, to now, "I'm more than a conqueror through Jesus Christ!"? [Clapping] I suggest to you that there is a conduit called prayer [Yeah!]. It is the privilege of the believer. It is the sanctuary of the saint. It is the refuge of the righteous. It is the comfort of the Christian, if you will pray.

But then, I remember, I remember, I was walking, I was walking in a major women's conference one day, Leo, and I was there with some of the "big name evangelists" and we were walking through this hotel packed with women everywhere and every few steps somebody would say, "Dr. Copeland, I'm so glad to see you!" "Dr. Copeland, your ministry is such a blessing!" praise the Lord, and we meandered on a few feet down through the crown then somebody else would say, "Evangelist Copeland, oh my goodness, I just love your

ministry! I've read all your books!" Speaking of which, they out there in the
hallway, ya'll better go get them after this service!" [Laughing & Clapping]
Praise the Lord, and we meandered on through the crowd and we got nearly to
the elevator, stopping three or four times, "Dr. Copeland," "Pastor Copeland,
I just love your ministry!" And way... yonder cross, way... yonder, I heard
somebody, Rev. Louisa, call out, "Hey Clyde!" Uh huh, I said, who up in here
know me? [Laughing & Clapping] For you see, Clyde is what they called me
in high school and college when I was more inclined toward Jesus than I was
immersed in Jesus [Laughing & Clapping]. Clyde was who they knew when
a little reefer was coming out from under the college dorm door [Laughing].
Clyde was who they knew when good and evil looked like twins and I got
the wrong one right [Laughing & Clapping]. Ain't nobody gonna talk to me
[Laughing & Clapping].

Jesus was talking to Simon Peter one day and he said, "Simon!" not Peter,
not your public persona, not who the people know on the pulpit, not who's
in the magazine and on TV, but "Simon!" your flesh man, personal man, the
one up underneath the, oh come on here, the one that ain't got no breasts, or
the one that's disfigured, the one that is apt to sabotage Peter if you let Simon
out. He said, look-a-here, in case you don't pray for yourself, and in case you
can't get nobody else to enter into prayer with you, I heard Jesus say, "Look-
a-here Simon, I have prayed for you!" When people forget you, when people
are embarrassed by your suffering, when people walk a wide circle around
you, this is your comfort, "Simon! With all of your disfigurements, with all
of your failures, with all of your weaknesses," I'm talking to somebody in
here today, "with all of your confusion about what is right, I have prayed for
you!" [Yeah!]

I'm so glad I found Christ before I found cancer! I'm so glad I have an
organizing principle in the midst of my life and it is founded upon the prayers
of the Great High Priest, who sits at the right hand of the Father praying for
me. Prayer, prayer, prayer, if you want to do something for me, let's join
together in prayer 'cause first of all, a saint who prays is Satan's greatest terror! [Shouting & Clapping] He is not afraid of believers, for the Bible said,
"demons believe and they tremble." He's not afraid of church members. The
Bible says, in Job 2, "When the folks came to Church, Satan came along
with them and walked up and down trying to see what he could check out!"
[Shouting & Clapping] He is not afraid of even you deep and wonderful
people who prophesy and heal and do mighty works because the Bible said,
"Jesus said, 'in that last day, some of ya'll, I'mmon tell you, I don't even
know you, depart from me!" Satan is not afraid of the deep wonder, but he
is afraid of saints who will pray! [Shouting & Clapping] Oh God, I don't
have no help in here, but I know of what I speak! [Shouting] You are Satan's
greatest terror! I say, I need you in my life. This is what I need you to do for

me. I need you to have my back in the realm and domain where principalities still want to take my life!

Oh, Mighty God, I understand that when I got sick, I realized that I got good friends all over the country, but I didn't call the ones who were talking about, "Now I lay me down to sleep [Laughing & Clapping] I pray the Lord my soul to keep" [Clapping]. I had to call somebody that knew their way around the prayer room [Clapping]. A saint who will pray is Satan's greatest terror! For when you pray, my God, when you get up in the morning and put your feet up on the floor, demons begin to get discombobulated [Shouting & Clapping]. When you have been in the throne room with God, oh . . . you can walk in and ain't got to say a word, you just change the atmosphere. A saint who will pray is Satan's greatest terror! [Clapping] Glory be to God forevermore! You see, he's afraid of you because when you pray, when you pray, when you pray, the Bible says, "The eyes of your understanding come open." [Shouting] When you pray, girl, you can see some things [Yeah!] There's nobody gonna help me, but I'm gonna help myself. I said, when you pray, you can see some things. Ah... I can discern spirits, I know whether it's an angel or a demon, I know whether it's human or Divine, I know whether it's going to be healing or death. When I pray I can see some things. Not only can I see some things when I pray, but my God, I can stop some things! [Shouting & Clapping] The Bible says, "Whatever I bind on the earth is gonna be bound in heaven." [Shouting & Clapping] When you pray, you become Satan's greatest nightmare! I don't mean any harm, but when we come to the altar, I don't need you to pat me. I don't need you to give me a Kleenex. I don't need you to pray pitiful prayers, but I need somebody who can boss some demons around [Shouting & Clapping] and say, "I bind your works. I bind the power of sickness and disease. You gonna live and not die." When you pray, you become Satan's greatest terror!

What can you do for your sister? Get a prayer life—you can see some things, you can stop some things, and you can set some things in motion! You can pull in some prophetic realities, can lay hold of some promises when you learn to pray. I've prayed for you that you will learn to join in this great warfare of prayer because you'll become Satan's nightmare, his greatest terror. Secondly, you'll become one of those who understand that prayer is self's greatest refiner. I did not know, somebody say, "refiner." I've been saved since I was fourteen, preaching since I was eighteen years old. I did not know until I got sick and I began to watch my body deteriorate. I did not know until I saw women start lining up to take my husband. I did not know what was still in me. I didn't know I could still cuss [Laughing & Clapping] like I could cuss [Laughing & Clapping]. Somebody say, "self's refiner." I did not know that I could actually go down to the state of Texas and apply for a license for a pistol permit to carry, put it in my pocketbook, bring it to church, and sit it right down by my pew [Laughing]. Somebody say, lift your hands and say, "Refine me Lord." [Yes He will!] 'Til I got sick and afflicted and had to fight with the enemy, I did not know I still had the capability on the inside to make up my mind, excuse me, I'mmon kill a negro [Laughing]. Oh yes I am, I'mmon kill a negro and I'm just gonna go sit in prison and have a prison ministry [Laughing, Shouting & Clapping]. I didn't know it was still in me! I didn't know it was still in me [Laughing]! I didn't know I could still be so angry with God [Preach], 'til I could shake my fists in His face. And say to Him, if this is how you treat your friends, I see why you have so few! [Shouting] I came to tell you that after you get finished railing and cursing God, after you get finished struggling against flesh and blood, finally you learn that prayer is self's greatest refiner [Amen!]. You'll find out that there are some things you can do without now [Shouting] when you learn how to pray [Shouting & Clapping]. Find some people that left you, you can kiss them goodbye and not be mad because I've learned how to pray. You've learned that whether I had to give up a man or a body part, I'm still victorious. Sometimes I have an aversion to my own appetite, I'm appalled by my own actions, I'm smothered by my own suffering, but now, since I've learned how to get in the face of God, thank you Jesus! Woe is me, I'm unclean and undone, but he touches the coal to my lips [Clapping], sanctifies me, cleanses me, and refines me.

What can you do for your little sister? You can learn to join me in the struggle of prayer because by prayer, you become Satan's greatest terror! While you're praying for me, some things will start happening for you [Clapping]. Satan's greatest terror, ourselves' greatest refiner. Give me five minutes and we'll all go home together. But, when you learn to pray, you find that a life of prayer becomes, listen to me, suffering's highest reward. I said, it becomes sufferings' highest reward. It takes me into an intimacy with God. I have suffered, you will suffer, there is a sorority in this sanctuary this morning of sufferers of many kind. Satan has come to kill and steal and destroy, but Jesus, I came that you might have life [Clapping]. And, I found out when I learn in the midst of my suffering to pray, something called serendipity happens. I don't know, I don't know if you quite understand it, but you heard a story about a man named Jed [Laughing], poor mountaineer, barely kept his family fed. Then one day, he was shooting at some food and up from the ground came some bubbling crude [Laughing], oil that is! I came to tell you that no matter what you're going through, no matter what you're doing without, no matter what life means for evil, God's got a way of turning that thing around and around and around! [Clapping] Kin folk said, "Jed move away from there! Head for the hills, Beverly Hills that is." [Clapping] Why? Because that which has come against you is now getting ready to work for you! [Clapping] It becomes suffering's highest reward.

What can you do for us? Learn to pray because not only do you become a terror to the devil and does your spiritual life become refined, not only do you find a great reward for all the suffering that you've been through. But prayer, survivors, we can testify, is the saint's surest refuge [Clapping & Shouting]. Daddy and them used to watch *Gunsmoke, The Rifleman, Paladin,* come on old school folks [Clapping]. Somebody lift your hands and say, "refuge." And at the end of, every, every single episode when the good guy would try to get somewhere against the bad guy, he would tell his buddies, "You cover me!" [Laughing] Bullets are flying, but cover me! I got somewhere to be, cover me! Ya'll ain't talking to me! [Clapping] I need a refuge in my life and when I can't pray for myself, I need somebody with some loaded guns [Shouting & Clapping]. I need a refuge so I can duck up under there in the time of trouble, he will hide me! It is the saint's surest refuge. Stand up on your feet, I've got to tell you one more thing before we go.

What shall be done for our sister? One day, there was a little doggie, don't start walking you gonna miss the good part [Laughing], she lived in an alley with a lot of her girlfriends. She had been a street doggie for a lot of years. She was mangy, her ribs were poking through. Her ear was torn off from a whole lot of doggie fights. Somebody say, "refuge." She had that look over your shoulder paranoid doggy walk for a dog that had lived outdoors for many years. She scrounged in garbage cans trying to survive. She was sick and she was dying. One day, one day, one day, down the street there was a gentleman driving a pick-up truck, he passed the alley and out of his peripheral view he saw a little doggie. He backed his truck up and looked down there, got gingerly out of his truck. Took a blanket from the back of the truck and tipped up on the little doggie and oh so carefully began to embrace her for you see, people who have been without help a long time sometime will bite you [Clapping] and misinterpret your intentions [Clapping]. He scooped her up in his arms and he put her in the back of the pick-up truck. Oh, did I tell you that the man was a veterinarian? [Laughing] And, he took her home with him. Gave her shelter. Gave her refuge. And, he dipped her and washed the flees off. And, he put salve in her mangy parts. He sewed up the torn ear, de-wormed her and deflead her, and gave her medicine to help her live. Not only that, but he bought some Purina Dog Chow [Laughing], put some meat on her bones. By and by, the veterinarian and the little doggie struck up a wonderful relationship. He loved her and she loved him and he said, "All I want you to do little girl is just stay!" Got along for a good little while, she had the run of the yard, huh-huh-huh. Every time she saw him coming her little tail was wagging and oh, she was a happy little dog. And, one day the veterinarian got up and called for the little doggie, he could find her nowhere. He began to whistle for her, he began to call her by name. He walked up and down the streets knocking on doors, "Have you seen my little doggie?" He drove up and down the neighborhood to make sure she had not been run over and could find her nowhere. He said, "Well, maybe to his sorrow, the street had probably reclaimed his little doggie." Then, bless the Lord, a long time later. One morning he got up out of his bed and he heard a commotion all out in the front yard. My God, it was doggies everywhere! [Laughing] It was big doggies, little doggies, Chihuahua doggies, Bull doggies, Pit Bull doggies, Collie doggies, Spaniel doggies, wuf-wuf doggies, and woof-woof doggies, big doggies everywhere! Oh, as far as the eye could see, nothing in his front yard but yards and acres of doggies! And then, bless the Lord, right down the middle aisle, here came his little doggie [Laughing & Clapping]. Came up to him with her tongue hanging out. He said, "Where you been? I thought I told you to stay!" She said, "I know you told me to stay, but all the while that I was up here in the shelter and the refuge of your house, I kept on thinking about my sister doggies that still live down in the alley and I had to go and tell them that I found a man that likes doggies, that gives doggies a refuge, that heals doggies, that restores doggies to life again!"

What can you do for your sister? Don't forget where you came from! Don't forget the refuge that has been offered to your life.

This version was delivered, October 7, 2007, at Mississippi Boulevard Christian Church, 70 North Bellevue, Memphis, TN 38104.

NOTE

1. Claudette A. Copeland, "What Shall We Do For Our Sister?" Reproduced by permission of the author.

Appendix F

Four Rhetorical Models

Table 6.1 Rhetorical Model 1. Radical Subjectivity Sermons (Victim to Victor)

Rhetorical Strategy	Purpose of Strategy	Example of Strategy
Focuses on self	To heighten maturity level—increase identity formation, self-love and self-worth	"God is calling for brave and determined women to adopt an attitude of intolerance for those things in their lives that abuse, confuse, and restrict"
Aim: Liberation	Moves a woman from being a victim to being a victor	"When she has a change of self-perception, she is able to move from a place of victimization to victory"
Identifies inner weakness and unhealthy relationships that consist of physical, emotional, and mental abuse. Then, pinpoints a woman's moment of epiphany	To affirm the power that exists in choosing to get out of destructive relationships	"Leah's emotional dependence upon Jacob robbed her of security and self-worth." "Leah had a reality check. She finally realized that she couldn't make Jacob love Leah, but she could love Leah . . ."
Rhetorical tool: Uses fight/war language and imagery*	To show the extremes of the abuse and the perversion of the abuser	". . . she wages a deliberate and systematic attack on him," "bludgeon her to death," "crush or be crushed"
Encourages a human agency and a rhetorical agency	So that women will change their oppressive situation and realize and proclaim to themselves that they do not have to live in an oppressive situation	"I do not have to settle for less. I do not have to participate in my own oppression." . . . "This time I will praise the Lord"
Sermonic values: Self-love, self-affirmation, self-worth	To affirm a woman's humanity in the midst of her oppression so she will stop looking for validation from others	"My value is not determined by anybody else. . . . My worth and my value come from God"
Names oppressive forces: Domestic abuse, infidelity, rejection, bondage, subordination, patriarchal domination, insecurity, wounded self-esteem, emotional dependence	To lead people to a type of self-transformation: physically, spiritually, mentally and/or emotionally	"He cheats on her but makes her feel that his cheating, like his beatings, is what she deserves." "She is clear that her husband is not going to give up or change, so the only way she is going to be free requires her to change"

Table created by Kimberly P. Johnson.

Table 6.2 Rhetorical Model 2. Traditional Communalism Sermons.
(Jeremiad – A calling back to original values)

Rhetorical Strategy	Purpose of Strategy	Example of Strategy
Focuses on self and community—has a both/and vantage point	To push people toward improving self so they can improve their relationships with others	"I challenge you to look and see, what is your call and are you still interested?" "God's people ought not suffer because we're bent over, busted up, and burned out"
Aim: Calling back to cultural beliefs and values, healing, and liberation	Moves a woman toward an individual healing, a communal healing, and calls us back to our original values	"Are you willing to be free so that you can help others to be free?"
Identifies our spiritual, pathological, and ideological infirmities along with our pathological behavior—performs a cultural critique	To encourage self-introspection and inspire women to free themselves from their illness by no longer practicing their sickness	"Racism mocks and violates God's precious, magnificent color and cultural palate of peoples;" "Faux churchism limits our experience of God and condemns the experiences of others"
Rhetorical tool: Uses a language of sickness and a Rhetorical Jeremiad*	To identify our current condition and what cripples self/community. Plus, it calls individuals/ communities back to their original values	"For you see, with all the 'isms,' each 'ism' cripples us in a very dynamic way;" "So the question is, are you living the message of the gospel before them?"
Encourages a human agency	Encourages individuals to make sure they are living the gospel message, so that the community as a whole can be the people God has called them to be	"To be church means discerning all the 'bent overness' and deal with them. Starting first with ourselves"
Sermonic values: Being the people of God, discerning "bent overness," freedom, salvation	To affirm a woman's humanity in the midst of her oppression so she will stop looking for validation from others	"We can't talk about being the people of God if we don't live the people of God"
Names oppressive forces: Crippling spirits, racism, sexism, heterosexism, patriarchy, misogyny, classism, faux churchism	To lead people to a type of self-transformation: physically, spiritually, and/ or emotionally	"How can we transform our passive aggressive behavior born out of patriarchy and misogyny? We must expose our internal societal oppressions if we want to be well"

*Rhetorical tools are not limited to what is reflected by the asterisk. Please refer to tables 2.1 and 2.2.
Table created by Kimberly P. Johnson.

Table 6.3   Rhetorical Model 3. Redemptive Self-Love Sermons. (Villain to Heroine)

Rhetorical Strategy	*Purpose of Strategy*	*Example of Strategy*
Focuses on one's ability to love herself regardless and the community's perception of her actions	To praise women who love themselves enough to resist being silenced or losing their dignity or self-worth so that it can begin to change society's negative perception of those women	"But Queen Vashti refused to come at the king's command . . . Queen Vashti's response often is overlooked for the more palatable story of Esther"
Aim: Redemption	Removes the socially perceived shame of a woman away from her actions to take her from being a villain to being a heroine	"Vashti's metaphorical response . . . became a model for all the women in Susa and a threat to those who would have found pleasure in her debasing display"
Identifies heroine qualities in women who are regarded as shameful, wicked, and/ or evil	To reveal the integrity that the woman has and the morals by which she lives	"Yet to gloss over this monumental moment of liberation is to miss the making of a model of leadership . . . following the sound of the genuine within one's self is paramount"
Rhetorical tool: Uses provocative language along with a metaphorical "Hell No!"*	To encourage women to go for the shock-and-awe value to help us retrieve our voice, our power, and our bodies	"Hell no!" "I'm sick and tired of being sick and tired;" "If I perish let me perish"
Encourages a rhetorical agency	Empowers a woman to match her human agency and moral agency with a rhetorical agency—an emphatic verbal response	"I think of Nez, who, if she had been with Vashti . . . surely would have looked at the queen and given her the royal nod to repeat after her and say, 'Hell no!'"
Sermonic values: Self-love, self-acceptance, self-development, revolution, reverence for one's self, righteous indignation	To affirm women in listening to their own voices in order to be true to self	". . . the sound of the genuine within one's self is paramount" "Outward success is not equal to inner worth"
Names oppressive forces: Objectification, silence, exile, pride of the powerful, patriarchal dominance	To encourage a woman not to submit to quiet conspiracy and lead them to actually start a revolution that reverences self by honoring the divinity that is inside of her	"A simple answer of 'No thank you,' or 'I'm sorry, I'll pass' just doesn't get it. We need to go for the shock-and-awe value and retrieve our voice, our power, and our bodies"

Table created by Kimberly P. Johnson.

Table 6.4   Rhetorical Model 4. Critical Engagement Sermons. (Cultural Critique)

Rhetorical Strategy	*Purpose of Strategy*	*Example of Strategy*
Focuses on self and community with a both/ and vantage point—but, primarily focuses on community	To push people to confront their internal system of beliefs in order to build community so they can collectively combat the external system of beliefs	"Cancer is not contagious, you can't catch it. I need partnership while I go through"
Aim: A cultural critique of society's oppressive forces	Offers a perspectival corrective that moves people toward partnership on devising a plan on how WE can fix/eliminate the problem	Asks: What shall/can we do?
Identifies society's normative view of oppression via its own cultural critique of a particular situation	To challenge the ways in which we view other people's struggles	"There's a rat trap in the farm house and if affects the whole farm" (What affects one, affects everyone)
Rhetorical tool: Uses a critical cognitive praxis*	To question the patterns and experiences by gathering and weighing evidence against cultural codes, signs, and hegemonic truths	"What shall we do for our little sister?" "What shall be done for her when men come to call?" "If God can speak through a donkey . . . God's gonna talk to you this morning through a breast"
Encourages a human/ rhetorical agency	Inspires people to collectively change their thoughts and behavioral practices so they can help fix/eliminate the problem	"What shall we do for our little sis? . . . if you want to do anything for your little sister": Partnership, acknowledgment, validation, understanding, prayer
Sermonic values: Prayer, joining others in their struggle, acknowledgment, understanding, compassion, doing for others, sharing our refuge	To affirm the power one has and the need for us to come together in support of each other	"I need somebody who can . . . say, 'I bind the power of sickness and disease. You gonna live and not die." "A saint who will pray is Satan's greatest nightmare"
Names oppressive forces: Breast cancer, struggle, wounds of the flesh, wounds of the spirit, becoming invisible	To reassure people who are struggling that Jesus has prayed for them and is with them, and to lead people to emulate that same type of behavior toward each other	"I heard Jesus say . . . 'I have prayed for you!' When people forget you, . . . are embarrassed by your suffering, . . . walk a wide circle around you, this is your comfort"

Table created by Kimberly P. Johnson.

Bibliography

Allen, Donna. *Toward a Womanist Homiletic: Katie Cannon, Alice Walker, and Emancipatory Proclamation: Katie Cannon, Alice Walker and Emancipatory Proclamation*. New York: Peter Lang, 2013.

Bridgeman, Valerie. "Womanist Criticism." In *The Oxford Encyclopedia of the Bible and Gender Studies*, Vol. 2. New York: Oxford University Press, 2014: 431–439.

Brown, Teresa Fry. "A Womanist Model for Proclamation of the Good News," *The African American Lectionary*, http://www.theafricanamericanlectionary.org/PopupCulturalAid.asp?LRID=73 (accessed April 24, 2010).

Burke, Kenneth. *A Grammar of Motives*. Berkeley: University of California Press, 1969.

Buttrick, David. *Homiletic Moves and Structures*. New York: Harcourt Brace & Company, 1983.

Campbell, Karlyn Kohrs. "Agency: Promiscuous and Protean." Paper presented at the Alliance of Rhetoric Societies 2003 Conference: 1–26. Rhetoric Society. http://www.rhetoricsociety.org/ARS/pdf/campbellonagency.pdf (accessed May 20 2008.

_____. "Agency: Promiscuous and Protean." In *Communication and Critical/Cultural Studies*, 2 (1 March 2005): 1–19.

_____. *Man Cannot Speak For Her: Key Texts of the Early Feminists, II*. New York: Praeger, 1989.

Campbell, Karlyn Kohrs and Kathleen Hall Jamiesonl "Form and Genre in Rhetorical Criticism: An Introduction." In Readings in Rhetorical Criticism. 3rd ed. State College: Strata Publishing, 2005: 400–416.

Cannon, Katie. *Katie's Canon: Womanism and the Soul of the Black Community*. New York: Continuum, 1995.

_____. "Structured Academic Amnesia: As If This True Womanist Story Never Happened." In *Deeper Shades of Purple: Womanism in Religion and Society*, ed. Stacey Floyd-Thomas. New York, NY: New York University Press, 2006: 19–28.

_____. "Womanist Interpretation and Preaching in the Black Church." *Searching the Scriptures: A Feminist Introduction 1*, ed. Elizabeth Fiorenza. New York, NY: Crossroad, 1993: 326–337.

Collins, Patricia Hill. *Black Feminist Thought: Knowledge, Consciousness, and the Politics of* Empowerment, 2nd ed. New York: Routledge, 2000.

Cone, James H. *Speaking the Truth: Ecumenism, Liberation, and Black Theology*. Grand Rapids: Wm. B. Eerdmans Publishing, 1986.

Copeland, Claudette. "What Shall We Do For Our Sister?" Sermon Delivered at Mississippi Boulevard Christian Church, Memphis, Tennessee, 2007. Transcribed by Kimberly P. Johnson.

_____. *Stories From Inner Space: Confessions of a Preacher Woman and Other Tales*. San Antonio: Red Nail Press, 2003.

Copeland, M. Shawn. "A Thinking Margin: The Womanist Movement as Critical Cognitive Praxis." In *Deeper Shades of Purple: Womanism in Religion and Society*, ed. Stacey Floyd-Thomas. New York, NY: New York University Press, 2006: 226–235.

Douglas, Kelly Brown. "Twenty Years a Womanist: An Affirming Challenge." In *Deeper Shades of Purple: Womanism in Religion and Society*, ed. Stacey Floyd-Thomas. New York, NY: New York University Press, 2006: 145–157.

Duncan, Carol B. "From "Force-Ripe" to "Womanish/ist:" Black Girlhood and African Diasporan Feminist Consciousness." In *Deeper Shades of Purple: Womanism in Religion and Society*, ed. Stacey Floyd-Thomas. New York, NY: New York University Press, 2006: 29–37.

Fiorenza, Elizabeth Schüssler. *But She Said: Feminist Practices of Biblical Interpretation*. Boston: Beacon Press, 1992.

_____. *Revelation: Vision of a Just World*. Minneapolis: Fortress Press, 1991.

Flake, Elaine M. "The Power of Enough" In *God In Her Midst: Preaching Healing to Wounded Women*. Valley Forge, PA: Judson Press, 2007: 41–47.

_____. *God In Her Midst: Preaching Healing to Wounded Women*. Valley Forge, PA: Judson Press, 2007.

Floyd-Thomas, Stacey M., ed. *Deeper Shades of Purple: Womanism in Religion and Society*. New York: New York University Press, 2006.

Foster, Francis Smith. *Written by herself: Literary production by African American Women, 1746–1892*. Bloomington: Indiana University Press, 1993.

Grant, Jacquelyn. *White Women's Christ and Black Women's Jesus: Feminist Christology and Womanist Response*. Atlanta: Scholars Press, 1989.

_____. "Black Theology and the Black Woman." In *Black Theology: A Documentary History, vol. 1 1966–1979*, eds. James H. Cone and Gayraud S. Wilmore. Maryknoll: Orbis Books, 1993.

Harding, Rosemary Freeney with Rachel Elizabeth Harding. "Hospitality, Haints, and Healing: A Southern African American Meaning of Religion." In *Deeper Shades of Purple: Womanism in Religion and Society*, ed. Stacey Floyd-Thomas. New York, NY: New York University Press, 2006: 98–114.

Hariman, Robert. "Prudence/Performance," in *Rhetoric Society Quarterly* 22. no. 2 (Spring 1991): 26–35.

Harris, Melanie L. "Womanist Humanism: A New Hermeneutic." In *Deeper Shades of Purple: Womanism in Religion and Society*, ed. Stacey Floyd-Thomas. New York, NY: New York University Press, 2006: 211–225.

Hayes, Diana L. "Standing in the Shoes My Mother Made: The Making of a Catholic Womanist Theologian." In *Deeper Shades of Purple: Womanism in Religion and Society*, ed. Stacey Floyd-Thomas. New York, NY: New York University Press, 2006: 54–76.

hooks, bell. *Ain't I A Woman: Black Women and Feminism*. Boston: South End Press, 1981.

_____. *Feminism is for Everybody: Passionate Politics*. Cambridge, South End Press, 2000.

Houston, Marsha and Olga Idriss Davis, eds. *Centering Ourselves: African American Feminist and Womanist Studies of Discourse*. Cresskill: Hampton Press, Inc., 2002.

Johnson, Kimberly P. "Womanism." In *The Wiley Blackwell Encyclopedia of Gender and Sexuality Studies*, ed. Nancy A. Naples. Oxford: John Wiley & Sons, Ltd., 2016: 1–3.

Kennedy, George. *The Art of Persuasion in Greece*. New Jersey: Princeton University, 1963.

Kirk-Duggan, Cheryl. *Exorcizing Evil: A Womanist Perspective on the Spirituals*. Maryknoll: Orbis Books, 1997.

_____. "Prophesied, Sanctified Performed Praxis: Womanist Preaching." Working paper, Womanist Preaching, Faculty of Theology and Women's Studies, Shaw University Divinity School, 1999.

_____. "Quilting Relations with Creation: Overcoming, Going Through, and Not Being Stuck." In *Deeper Shades of Purple: Womanism in Religion and Society*, ed. Stacey Floyd-Thomas. New York, NY: New York University Press, 2006: 176–190.

_____. "Women of the Cloth." Sermon Delivered at Austin Presbyterian Theological Seminary, Austin, Texas, 2006. Transcribed by Kimberly P. Johnson.

Logan, Shirley Wilson. *With Pen and Voice: A Critical Anthology of Nineteenth-Century African American Women*. Carbondale: Southern Illinois University Press, 1995.

Lonergan, Bernard. "Cognitional Structure." In *Collection: Papers by Bernard Lonergan*, ed. Frederick E. Crowe. Montreal: Palm Publishers, 1967: 221–239.

Lorde, Audre. "The Uses of Anger: Women Responding to Racism." In *Sister Outsider: Essays and Speeches*. Berkeley: The Crossing Press, 1984:124–133.

Lowery, Eugene L. *The Homiletical Plot, Expanded Edition: The Sermon as Narrative Art Form*. Louisville: Westminister John Knox Press, 2001.

Majeed, Debra Mubashshir. "Womanism Encounters Islam: A Muslim Scholar Considers the Efficacy of a Method Rooted in the Academy and the Church." In *Deeper Shades of Purple: Womanism in Religion and Society*, ed. Stacey Floyd-Thomas. New York, NY: New York University Press, 2006: 38–53.

Massey, James Earl. *Designing the Sermon: Order and Movement in Preaching*. Nashville: Abingdon Press, 1980.

McMickle, Marvin A. *Where Have All the Prophets Gone?: Reclaiming Prophetic Preaching in America?* Cleveland: Pilgrim Press, 2006.

Mitchem, Stephanie Y. *Introducing Womanist Theology.* Maryknoll: New York, 2005.

Osborn, Michael. "Archetypal Metaphor in Rhetoric: The Light-Dark Family." In *Readings in Rhetorical Criticism Third Edition*, ed. Carl R. Burgchardt. State College, PA: Strata Publishing, Inc, 2005.

Ogunyemi, Chikwenye Okonjo. "Chikwenye Okonjo Ogunyemi's African Womanism." In *Deeper Shades of Purple: Womanism in Religion and Society*, ed., Stacey M. Floyd-Thomas. New York: New York University Press, 2006: 26.

Phillips, Layli, ed. *The Womanist Reader.* New York: Routledge, 2006.

Ross, Rosetta E. "Lessons and Treasures in Our Mothers' Witness: Why I write about Black Women's Activism." In *Deeper Shades of Purple: Womanism in Religion and Society*, ed. Stacey Floyd-Thomas. New York, NY: New York University Press, 2006: 115–127.

Sampson, Melva L. "Hell No!" In *Those Preaching Women: A Multicultural Collection*, eds. Ella Pearson Mitchell and Valerie Bridgeman Davis. Valley Forge: Judson Press, 2008: 27–31.

Settles, Shani. "The Sweet Fire of Honey: Womanist Visions of Osun as a Methodology of Emancipation." In *Deeper Shades of Purple: Womanism in Religion and Society*, ed. Stacey Floyd-Thomas. New York, NY: New York University Press, 2006: 191–206.

Spelman, Elizabeth V. *Inessential Woman: Problems of Exclusion in Feminist Thought.* Boston: Beacon Press, 1988.

Stanton, Elizabeth Cady. "National Woman's Rights Convention Debate, New York City, 1860." In *Man Cannot Speak For Her: Key Texts of the Early Feminists*, Volume II, ed. Karlyn Kohrs Campbell. New York: Praeger, 1989: 187–234.

_____. *The Woman's Bible.* New York: Europian Publishing Company, 1895–1898.

Stewart, Dianne M. "Dancing Limbo: Black Passages through the Boundaries of Place, Race, Class, and Religion." In *Deeper Shades of Purple: Womanism in Religion and Society*, ed. Stacey Floyd-Thomas. New York, NY: New York University Press, 2006: 82–97.

Stewart, Gina. "Enough is Enough!" In *Those Preaching Women: A Multicultural Collection*, eds. Ella Pearson Mitchell and Valerie Bridgeman Davis. Valley Forge: Pennsylvania, 2008: 9–13.

Thomas, Frank A. *Introduction to the Practice of African American Preaching.* Nashville: Abingdon Press, 2016.

_____. *They Like To Never Quit Praisin' God: The Role of Celebration in Preaching.* Cleveland: Pilgrim Press, 2013.

Thomas, Linda. "Womanist Theology, Epistemology, and a New Anthropological Paradigm." *CrossCurrents* 48, (Winter 1998): 488–499.

Townes, Emilie M. "Ethics as an Art of Doing the Work Our Souls Must Have." In *The Arts of Ministry: Feminist-Womanist Approaches*, ed. Christie Cozad Neuger. Louisville: Westminister John Knox Press, 1996: 143–161.

Travis, Sarah. *Decolonizing Preaching: The Pulpit as Postcolonial Space*. Eugene: Cascade Books, 2014.

Turner, Mary Donovan and Mary Lin Hudson. *Saved from Silence: Finding Women's Voice in Preaching*. St. Louis: Chalice Press, 1999.

Walker, Alice. *In Search of Our Mother's Gardens: Womanist Prose*. Orlando: Harcourt Inc, 1983.

Weems, Renita. *Battered Love: Marriage, Sex, and Violence in the Hebrew Prophets*. Minneapolis: Fortress Press, 1995.

_____. "How Will Our Preaching Be Remembered? A Challenge to See the Bible from a Woman's Perspective." In *The African American Pulpit 9*, no. 3 (Summer 2006): 26–29.

_____. *Just a Sister Away: A Womanist Vision of Women's Relationships in the Bible*. Philadelphia: Innisfree Press Inc., 1988.

Westfield, Nancy Lynne. "'Mama Why...?' A Womanist Epistemology of Hope." In *Deeper Shades of Purple: Womanism in Religion and Society*, ed. Stacey Floyd-Thomas. New York, NY: New York University Press, 2006: 128–139.

Williams, Delores S. *Sisters in the Wilderness: The Challenge of Womanist God—Talk*. Maryknoll: Orbis Books, 1993.

BIBLIOGRAPHY OF SERMONS BY WOMANIST PREACHERS

Bridgeman, Valerie. "It Is Finished." In *Those Preaching Women: A Multicultural Collection*, eds. Ella Pearson Mitchell and Valerie Bridgeman Davis. Valley Forge: Pennsylvania, 2008: 126–128.

Cannon, Katie. "On Remembering Who We Are." In *Those Preaching Women: Sermons By Black Women Preachers Volume 1*, ed. Ella Pearson Mitchell. Valley Forge: Judson Press, 1985: 43–50.

_____. "A Catechism for Prophetic Living." In *The African American Pulpit*, 3 no.1 (Winter 1999/2000): 14–20.

_____. "Prophets for a New Day." In *The African American Pulpit*, 1 no. 2 (Spring 1998): 13–18.

_____. "To Tell the Truth." In *The African American Pulpit*, 1 no. 3 (Summer 1998): 29–35.

Copeland, Claudette. "What Shall We Do For Our Sister?" Sermon Delivered at Mississippi Boulevard Christian Church, Memphis, Tennessee, 2007.

_____. "Tamar's Torn Robe." In *This is My Story: Testimonies & Sermons of Black Women in Ministry*, ed. Cleophus J. LaRue. Louisville: Westminister John Knox Press, 2005: 113–118.

_____. "Remember Lot's Wife." In *The African American Pulpit*, 3 no. 3 (Summer 2000): 17–23.

_____. "Why Are You Here?" In *The African American Pulpit*, 8 no. 4 (Fall 2005): 33–37.

_____. "Live on What's Left." In *The African American Pulpit*, 6 no. 2 (Spring 2003): 41–46.

Flake, Elaine M. *God In Her Midst: Preaching Healing to Wounded Women*. Valley Forge, PA: Judson Press, 2007.

———. "This is the Day to Walk Away." In *The African American Pulpit*, 5 no. 4 (Fall 2002): 62–66.

Gilkes, Cheryl Townsend. "A Cry, a Gift, and a Song." In *The African American Pulpit*, 2 no. 2 (Winter 1998–1999): 21–26.

———. "A Total God for Total Liberation." In *The African American Pulpit*, 2 no. 4 (Fall 1999): 25–32.

Grant, Jacqueline. "On Containing God." In *The African American Pulpit*, 3 no. 3 (Summer 2000): 24–31.

———. "When Standing Up Means Sitting Down." In *The African American Pulpit*, 5 no. 4 (Fall 2002): 70–73.

Johnson, Allison P. Gise. "When the Miraculous Happens." In *This is My Story: Testimonies & Sermons of Black Women in Ministry*, ed. Cleophus J. LaRue. Louisville: Westminister John Knox Press, 2005:146–148.

Kirk-Duggan, Cheryl. "Women of the Cloth." Sermon Delivered at Austin Presbyterian Theological Seminary, Austin, Texas, 2006.

———. "From the Wilderness to the Light." In *This is My Story: Testimonies & Sermons of Black Women in Ministry*, ed. Cleophus J. LaRue. Louisville: Westminister John Knox Press, 2005: 186–190.

McSwine-Harris, Charlotte. "At the Table." In *This is My Story: Testimonies & Sermons of Black Women in Ministry*, ed. Cleophus J. LaRue. Louisville: Westminister John Knox Press, 2005: 200–203.

Mitchell, Ella Pearson. "Redigging the Wells." In *The African American Pulpit*, 2 no. 4 (Fall 1999): 40–46.

Sampson, Melva L. "Hell No!" In *Those Preaching Women: A Multicultural Collection*, eds. Ella Pearson Mitchell and Valerie Bridgeman Davis. Valley Forge: Pennsylvania, 2008:27–31.

Stewart, Gina. "Enough is Enough!" In *Those Preaching Women: A Multicultural Collection*, eds. Ella Pearson Mitchell and Valerie Bridgeman Davis. Valley Forge: Pennsylvania, 2008: 9–13.

———. "An Unfinished Agenda." In *The African American Pulpit*, 3 no. 3 (Summer 2000): 86–89.

Weems, Renita. "Not . . . Yet." In *The African American Pulpit*, 7 no. 4 (Fall 2004): 79–84.

Index

Note: Page references for figures are italicized

Jacob, *18*, 21–22, 26–28, 30, 32–33, 54,
   120, 131, 132, 135–38, *162*
Jamieson, Kathleen Hall, 127n17
Jeremiad, 37, *42*, 55, 111, 118, *121*,
   124, 126, 163
   Jesus, xix, xxiv, 6–8, 23, 29, 40–41,
      44–45, 47–51, 62, 82, 84, *85*, 90,
      92–3, 108, 110, 116, *123*, 125,
      139–43, 149, 153–56, 158, *165*
   Johnson, Kimberly P., xxvin4, 18,
      26, 42, 56n24, 67, 85, 101n35,
      120–23, 127n6, 162–65

Kennedy, George, 10n8
King Ahasuerus, 64–71, 73–75, *122*,
   145–48, *164*
King, Martin Luther, Jr., xv–xvi
Kirk-Duggan, Cheryl, xxiv–xxvi, 40–54,
   62, 98–99, 105, 108–12, 115,
   125, 139–44

Laban, 26–27, 32, 131, 135–37
language:
   emotional prison, 17–18, 22, *26*, 29,
      31–32, 50, 70, 94, 129–30, 133,
      135, 143, 158;
   erotic, *85*, 87, 112, 152;
   fight, xvi–xix, *18*, 19, 22–24, 32, 40,
      45, 54, 60, 65–66, 69, 73, 80–81,
      83, 93–94, 107, 110, 112, *120*,
      124, 126, 130, 133, 141, 145, 147,
      158–59, *162*;
   inclusive language, 5–6, *42*, 45, 53,
      108, 115;medical terminology,
      85;
   Adriamycin, 153;Cytoxan, 153;fatty
      tissue and ligaments, 87, 112,
      151;5-FU, 153;HIV positive,
      88, 96, 152;infiltrating ductal
      adenocarcinoma, 89;lymphatic
      fluid, 87, 112, 151;pectoral
      muscles, 87, 112, 151;Struma, 87,
      112, 151;sickness, *42*, 94, 96–98,
      121, *123*, 143, 157, *163*, *165*;
   prisoner, 17, 18, 22, 31–32, 94,
      129–130, 158 ;

provocative, *67*, *122*, *164*;
Common vernacular names for
   breasts, 87, 151–52;psychological
   prison, *26*, 29, 31–32, 50, 129,
   130, 133, 135, 143;
scenic language describing breasts,
   87, 112, 151;
war, *18*, 22, 32, 54, 94, 114, *120*,
   157, *162*
Leah, 15, *18*, 21–30, 32–33, 105, *120*,
   131–138, *162*
liberation, xvi, xviii–xix, xxiii, 1–4, 7,
   24, 29, 37–40, 63, 68, 80–81,
   105, 110–11, 113, *120–22*,
   124, 126, 133, 146, *162–64*;
   theology, xviii–xix, 81
linguistics, xx, *18*, *26*
little sister with no breasts, 82, 84, *85*,
   88–90, 96–99, 106, *123*, 149,
   151–53, 155, 158, 165
Logan, Shirley Wilson, 128n30
logical appeal. *See* Aristotle; logos
Lonergan, Bernard, 100n11
Lorde, Audre, xvii
Lowery, Eugene L., 114

McMickle, Marvin A., 114
Majeed, Debra Mubashshir, 14, 107
Martin, Clarice, 5
Massey, James Earl, 114
metaphors, xxi, 17, *18*, 20, *26*, 27,
   32–33, 54, 83, 87, 108;
   breast metaphor, 85, 88–89;
   crippling spirit metaphor, xxiv,
      41–45, 49, 51–52, 54, 98, 106,
      109–12, *121*, 139–40, *163*;
   dark-light metaphors, 20;
   hell no! metaphor, 64–74, 110, *122*,
      145–48;
   Jacob(s) metaphor, 18, 22, *26–28*,
      32, 54, 132, 137–38;
   Laban(s) metaphor *26*, 27, 32, 137;
   light-dark metaphors, 17, *18*, 20, 54;
   little sister metaphor, 85, 88–90, 96,
      98, *123*, 149, 151–53, 155, 158,
      165

Index

About the Author

Kimberly P. Johnson is an assistant professor of Communications at Tennessee State University, in Nashville, Tennessee. She received her PhD in communication along with a graduate certificate in women's and gender studies from the University of Memphis. She received her MDiv from McCormick Theological Seminary, and a BS in speech from Northwestern University. She is also an ordained minister in the Christian Church (Disciples of Christ).